All in One

COMPLETE STUDY | COMPLETE PRACTICE | COMPLETE ASSESSMENT

Information Technology

CBSE Class 10

As Per Latest CBSE Syllabus 2022-23
Issued on 21 April, 2022

COMPLETE STUDY | COMPLETE PRACTICE | COMPLETE ASSESSMENT

Information Technology

CBSE Class 10

Authors
Neetu Gaikwad
Shweta Agarwal

ARIHANT PRAKASHAN (School Division Series)

ARIHANT PRAKASHAN
(School Division Series)
All Rights Reserved

ॐ **ADMINISTRATIVE & PRODUCTION OFFICES**

Regd. Office

'Ramchhaya' 4577/15, Agarwal Road, Darya Ganj, New Delhi -110002
Tele: 011- 47630600, 43518550; Fax: 011- 23280316

ॐ **Head Office**

Kalindi, TP Nagar, Meerut (UP) - 250002, Tel: 0121-7156203, 7156204

ॐ **SALES & SUPPORT OFFICES**

Agra, Ahmedabad, Bengaluru, Bareilly, Chennai, Delhi, Guwahati, Hyderabad, Jaipur, Jhansi, Kolkata, Lucknow, Nagpur & Pune.

PO No : TXT-XX-XXXXXXX-X-XX

Published By Arihant Publications (India) Ltd.

For further information about the books published by Arihant, log on to www.arihantbooks.com or e-mail at info@arihantbooks.com

Follow us on

PRODUCTION TEAM

Publishing Managers
Mahendra Singh Rawat & Keshav Mohan

Project Coordinator
Er. Ashwani

Cover Designer
Shanu Mansoori

Inner Designer
Ankit Saini

Page Layouting
Ravinder Kumar

Proof Reader
Shruti Agarwal

A WORD
WITH THE READERS

All*in*one Information Technology Class 10th has been written keeping in mind the needs of students studying in Class 10th CBSE (Under Skill Subjects). This book has been made in such a way that students will be fully guided to prepare for the exam in the most effective manner, securing higher grades.

The purpose of this book is to aid a CBSE Student to achieve the best possible grade in the exam. This book will give you support during the course as well as advice you on revision and preparation for the exam itself.

Key Features

- Each chapter starts with the detailed Study Material well supported with Definitions, Remarks, Figures, Snapshots etc.

- Exam Practice Section of each chapter contains questions in that format in which these are asked in the examinations. Questions have been divided into **Multiple Choice Questions, Fill in the Blanks, True and False, Very Short Answer Type Questions, Short Answer Type Questions, Long Answer Type Questions** and **Application Oriented Type Questions.**

- Each chapter has an unsolved **Self Assessment Test**.

- There are **5 Sample Question Papers** to make students practice for the examination as well as they will be able to learn Time Management during the examination.

- **Abbreviations & Glossary** are also given in the end of the book.

All-in-One Information Technology for CBSE Class 10th has all the material for examination and will surely guide students to their way to Success.

We are highly thankful to ARIHANT PRAKASHAN, MEERUT for giving us such an excellent opportunity to write this book. The role of Arihant DTP Unit and Proofreading team is praiseworthy in the making of this book. Suggestions for further improvement of the book will be welcomed & incorporated in further editions.

In the end, we would like to wish BEST OF LUCK to our readers!

Authors
Neetu Gaikwad
Shweta Agarwal

All in One
COMPLETE STUDY | COMPLETE PRACTICE | COMPLETE ASSESSMENT

PREVIEW

THEORY SECTION

Contains the necessary study material for both parts, well supported by Definitions, Remarks, Figures, Snapshots etc. This section provides all the essentials needed to prepare you for the exam, even if you have not gone through the textbook.

Communication Skills-II

Chapter Checklist

- Methods of Communication
- Providing Feedback
- Barriers to Communication
- Principles of Communication
- Basic Writing Skills

Communication skills are important to everyone, they are how we give and receive information and convey our ideas and opinions to those around us. Communication comes in various forms such as:

- Verbal (sounds, language and tone of voice)
- Aural (listening and hearing)
- Non-verbal (facial expressions, body language and posture)
- Written (journals, e-mails, blogs and text messages)
- Visual (signs, symbols and pictures)

We must develop a variety of skills for both communicating to others and learning how to interpret the information received from others. Good communication skills are essential for working in an organisation. For example, during a personal interview, employers are impressed by a job candidate who answers questions with more than one-word answers, demonstrates that he is listening, and shares information and ideas by asking questions for clarification and follow-up. Further, non-verbal communication, such as good eye contact, good posture and 'active' listening, is also critical in an interview.

Methods of Communication

Verbal Communication

Verbal communication means communication through spoken oral and written words. It implies use of words which make up a language. It is the ability to communicate using words in understandable language i.e. English, Hindi, French, Urdu etc. Language play a significant role in verbal communication. The effectiveness of the verbal communication depends on the tone of the speaker, clarity of speech, volume, speed, body language and the quality of words used in conversation.

Verbal communication are two types. These are :

1. **Oral communication** It means communication through the mouth (speaking) and the ears (listening). Two individuals conversing with each other, either face-to-face or through the telephone is an example of oral communication. Interviews, speeches, presentations, to conferences, workshops and group discussions are also forms of oral communication.
2. **Written communication** This is a medium of communication that entails the written word. Letters, e-mails, websites, memorandums, reports, notices, manuals, quotations, newsletters, newspapers etc., are forms of written communication.

- Eye contact
- Gestures
- Body language
- Proximity
- Touch
- Personal appearance
- Visual communication
- Para-linguistic (tone/ pitch/ inflection)

- Facial expressions
- Posture and body orientation
- Space and Distance
- Humour
- Silences
- Symbols

Components of Verbal Communication

Hand Gestures

For the feedback to be effective, it must be clear, well in time, specific, having the right attitude, true and honest, impersonal and informative. It is important because proper feedback helps avoid misunderstandings. Thus, if the receiver has interpreted the message incorrectly, the sender has a chance to correct it. Whether the communication has created the desired effect or not can be determined by analysing the receiver's feedback.

Descriptive Feedback

This form of feedback is most suited to teacher-student interactions when the students are attending a course taught by the teacher. In such a case, it has the specific purpose of helping students improve while they are still gaining knowledge and practising their skills in the subject.

It means that descriptive feedback helps in supporting student development from their current level of achievement. It should make clear to them how to achieve the learning goals of a subject. Descriptive feedback can be written, oral or may even be the response of students to a question while they are working. It is relevant to the task students are performing, and allows them to re-focus and improve their mastery of the subject.

Specific/ Non-specific Feedback

Specific feedback from a teacher to a student provides detailed information about the student's performance on a subject.

For example, a teacher may tell a student, "you wrote the descriptions very well, but your diagrams were made untidily and missed some details." This is specific feedback to the student so as to enable him to improve his performance.

However, a non-specific or generic feedback may be, "you did very poorly in the text" or "you could have done better." Some other examples of specific and non-specific feedback are:

Examples of Specific Feedback	Examples of Non-specific Feedback
I like the way you described your grandfather. It makes me feel like I know him too.	I like your story. It's good.
I like the part where you fell. It made me laugh.	I like your topic. I want to write about that too.

SUMMARY

- Communication comes in various forms such as verbal, aural, non-verbal, written and visual.
- Good communication skills, both verbal and non-verbal, are essential for working in an organisation.
- Verbal communication consists of oral and written communication.
- Non-verbal communication relies on various non-verbal cues and includes visual communication.
- The main steps in a communication are in the form of a cyclic process, which is completed by a feedback from the receiver of the communication to the sender.
- For the feedback to be effective, it must be clear, well in time, specific, having the right attitude, true and honest, impersonal and informative.
- A barrier to communication is anything that prevents or disturbs the sending or receiving of a communication.
- Barriers to communication may be physical, personal or semantic.
- Barriers to communication can be overcome or will not arise if suitable steps related to the factors causing the barriers are taken.
- To ensure that the intended message of the sender and the interpreted message of the receiver are identical, the principles called 'The 7 C's of Effective Communication' should be followed.
- As writing skills form an important part of communication, we should know what the kinds of sentences are, their parts (subject and predicate) and the parts of speech used in sentences.
- We should also know the construction of a paragraph for our writing to be effective.

Check Point 02

1. Which one of the following is not a step in the communication cycle?
 (a) Encoding (b) Medium (c) Noise (d) Feedback
2. Which one of the following is not a medium of communication?
 (a) A verbal conversation (b) Writing on paper
 (c) The Internet (d) The telephone
3. Without feedback, the communication cycle remains ....
4. The .... form of feedback is most suited to teacher-student interactions.
5. How do errors in decoding occur in a communication cycle?
6. Why is feedback important in a communication cycle?

Barriers to Communication

Anything that prevents or disturbs the sending or receiving of a communication or message is considered as a barrier to communication. Such barriers can retard or distort the message or intention of the message being conveyed. It may result in failure of the communication process or cause an effect that is undesirable. Speaking louder to drown out the noise is a measure to overcome a barrier to communication.

Types of Barriers

The types of barriers to communication include:

Physical and Environment Based Barriers

These are environmental factors which prevent or reduce the sending and receiving of communications. They include physical distance, distracting noises and similar interferences.

Interpersonal Barriers

They arise from the judgements, emotions and social values of people. They cause a psychological distance between people similar to the physical distance. Thus, sometimes the message may not be understood at all. At other times, part of the communication is only understood. In other cases, the message may be wrongly interpreted.

Our emotions also affect nearly all our communications. For example, if we are feeling angry, we may say something which we would say differently if we were not angry. In such a situation, we are communicating what we are feeling is correct. However, this may not be the case actually. Thus, our emotions affect our communications.

Semantic Barriers

These refer to symbols or visuals used in the message. The barrier may arise due to the symbol we use, as it may mean different things to different people. For example, the 'thumbs up' gesture is recognised as a sign of approval or agreement in European countries, but it may be interpreted as an indecent gesture in rural areas of India.

CHECK POINT

To assess your step-by-step learning of chapter, Check Point Questions are incorporated in between the theory.

for CBSE Class 10th Examination is a complete book which can give you all study, practice and assessment. It is hoped that this book will reinforce and extend your ideas about the subject and finally will place you in the ranks of toppers.

EXAM PRACTICE

Exam Practice have questions in that format in which these are asked in the examinations, i.e. Multiple Choice Questions, Fill in the Blanks, True and False, Very Short Answer Type Questions, Short Answer Type Questions, Long Answer Type Questions & Application Oriented Type Questions. All the questions are fully solved. The explanations given here teach the students, how to write the answer in the examination to get full marks. Students can use these questions for practice and assess their understanding & recall of the chapter.

Exam Practice

Multiple Choice Questions [1 Mark each]

1. Aural communication is based on ....
   (a) Facial expressions
   (b) Listening and Hearing
   (c) Body language
   (d) Language and tone of voice
   Ans. (b) Listening and Hearing

7. It is a word used in place of noun that is ....
   (a) Adverb (b) Verb
   (c) Pronoun (d) Preposition
   Ans. (c) Pronoun

Fill in the Blanks [1 Mark each]

1. To indicate .... we use a skull placed between two bones put in crosswise fashion.
   Ans. danger to human life

2. .... form of feedback is most suited to teacher-student interactions when the students are attending a course taught by the teacher.
   Ans. Descriptive

   Ans. receiver's, sender

5. The noun for which a pronoun is substituted is called its ....
   Ans. antecedent

6. Absence of .... leads to misunderstanding in the communication.
   Ans. feedback

True and False [1 Mark each]

1. Good communication skills are essential for working an organisation.
   Ans. True

2. A communication is complete without the feedback.
   Ans. False

6. The sender must try to eliminate unnecessary information.
   Ans. True

7. Concreteness is one of the principle of effective communication.
   Ans. True

Very Short Answer (VSA) Type Questions [2 Marks each]

1. Define verbal communication
   Ans. Verbal communication means communication through spoken and written words. It implies use of words which make up a language. It is the ability to communication by using words.

9. What does a predicate in a sentence refer to?
   Ans. The predicate part of a sentence includes the verb and the words that relate to it. It tells what the subject does with an action verb or describes the subject.

Short Answer (SA) Type Questions [3 Marks each]

1. Describe the term descriptive feedback.
   Ans. Descriptive feedback can be written, oral or may even be the response of students to a question while they are working. It is relevant to the task students are performing, and allows them to re-fours and improve their mastery of the subject. This form of feedback is most suited to teacher-student interactions when the students are attending a course taught by the teacher.

6. What are the various forms of communication? Describe them in one sentence each with examples.
   Ans. The various forms of communication are:
   (i) Verbal This is communication through spoken and written words such as making sounds, using language and changing tone of voice etc.

Long Answer (LA) Type Questions [5 Marks each]

1. Explain the communication cycle briefly.
   Ans. The main steps in a communication are in the form of a cyclic process and these are explained below:
   • The First step is initiated by the communicator or sender or organisation originating the communication.

   (i) Noun It is a word for a person, place, thing or idea. Nouns are sometimes used with an article (the, a, an). Nouns can be singular or plural, concrete or abstract. e.g. The young girl brought me a very long letter from the teacher.

Application Oriented (AO) Type Questions

1. The following paragraph describes the term computer network.
   A computer network is a group of (i) .... that are (ii) .... to each other for the purpose of (iii) .... A computer (iv) .... allows computers to communicate with

4. Anila works in a Multi National Company (MNC) and needs to work online from home also. She requires fast Internet connection. Which type of Internet connection in your view would be best suited for her?

Self Assessment

Multiple Choice Questions [1 Mark each]

1. .... is an instance of visual communication.
   (a) An e-mail (b) A speech
   (c) Eye contact (d) Bar chart

2. Which of the following is not a factor causing a barrier in oral communication?
   (a) Preconceived notions (b) Physical hearing problem
   (c) Emotions (d) Semantics

Fill in the Blanks [1 Mark each]

1. Requesting clarification is part of a good .... phase of a communication cycle.

True/False [1 Mark each]

1. Non-verbal communication does not occur without using any written or oral word.
2. Feedback is essential to complete the cycle of communication.

Very Short Answer (VSA) Type Questions [2 Marks each]

1. What is a semantic barrier to communication?
2. What is the function of an adjective in a sentence?

Short Answer (SA) Type Questions [3 Marks each]

1. Explain the difference between specific feedback and non-specific feedback by giving examples of each.

Long Answer (LA) Type Questions [5 Marks each]

1. Explain the types of barriers to effective communication in detail.

Abbreviation and Glossary

Abbreviation

ADSL	Asymmetric Digital Subscriber Line	ICT	Information and Communication Technology
AMV	Animated Music Video	IE	Internet Explorer
ARPANET	Advanced Research Projects Agency NETwork	IETF	Internet Engineering Task Force
ASCII	American Standard Code for Information Interchange	IIS	Internet Information Server
		IMAP	Internet Message Access Protocol
ATM	Automated Teller Machine	InterNIC	Internet Network Information Center
B2B	Business to Business	IP	Internet Protocol

SELF ASSESSMENT

At the end of the Unit, these unsolved questions are for practice of students. By practising these questions, students can assess their preparation level for the chapter.

ABBREVIATION & GLOSSARY

With the theory of the chapter, important terms are highlighted and described at the end of book.

CONTENTS

Course Structure
Information Technology

This course is a planned sequence of instructions consisting of units meant for developing employability and vocational competencies of students of Class X opting for vocational subject along with general education subjects. The unit-wise distribution of hours and marks for class X is as follow:

	Units	No. of Hours for Theory and Practical 200		Max. Marks for Theory and Practical 100
	Employability Skills			
	Unit 1: Communication Skills-II*	10		-
	Unit 2: Self-Management Skills-II	10		3
PART A	Unit 3: ICT Skills-II	10		3
	Unit 4: Entrepreneurial Skills-II	15		4
	Unit 5: Green Skills-II*	05		-
	Total	50		**10**
	Subject Specific Skills	**Theory (In Hours)**	**Practical (In Hours)**	**Marks**
	Unit 1: Digital Documentation (Advanced)	12	18	8
	Unit 2: Electronic Spreadsheet (Advanced)	15	23	10
PART B	Unit 3: Database Management System	18	27	12
	Unit 4: Web Applications and Security	15	22	10
	Total	**60**	**90**	**40**
	Practical Work			**Marks**
	Practical Examination			
	• Advanced Documentation	5 Marks		
PART C	• Advanced Spreadsheets	5 Marks		20
	• Databases	10 Marks		
	• Viva Voce	10 Marks		10
	Total			**30**

	Project Work/Field Visit		Marks
PART D	Any Interdisciplinary Real World Case Study to be taken. Summarized data reports of same can be presented in base. Input should be taken using forms and output should be done using reports using base. Documentation of the case study should be presented using writer.		10
	PORTFOLIO/ PRACTICAL FILE: (Portfolio should contain printouts of the practical done using Writer, Calc and Base with minimum 5 problems of each)		10
	Total		20
	Grand Total	200	100

Note: * marked units are to be assessed through Internal Assessment/ Student Activities.
They are not to be assessed in Theory Exams

PART A

Employability Skills

Communication Skills-II

Communication skills are important to everyone, they are how we give and receive information and convey our ideas and opinions to those around us. Communication comes in various forms such as:

- Verbal (sounds, language and tone of voice)
- Aural (listening and hearing)
- Non-verbal (facial expressions, body language and posture)
- Written (journals, e-mails, blogs and text messages)
- Visual (signs, symbols and pictures)

We must develop a variety of skills for both communicating to others and learning how to interpret the information received from others. Good communication skills are essential for working in an organisation. For example, during a personal interview, employers are impressed by a job candidate who answers questions with more than one-word answers, demonstrates that he is listening, and shares information and ideas by asking questions for clarification and follow-up. Further, non-verbal communication, such as good eye contact, good posture and 'active' listening, is also critical in an interview.

One of the challenges in the workplace is learning the specific communication styles of others and how and when to share your ideas or concerns. Knowing how to listen carefully and when to ask for help is important. If an employee and a supervisor learn to communicate well (in whatever method that works), there is a greater likelihood of the employee doing an excellent job.

Methods of Communication

Verbal Communication

Verbal communication means communication through spoken oral and written words. It implies use of words which make up a language. It is the ability to communicate using words in understandable language i.e. English, Hindi, French, Urdu etc. Language play a significant role in verbal communication. The effectiveness of the verbal communication depends on the tone of the speaker, clarity of speech, volume, speed, body language and the quality of words used in conversation.

Verbal communication are two types. These are :

1. **Oral communication** It means communication through the mouth (speaking) and the ears (listening). Two individuals conversing with each other, either face-to-face or through the telephone is an example of oral communication. Interviews, speeches, presentations, to conferences, workshops and group discussions are also forms of oral communication.

2. **Written communication** This is a medium of communication that entails the written word. Letters, e-mails, websites, memorandums, reports, notices, manuals, quotations, newsletters, newspapers etc., are forms of written communication.

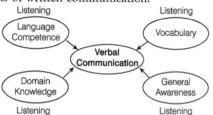

Components of Verbal Communication

Advantages of Verbal Communication

- It is quick in obtaining feedback once delivered.
- It saves time in communication.
- It is more reliable method of communication.
- It is cheaper way of communication and hence saves money.
- It provides complete understanding of communication delivered and there is chance to make it more clear in case of doubts in interpretation of words or ideas. .

Disadvantages of Verbal Communication

- It has no legal validity and hence will lead to problems in certain situations. Emotions are visible and hence leads to trouble in certain cases.
- It has issues when communicating with distant people. It does not provide permanent record unless it is recorded with modern means of storage.
- This form of communication is not suitable for lengthy message.

Non-Verbal Communication

Non-verbal communication occurs without using any oral or written word. Instead, it relies on various non-verbal cues such as physical movements, colors, signs, symbols, body language etc., to express feelings, attitudes or information. Although no word is used in non-verbal communication, this form of communication can effectively communicate many human feelings more accurately than verbal methods of communication. Various components or forms of non-verbal communication are:

- Eye contact
- Gestures
- Body language
- Proximity
- Touch
- Personal appearance
- Visual communication
- Para-linguistic (tone/ pitch/ inflection)

- Facial expressions
- Posture and body orientation
- Space and Distance
- Humour
- Silences
- Symbols

Hand Gestures

Advantage of Non-Verbal Communication

- It conveys clear and precise meaning to the receiver.
- It is presentable through visuals, audio-visual and silent means.
- This type of communication serves as substitute for verbal communication.
- It is helpful in communicating with illiterate people.
- It is attractive in nature as visual, pictures, graphs attract everybody's attention.
- It is very impactful as visuals greatly affect minds of people.

Disadvantages of Non-Verbal Communication

- In the absence of language, this type of communication do not convey actual meaning of the message. This makes this communication imprecise.
- It can be confusing as no clear message is conveyed.
- Long conversation are not possible in non-verbal communication.
- It can costly as Neon signs, PowerPoint presentation movies involve huge cost.

Visual Communication

Visual communication conveys ideas and information in forms that can be seen. It is also known as graphic communication.

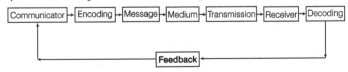

Public Signs and Icons

Check Point 01

1 Which of the following is not a form of oral communication?
   (a) Listening carefully   (b) An e-mail
   (c) An interview   (d) A group discussion
2 Which of the following is not a form of written communication?
   (a) A newspaper   (b) A website
   (c) A notices   (d) A telephone conversation
3 Verbal communication consists of .... communication and .... communication.
4 During a personal interview, employers are impressed by a job candidate who answers questions with .... answers.
5 What are communication skills?
6 What visual communication is used to indicate an area which is dangerous to human life?

Providing Feedback

A communication is complete when feedback is provided, as it enables us to understand whether our message has reached the intended person and has been understood. Thus, feedback is essential to complete the cycle of communication. If there is absence of feedback then it will lead to a communication barrier.

The Communication Cycle

The main steps in a communication form is communication cycle. These steps are shown and explained below:

Communicator → Encoding → Message → Medium → Transmission → Receiver → Decoding → Feedback

Components of a Communication Cycle

- The **Communicator** or **Sender** is the person or organisation originating the communication. It decides what the message is, how it will be expressed and sent, and who it is to be sent to.

- **Encoding** means to change the message into a form suitable for sending. The factors which must be considered when a encoding messages are language, cultural differences etc.
- The **Message** is the actual information that the sender wishes to convey to the receiver.
- The **Medium** or **Channel** is the means by which the message is sent. Some messages are more effective in written form, others may be more effective on the telephone (e.g. urgent messages), while others may be more effective if sent *via* electronic means such as e-mail. Noise introduced by a communication medium is anything that interferes with communication. It may cause misunderstanding of the message or even disrupt the message completely so that it is not even received.
- **Transmission** of message describes one-way, linear process in which a sender encodes a message and transmits it through a channel to a receiver who decodes it. The transmission of message may be distrupted by environmental or semantic noise.
- The **Receiver** is the person or organisation to whom the message is sent.
- **Decoding** is the process in which the receiver interprets and understands the message. Sometimes errors in decoding occur if the receiver isn't sure it understands the message but doesn't make the effort to ask for a clarification.
- **Feedback** is the receiver's response to the message. Requesting clarification is part of a good feedback phase of a communication cycle. Without feedback, the communication cycle remains incomplete.

Meaning and Importance of Feedback

Feedback is the final step in the communication cycle. It is the receiver's response to the message, which enables the sender to evaluate the effectiveness of the message sent. Thus, feedback plays a very important role in communication cycle. For example, if the receiver doesn't understand the meaning of the message, the sender can know this by the feedback received and can improve the message accordingly. Thus, the sender must create an environment that encourages feedback.

For instance, after explaining the job to be done by a worker, the supervisor must ask the worker questions such as "Do you understand?", "Do you have any doubts?" etc. At the same time, the supervisor must allow the worker to express his views also.

For the feedback to be effective, it must be clear, well in time, specific, having the right attitude, true and honest, impersonal and informative. It is important because proper feedback helps avoid misunderstandings. Thus, if the receiver has interpreted the message incorrectly, the sender has a chance to correct it. Whether the communication has created the desired effect or not can be determined by analysing the receiver's feedback.

Descriptive Feedback

This form of feedback is most suited to teacher-student interactions when the students are attending a course taught by the teacher. In such a case, it has the specific purpose of helping students improve while they are still gaining knowledge and practising their skills in the subject.

It means that descriptive feedback helps in supporting student development from their current level of achievement. It should make clear to them how to achieve the learning goals of a subject. Descriptive feedback can be written, oral or may even be the response of students to a question while they are working. It is relevant to the task students are performing, and allows them to re-focus and improve their mastery of the subject.

Specific/ Non-specific Feedback

Specific feedback from a teacher to a student provides detailed information about the student's performance on a subject.

For example, a teacher may tell a student, "you wrote the descriptions very well, but your diagrams were made untidily and missed some details." This is specific feedback to the student so as to enable him to improve his performance.

However, a non-specific or generic feedback may be, "you did very poorly in the test" or "you could have done better." Some other examples of specific and non-specific feedback are:

Examples of Specific Feedback	Examples of Non-specific Feedback
I like the way you described your grandfather. It makes me feel like I know him too.	I like your story. It's good.
I like the part where you fell. It made me laugh.	I like your topic. I want to write about that too.
I like the part where you and your sister were fighting. I fight with my brother too.	I like the ending. It was different than I expected.

Check Point 02

1. Which one of the following is not a step in the communication cycle?
   (a) Encoding   (b) Medium   (c) Noise   (d) Feedback
2. Which one of the following is not a medium of communication?
   (a) A verbal conversation   (b) Writing on paper
   (c) The Internet   (d) The telephone
3. Without feedback, the communication cycle remains ....
4. The .... form of feedback is most suited to teacher-student interactions.
5. How do errors in decoding occur in a communication cycle?
6. Why is feedback important in a communication cycle?

Barriers to Communication

Anything that prevents or disturbs the sending or receiving of a communication or message is considered as a barrier to communication. Such barriers can retard or distort the message or intention of the message being conveyed. It may result in failure of the communication process or cause an effect that is undesirable. Speaking louder to drown out the noise is a measure to overcome a barrier to communication.

Types of Barriers

The types of barriers to communication include:

Physical and Environment Based Barriers

These are environmental factors which prevent or reduce the sending and receiving of communications. They include physical distance, distracting noises and similar interferences.

Interpersonal Barriers

They arise from the judgements, emotions and social values of people. They cause a psychological distance between people similar to the physical distance. Thus, sometimes the message may not be understood at all. At other times, part of the communication is only understood. In other cases, the message may be wrongly interpreted.

Our emotions also affect nearly all our communications. For example, if we are feeling angry, we may say something which we would say differently if we were not angry. In such a situation, we are communicating what we are feeling is correct. However, this may not be the case actually. Thus, our emotions affect our communications.

Semantic Barriers

These refer to symbols or visuals used in the message. The barrier may arise due to the symbol we use, as it may mean different things to different people. For example, the 'thumbs up' gesture is recognised as a sign of approval or agreement in European countries, but it may be interpreted as an indecent gesture in rural areas of India.

Symbols are of the following three types:

1. **Linguistic or Related to Language** Language, whether spoken or written, is the most used method of communication. However, a major difficulty with language is that nearly every common word has several meanings, depending on the context in which it is used. In fact, the Oxford Dictionary records an average of 28 separate meanings for each of the 500 most used words in the English language.

2. **Pictures** Organisations make extensive use of pictures such as blueprints, charts, maps, films, three-dimensional models and other similar devices for communication in their normal work, which would otherwise require many words for describing each visual.

3. **Action** A person communicates his intentions and meaning of his communication through his actions.

Intra-Personal Barriers

It refers to the elements within the individuals personality which acts as a barrier in receiving, analysing and interpreting the information that is available. There are different types of intra-personal barriers in an individuals's personality like selective perception, individual differences in communication skills, emotions, preconceived ideas etc.

Factors Causing Barriers

There are a number of factors which may cause the barriers to communication mentioned above. Very often the factors are related to culture, especially if the sender and receiver of the communication belong to different cultures.

Thus, the factors causing barriers to communication include:

- **Poor Planning** Without adequate planning of the message to be sent, the result desired due to the communication may not be achieved. So, we need to properly plan what message we want to send before actually sending it.

- **Mistrust** If the sender and receiver of the communication do not trust each other, it may lead to disbelief of the message sent, causing a barrier.

- **Differences in Meaning/Ambiguity** Sometimes the receiver of the message does not correctly understand the meaning intended by the sender, as the message may have more than one meaning due to being worded in a vague manner.

- **Distortion** Sometimes the message may be distorted by the receiver to suit his own convenience. Although the sender may believe that his message will get the desired action, it may not follow due to the receiver changing it according to his own requirement.

- **Implied Meaning** Some messages have a particular meaning in one culture and a different meaning in another culture. Thus, if such a message is sent by a person in the first culture to a person in the second culture, it will cause a barrier in communication.

- **Noise** As mentioned earlier, noise is added in the channel or medium of communication. Noise can make the communication difficult to be understood. Besides, physical interference, noise can also include illegible handwriting, a poor photocopy, a slow internet connection etc.

- **Absence of Feedback** Feedback is one of the best tool to improve communication, as it ensures that both the sender and the receiver are having a common understanding. If it is absent, a misunderstanding may occur, thus causing a communication barrier.

- **Time and Distance** Time and distance act as barriers to the smooth flow of communication. Use of mobiles, along with computer technology, has made communication very fast. However, technical fault sometime may take these facilities ineffective. In such cases the physical distance between the sender and the receiver becomes a strong barrier. Even where the physical distance does not matter much, such as a closed room a useless seating can also become a barrier to effective communication.

Measures to Overcome Barriers

To ensure that barriers to communication do not arise or can be overcome, we can take some steps related to the factors causing the barriers. The steps to be taken for overcoming some of these factors are:

- **Be Prepared before Communicating** Often we are not properly prepared for communicating a message because we do not have enough information or knowledge of what we want to communicate. At other times, we are not the behaviour expected of the receiver of the communication. Either of these creates a barrier between us and the receiver.

- **Give Sufficient Time** The message should not be communicated too fast; this is particularly true for oral messages. If it is not done at a suitable speed the receiver may miss its important points or may not understand it at all. Thus, oral communication in a group, such as a speech, debate or group discussion, must be done at a measured rate so that the entire audience is able to grasp what is being said.

- **Simplify the Language** Both the sender and receiver of the communication must have sufficient knowledge of the language in which they are communicating. If this is not confirmed, it is better to use simplified language with easily understood words and simple ideas.

- **Don't Assume Anything** Without appropriate feedback, the sender of the message should not assume that his message has been understood. He should only rely on suitable feedback about the understanding of the message.
- **Avoid Overconfidence** Have a humble attitude when communicating a message. Similarly, the receiver should not be egocentric, otherwise he may fail to understand some important points of the message he has received.
- **Preconceived Notions/Expectations, Perceptions and Assumptions** When the receiver has a different perception from that of the sender, communication is affected. This can be overcome by thinking from the speaker's point of view. In addition, if the communication is not clear, the receiver must ask for clarifications instead of assuming anything.
- **Avoid Making Judgements** Communication can fail if the message communicated passes some judgement against the receiver, as then the content of the message is not understood in its real sense. It makes the receiver defensive, thus creating a barrier. So, this kind of situation should be avoided.
- **Respect the Receiver** There should be mutual respect for each other by the sender and the receiver for a message to be successfully communicated. This will motivate each of them to take out some time for the other person.
- **Improve the Attitude** The receiver should not have apathy towards the sender and *vice-versa*, otherwise there will be a breakdown in communication. Important points in the communication may be missed in such a case.
- **Information Overload/ Attention Span** Overload of information or giving too many details reduces the receiver's ability to concentrate on the important parts of the message. It also reduces his attention span. So, the sender must try to eliminate unnecessary information and stick to important information only.

Check Point 03

1. Symbols may be related to which of the following?
   (a) Pictures   (b) Action   (c) Language   (d) All of these
2. Which one of the following is not a factor causing a barrier to communication?
   (a) Wordiness   (b) Physical
   (c) Emotions   (d) Noise in the medium
3. Symbols may reach a person's brain through any of his senses, such as .... or ....
4. Information .... reduces the receiver's ability to concentrate on the important parts of the message.
5. What are the barriers to communication?
6. What are the factors that cause barriers to communication?

Principles of Communication

For a communication to be effective, it must fulfil certain conditions. These basic principles are named in various ways which are easy to remember.

Basic Principles of a Effective Communication

The most basic principle for a communication to be effective is that the intended message of the sender and the interpreted message of the receiver are one and the same. Although this should be the goal in any communication, it is not always achieved. Thus, a set of principles needs to be followed to ensure it. The most popular name of these basic principles is known as 7C's of Effective Communication.

The 7 C's of Effective Communication

We communicate at home, at work, with our neighbour etc. We communicate in written or oral, audio or visual, so it is important that we follow the 7C's of effective communication.

These principles of effective communication are:

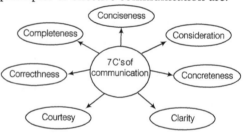

1. **Completeness** The message must be complete, meaning that it should convey all the information required by the receiver. Nothing which may be required by the receiver should be left out of the message. The sender of the message must take into consideration the requirements of the receiver while making the message. For instance, if there is a query by a customer, he must be provided complete information about his query in a short span of time. Your prompt and complete reply will enable you to maintain a good business relation with the customer.

   One way to make your message complete is to answer the five W's: 'Who?', 'What?', 'When?', 'Where?' and 'Why'? The five question method is useful when you write requests, announcements or other informative messages. For instance, to order (request) some items, make clear 'what' you want, 'when' you need it/ them, and 'where' it is to be sent.

2. **Conciseness** It means communicating what you want to convey in the least possible words so that there are no unnecessary bits of information in it. A concise communication is both time-saving as well as cost-saving. It highlights the main message, thus making it more appealing and comprehensible to the audience. For instance, instead of saying 'at this time', we can use the single word 'now'.

3. **Consideration** The sender should have consideration for the receiver of the message while making the communication to be sent. The sender should focus on 'you' instead of 'I' or 'we'. The receiver's viewpoint, background, mindset, culture, educational level etc., should be understood by the sender. Thus, a written message should not be sent to an illiterate person. Similarly, a person who is hearing-impaired should not be conveyed a message orally. Also, the sender must ensure that the tone of the communication should be such that the self-respect of the receiver is maintained and his emotions are not harmed.

4. **Concreteness** It implies being objective and clear, rather than vague, confused or obscure. A concrete message will have specific facts and figures. Thus, for example, if you are a salesperson talking to your client, always use facts and figures instead of generic or irrelevant information. Concrete information makes use of words that are clear. It will build up the reputation of the sender as one who knows what he wants to say. Further, concrete messages are not misinterpreted.

5. **Clarity** It implies emphasising a specific message in a communication instead of trying to cover too many items in one communication. It makes understanding of the message easier by the receiver. Complete clarity of thoughts and ideas enhances the meaning of the message. For achieving complete understanding, the message must make use of exact, appropriate and precise words which are familiar and easy to understand.

6. **Courtesy** A courteous message is politely worded. It implies that the message should use words which show the sender's respect for the receiver. Thus, the sender of the message should be sincerely polite and well-mannered. Knowing the person who you are sending the communication to allow you to use appropriate statements of courtesy. Using socially accepted manners is a form of courtesy. It is politeness that grows out of respect and concern for others. Courtesy implies taking into consideration both the viewpoints as well as the feelings of the receiver.

7. **Correctness** It implies that there are no grammatical, spelling or punctuation errors in the communication being sent. Further, use the level of language appropriate to the status of the receiver. The three levels of language are formal (e.g. Respected Sir), informal (e.g. Hi there!) and sub-standard. Avoid substandard language. Using incorrect words (e.g. 'ain't' for 'isn't'), incorrect grammar, faulty pronunciation etc., all suggest as inability to use good English.

The message should also be sent at the correct time, i.e. it is correctly timed. A correct message has a greater impact on the receiver if the facts and figures mentioned in the communication are also accurate and true.

Check Point 04

1 .... is not one of the 7 C's of effective communication.
   (a) Completeness   (b) Correctness
   (c) Comprehensiveness   (d) Clarity

2 Which one of the following is not one of the five W's whose answers will make a communication complete?
   (a) Where   (b) When   (c) What   (d) Which

3 A .... communication is both time-saving as well as cost-saving.

4 Courtesy implies taking into consideration both the viewpoints as well as the feelings of the ....

5 What is the most basic principle for a communication to be effective?

6 What is an instance of a communication which does not follow the principle of 'Consideration'?

Basic Writing Skills

Writing skills are an important part of communication. Good writing skills allow you to communicate your message clearly and easily to a large audience. You may be asked to write a report, plan or strategy at work; write an application for granting something; or a press release; or a well written CV or résumé; all with no spelling, punctuation or grammatical mistakes. In any of these, poor writing skills create poor first impressions and many readers will have an immediate negative reaction if they spot a spelling or grammatical mistake in what you have written.

So, to ensure that we write correctly, we should understand some basic parts of a document such as **kinds of sentences**, **parts of a sentence**, **parts of speech** and **construction of a paragraph**.

The Sentence

A sentence is a set of words that is complete in itself and which contains a subject and a predicate part. It conveys a statement, question, exclamation or command. It consists of a main clause and sometimes one or more subordinate clauses.

Examples of sentences are:

- Lions roar.
- The house behind my home is the one where you have to go, isn't it?
- What a lovely shot that was!
- Go to the end of the road and turn right.

Kinds of Sentence

There are four types of sentences. These are:

1. **Simple** It consists of an independent clause with no conjunction or dependent clause. For example, kind of sentences "My home has four rooms."
2. **Complex** It contains one independent clause and atleast one dependent clause. For example "Because it was chasing a rabbit, the dog jumped over the fence."
3. **Compound** It contains two independent clauses joined by a conjunction (e.g. and, but, or, as etc.). For example, "My home is very big and it has four rooms."
4. **Compound-complex** It contains more than one independent clause and atleast one dependent clause joined by conjunctions. For example, "The sun is shining now, so I think that we can go for swimming."

Parts of a Sentence

A sentence consists of two parts, a **subject part** and a **predicate part**. Each part of a sentence has a particular function, though sometimes both parts may not be written for it to be complete. The subject refers to that part of the sentence which tells who or what the sentence is about. The subject is a noun, pronoun or noun phrase. Instances of typical sentences with such subjects are:

- Kailash ran across the road.   ('Kailash' is a noun)
- They went to the market.   ('They' is a pronoun)
- The brown dog is sleeping.
  ('The brown dog' is a noun phrase)

The predicate part of a sentence includes the verb and the words that relate to it. It tells what the subject does with an action verb or describes the subject. Predicates can contain much information and may be quite long. Predicates often have several parts in addition to the verb, including objects and complements. Instances of predicates are underlined in the sentences given below:

- The letter <u>contained exciting news.</u>
- The army officers <u>are experienced persons who acquired their experience in the Kargil War.</u>
- I <u>am going to outside and may take some time to return.</u>

Parts of Speech

According to their function in a sentence, words in the English language are classified as different parts of speech. These are disussed below:

- **Noun** It is a word for a person, place, thing or idea. Nouns are sometimes used with an article (the, a, <u>an</u>). Proper nouns always start with a capital letter; common nouns do not. Nouns can be singular or plural, concrete or abstract. Example of nouns are underlined in the sentences given below:
  - The young <u>boy</u> brought me a very long <u>letter</u> from the <u>teacher</u>.
  - He went to <u>Rashid</u> and told him the <u>secret</u> of his happiness.
- **Pronoun** It is a word used in place of a noun. A pronoun is usually substituted for a specific noun, which is called its antecedent. The types of pronouns are personal, possessive, reflexive, relative and demonstrative.

Examples of pronouns are underlined in the sentences given below:

  - Jagdish was in a hurry, so <u>he</u> washed the car <u>himself</u>.
  - <u>He</u> went to Rashid and told <u>him</u> the secret of his happiness.

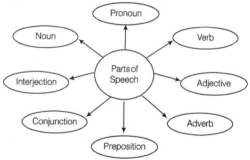

- **Verb** In a sentence, the verb expresses an action or the state of the subject in the sentence. There is a main verb and sometimes one or more helping verbs in a sentence. Verbs also take different forms to express tense. Instances of verbs are underlined in the sentences given below:
  - Jagdish <u>was</u> in a hurry, so he <u>washed</u> the car himself.
  - He <u>went</u> to Rashid and <u>told</u> him the secret of his happiness.
- **Adjective** It is a word used to modify or describe a noun or a pronoun. It usually answers the question of which one, what kind, or how many. Examples of adjectives are underlined in the sentences given below:
  - The <u>young</u> boy brought me a <u>very long</u> letter from the class teacher.
  - I have <u>two large brown</u> dogs in my <u>spacious</u> home.

- **Adverb** It describes or modifies a verb, an adjective, or another adverb, but never a noun. It usually answers the questions of when, where, how, why, under what conditions, or to what degree. Examples of adverbs are underlined in the sentences given below:
  - She laughed <u>loudly</u>.
  - Harish forgot to bring his lunch <u>yesterday</u> and again <u>today</u>.
  - I started running <u>so that</u> I wouldn't be late.
- **Preposition** It is a word placed before a noun or pronoun to link it to another word in the sentence.
  Examples of prepositions are underlined in the sentences given below:
  - The mouse jumped <u>off</u> the table <u>onto</u> the floor <u>of</u> the room.
  - The members <u>of</u> the environment club were standing <u>around</u> the tree <u>in</u> a circle.
- **Conjunction** It joins words, phrases, or clauses and indicates the relationship between them.
  Examples of conjunctions are underlined in the sentences given below:
  - You can have <u>either</u> chocolate <u>or</u> vanilla ice-cream.
  - He <u>not only</u> plays the guitar <u>but also</u> the drums.
  - <u>Such</u> was his strength <u>that</u> he was able to break the chains on his arms.
- **Interjection** It is a word used to express emotion. It is often followed by an exclamation mark.
  Examples of interjections are underlined in the sentences given below:
  - <u>Oh God</u>! I don't know what to do about this mess.
  - <u>Congratulations</u>! So, you have finally got your master's degree.

Articles

An article is a kind of adjective which is always used with a noun and gives some information about it. The words 'a' (used before a word beginning with a consonant sound while speaking) and 'an' (used before a word beginning with a vowel sound while speaking) are called indefinite articles because the noun they go with is indefinite or general. Instances of indefinite articles used in sentences are:

- I will reach home within <u>an</u> hour.
- It is difficult to find <u>a</u> one-rupee currency note in the present day.

The word "the" is known as a definite article because it refers to a specific noun. The difference between the sentences, "I sat on a chair." and "I sat on the chair." is that the second sentence refers to a particular, specific chair, not just any chair.

Whenever we see an article, we will find a noun after it. The noun may be the next word as in "the man" or there may be adjectives and perhaps adverbs between the article and the noun as in "the very angry, young man".

Construction of a Paragraph

A paragraph is a group of sentences dealing with a particular topic. Paragraphs can be of any length and can vary from only one sentence to even more than ten sentences. However, for maintaining clarity, paragraphs should be as short as possible.

For instance, the paragraph you are reading has only four sentences. The first sentence of a paragraph is usually the topic sentence, as it states the main point to be developed or explained in the paragraph. Each sentence following it should be relevant to that topic, giving the paragraph a look of unity.

Each sentence in a paragraph should also be connected to the sentence that comes before it. This can be done by:

- Inserting transition words and phrases such as 'In addition', 'Further', 'Next', 'Finally' etc.
- Repeating key words or their synonyms, such as 'rewriting' may change to 'revising' in the next sentence, 'writer' may change to 'he' in the next sentence, and so on.

An instance of a typical paragraph with comments added in brackets is given below: Good writing comes from hard work (*topic sentence*). But (*transition word*) hard work (*repeating a key word*) has never scared me. In fact (*transition word*), I relish the challenge of creating something new, no matter how difficult (*key word synonym*) or time consuming. I have spent weeks on a few pages, months on an essay, and years on a book (*parallel structure for similar items*).

Check Point 05

1. The sentence "A paragraph has many sentences which are about a single, clearly-defined topic." is a .... sentence.
   (a) simple   (b) complex
   (c) compound   (d) compound-complex

2. In the sentence "He ate the <u>chocolate</u> cake greedily.", the underlined word is a/ an ....
   (a) adjective   (b) adverb
   (c) noun   (d) verb

3. A .... expresses an action or the state of the subject in the sentence.

4. The first sentence of a paragraph is usually the ....

5. What does the subject in a sentence refer to?

6. What questions does an adverb answer?

SUMMARY

- Communication comes in various forms such as verbal, aural, non-verbal, written and visual.
- Good communication skills, both verbal and non-verbal, are essential for working in an organisation.
- Verbal communication consists of oral and written communication.
- Non-verbal communication relies on various non-verbal cues and includes visual communication.
- The main steps in a communication are in the form of a cyclic process, which is completed by a feedback from the receiver of the communication to the sender.
- For the feedback to be effective, it must be clear, well in time, specific, having the right attitude, true and honest, impersonal and informative.
- A barrier to communication is anything that prevents or disturbs the sending or receiving of a communication.
- Barriers to communication may be physical, personal or semantic.
- Barriers to communication can be overcome or will not arise if suitable steps related to the factors causing the barriers are taken.
- To ensure that the intended message of the sender and the interpreted message of the receiver are identical, the principles called 'The 7 C's of Effective Communication' should be followed.
- As writing skills form an important part of communication, we should know what the kinds of sentences are, their parts (subject and predicate) and the parts of speech used in sentences.
- We should also know the construction of a paragraph for our writing to be effective.

Exam Practice

Multiple Choice Questions

1 Aural communication is based on ....
(a) Facial expressions
(b) Listening and Hearing
(c) Body language
(d) Language and tone of voice

Ans. (*b*) Listening and Hearing

2 Visual communication among the people are dependent on ....
(a) Signs, symbols and pictures
(b) Text messages
(c) Posture
(d) Body language

Ans. (*a*) Signs, symbols and pictures

3 _____feedback is specific information, in the form of written comments or verbal conversations that help the learner understand what she or he needs to do in order to improve.   **[CBSE SQP Term-I]**
(a) Descriptive
(b) Specific
(c) General
(d) Sign

Ans. (*a*) Descriptive

4 _____communication is the use of body language, gestures and facial expressions to convey information to others.   **[CBSE SQP Term-I]**
(a) Verbal
(b) Written
(c) Non-verbal
(d) Visual

Ans. (*c*) Non-verbal

5 There are many reasons why interpersonal communications may fail. While communicating, the message may not be received exactly the way, the sender intended and therefore it is important that the communicator seeks .... to check that their message is clearly understood.   **[CBSE 2021 Term-I]**
(a) description
(b) feedback
(c) channel
(d) sign

Ans. (*b*) feedback

6 Which one of the following is not a barrier to effective communication? **[CBSE 2021 Term-I]**
(a) Physical barrier
(b) Linguistic barrier
(c) Interpersonal barrier
(d) Subjective barrier

Ans. (*d*) Subjective barrier

7 It is a word used in place of noun that is ....
(a) Adverb
(b) Verb
(c) Pronoun
(d) Preposition

Ans. (*c*) Pronoun

8 A word used to express emotion and is often followed by an exclaimation mack is called ....
(a) Preposition
(b) Conjunction
(c) Interjection
(d) Adverb

Ans. (*c*) Interjection

9 Which part of sentence contains two independent clauses joined by a conjunction?
(a) Compound Sentences
(b) Simple Sentences
(c) Complex Sentences
(d) Compound-Complex Sentences

Ans. (*a*) Compound Sentences

10 The sentence "The Sun is shining now, so I think that we can go shopping" which of the following types of sentences is this?
(a) Simple
(b) Complex
(c) Compound
(d) Compound-Complex

Ans. (*d*) Compound-Complex

11 .... is an instance of non-verbal communication.
(a) A speech
(b) Proximity
(c) A notice
(d) An e-mail

Ans. (*b*) Proximity

12 Which of the following is the process in which the receiver interprets and understands the message?
(a) Decoding
(b) Encoding
(c) Feedback
(d) None of these

Ans. (*a*) Decoding

13 Speaking louder to drown out the noise is a .... barrier to communication.
(a) type of
(b) factor causing a
(c) measure to overcome a
(d) None of these

Ans. (*c*) measure to overcome a

14 If we take into consideration both the viewpoints as well as the feelings of the receiver of a communication, which of the 7 C's are we fulfilling?

(a) Clarity   (b) Consideration
(c) Courtesy   (d) Correctness

Ans. (*c*) Courtesy

15 The sentence "I am going to outside and may take some time to return." which of the following types of sentence is this?

(a) Simple   (b) Complex
(c) Compound   (d) Compound-complex

Ans. (*c*) Compound

Fill in the Blanks

1 To indicate .... we use a skull placed between two bones put in crosswise fashion.

Ans. danger to human life

2 .... form of feedback is most suited to teacher-student interactions when the students are attending a course taught by the teacher.

Ans. Descriptive

3 A major difficulty with .... is that nearly every common word has several meanings, depending on the .... in which it is used.

Ans. language, context

4 Consideration means that the .... viewpoint, background, mindset, culture, educational level etc., should be understood by the ....

Ans. receiver's, sender

5 The noun for which a pronoun is substituted is called its ....

Ans. antecedent

6 Absence of .... leads to misunderstanding in the communication.

Ans. feedback

7 .... is a word placed before a noun or a pronoun to link it to another word in a sentence.

Ans. Preposition

8 .... is a word that expresses emotion.

Ans. Interjection

True and False

1 Good communication skills are essential for working an organisation.

Ans. True

2 A communication is complete without the feedback.

Ans. False

3 Descriptive form of feedback is suited to teacher-student interactions.

Ans. True

4 Interpersonal barriers did not arise from the judgements, emotions and social values of people.

Ans. False

5 The message should be communicated too fast.

Ans. False

6 The sender must try to eliminate unnecessary information.

Ans. True

7 Concreteness is one of the principle of effective communication.

Ans. True

8 Language is not important for both the sender and receiver of the information.

Ans. False

9 Good writing skills allows you to communicate your message clearly.

Ans. True

10 Pronoun is a word used in place of a Noun.

Ans. True

Very Short Answer (VSA) Type Questions

1 Define verbal communication

Ans. Verbal communication means communication through spoken and written words. It implies use of words which make up a language. It is the ability to communication by using words.

2 Explain the process of decoding.

Ans. Decoding is the process in which the receiver interprets and understands the message. Although sometimes errors in decoding occur if the receiver is not sure in understanding the message.

3 What do you understand by feedback?

Ans. Feedback is the final step in the communication cycle. It is the receiver's response to the message, which enables the sender to evaluate the effectiveness of the message sent.

4 How interpersonal barriers arises?

Ans. Interpersonal barriers arise from the judgements, emotions and social values of people. They cause a psychological distance between people similar to the physical distance.

5 How poor planning act as a barrier to communication?

Ans. Poor planning act as a barrier to communication as without adequate planning the result desired due to the communication may not be achieved. So, we need to properly plan what message we want to send before actually sending it.

6 Describe the principle of completeness of effective communication.

Ans. The principle of completeness implies that the message must be complete, means that it should convey all the information required by the receiver. Nothing which may be required by the receiver should be left out of the message.

7 What does concrete information implies?

Ans. It implies being objective and clear, rather than vague, confused or obscure. A concrete message will have facts and figures instead of irrelevant information.

8 How writing skills are important part of communication?

Ans. Writing skills are important part of communication as good writing skills allow you to communicate your message clearly and easily to a large audience.

9 What does a predicate in a sentence refer to?

Ans. The predicate part of a sentence includes the verb and the words that relate to it. It tells what the subject does with an action verb or describes the subject.

10 What do you mean by specific feedback?

Ans. Specific feedback from a teacher to a student provides detailed information about the student's performance on a subject.

11 During a personal interview, employers are impressed by a job candidate with what qualities?

Ans. During a personal interview, employers are impressed by a job candidate with the qualities of answering questions with more than one-word answers, demonstrating that he is listening and sharing information and ideas by asking questions for clarification and follow-up.

12 Describe what we mean by encoding a message.

Ans. Encoding a message means to change the message into a form suitable for sending. The factors which must be considered when encoding messages are language, cultural differences etc.

13 How should the sender of a communication overcome the barrier of information overload?

Ans. To overcome the barrier of information overload, the sender of a communication must try to eliminate unnecessary information and stick to only important information in the communication.

14 How can the sender of a communication improve its clarity?

Ans. The sender of a communication can improve its clarity by making use of exact, appropriate and precise words which are familiar and easy to understand.

15 What is a compound-complex sentence?

Ans. A compound-complex sentence is one which contains more than one independent clause and atleast one dependent clause joined by conjunctions.

Short Answer (SA) Type Questions

1 Describe the term descriptive feedback.

Ans. Descriptive feedback can be written, oral or may even be the response of students to a question while they are working. It is relevant to the task students are performing, and allows them to re-fours and improve their mastery of the subject. This form of feedback is most suited to teacher-student interactions when the students are attending a course taught by the teacher.

2 What are the factors that causes barriers to communication? Explain any three.

Ans. There are number of factors which may cause the barriers to communication and they are as follows:
(i) **Poor Planning** Without adequate planning of the message to be sent, the result desired due to the communication may not be achieved.
(ii) **Distortion** Sometimes the message may be distorted by the receiver to suit his own convenience.
(iii) **Noise** It can make the communication difficult to be understood. Besides physical interference, noise can also include illegible handwriting, a poor photocopy, a slow internet connection etc.

3 Which measures must be adopted to overcome the factors causing communication barriers?

Ans. Some measures must be adopted to overcome the factors causing communication barriers and these include:
(i) Be prepared before communicating the message to the receiver.
(ii) The message should not be communicated fast so sufficient time must be taken to communicate the message correctly to the receiver.
(iii) It is better to use simplified language with easily understood words and simple ideas.
(iv) There should be mutual respect for each other by the sender and the receiver for a message to be successfully communicated.

4 Explain the principle of conciseness and correctness in detail.

Ans. • **Conciseness** It means communicating what you want to convey in the least possible words so that there are no unnecessary bits of information in it. A concise communication is both time-saving as well as cost-saving. It highlights the main message, thus making it more appealing and comprehensible to the audience.
• **Correctness** It implies that there are no grammatical, spelling or punctuation errors in the communication being sent. The message should also be sent at the correct time. A correct message has a greater impact on the receiver if the facts and figures mentioned in the communication are also accurate and true.

5 What are the various forms of communication? Describe them in one sentence each with examples.

Ans. The various forms of communication are:
(i) **Verbal** This is communication through spoken and written words such as making sounds, using language and changing tone of voice etc.
(ii) **Aural** It is the listening and hearing part of verbal communication, whether it is directly listening to a person, face-to-face, as the audience to a speech in a gathering, on the telephone or hearing a radio or TV programme.
(iii) **Non-verbal** It consists various non-verbal cues such as physical movements, gestures, colours, signs, symbols, body language etc., to express feelings, attitudes or information.
(iv) **Written** It is a medium of communication that involves the written word, such as letters, e-mails, websites, memorandums, reports, notices, manuals, quotations, newsletters and newspapers.
(v) **Visual** It conveys ideas and information in forms that can be seen, such as facial expressions, personal appearance, gesture, posture, printed picture, sign, signal, symbol, map, poster etc.

6 In a communication cycle, explain the term 'medium'. What problems may the medium create and how?

Ans. In a communication cycle, the term 'medium' means the channel through which the message is sent. Some messages are more effective if sent through the medium of being in written form, others may be more effective if given verbally on the telephone, while some others may be more effective if sent *via* the electronic media such as e-mail. The medium may create a problem such as noise, which may interfere with the communication. The noise introduced may cause misunderstanding of the message or even disrupt the message completely so that it is not even received.

7 Describe the three types of barriers to communication in one sentence each with examples.

Ans. The three types of barriers to communication are:
(i) **Physical** These are environmental factors which prevent or reduce the sending and receiving of communications, such as physical distance, distracting noises and similar interferences.
(ii) **Personal** These cause a psychological distance between people similar to the physical distance, as they include judgements, emotions and social values of people, which change or distort the communication.
(iii) **Semantic** These barriers refer to symbols or visuals used in the message, such as those related to languages, pictures and actions.

8 Which principle of effective communication is covered by the five question method? List three aspects of this principle which need to be covered by these questions.

Ans. The communication principle of 'Completeness' is covered by the five question method. Three aspects of this principle which need to be covered by these questions are:

(i) The message should convey all the information required by the receiver.

(ii) Nothing which may be required by the receiver should be left out of the message.

(iii) The sender of the message must take into consideration the requirements of the receiver while making the message.

9 Describe, by giving some examples of each, the following three parts of speech: pronoun, adverb and conjunction.

Ans. The three parts of speech are described below:

(i) **Pronoun** It is usually substituted for a specific noun, which is called its antecedent, such as he, yourself, we, my etc. The types of pronouns are personal, possessive, reflexive, relative and demonstrative.

(ii) **Adverb** It describes or modifies a verb, an adjective, or another adverb, but never a noun. Instances of adverbs are loudly, yesterday, fast, slowly etc. It usually answers the questions of when, where, how, why, under what conditions, or to what degree.

(iii) **Conjunction** It joins words, phrases, or clauses and indicates the relationship between them. Instances of conjunctions are and, but or etc.

Long Answer (LA) Type Questions

1 Explain the communication cycle briefly.

Ans. The main steps in a communication are in the form of a cyclic process and these are explained below:

• The First step is initiated by the communicator or sender or organisation originating the communication. It decides what the message is, how it will be expressed and sent and who it is to be sent to.

• The Second step is encoding which means to change the message into a form suitable for sending. The factors which must be considered when a encoding messages are cultural differences etc.

• The Third step is the message that is the actual information that the sender wishes to convey to the receiver.

• The Fourth step is the medium or channel by which the message is sent. Some messages are more effective in written form, others may be more effective on the telephone. Noise introduced by a communication medium is anything that interferes with the communication.

• Another step includes the receiver who is the person or organisation to whom the message is sent.

• Decoding is another step in the process in which the receiver interprets and understands the message. Sometimes errors in the decoding occurs if the receiver is not sure in understanding the message.

• The Last step is the feedback means receiver's response to the message. Requesting clarification is a part of good feedback phase of communication cycle. Without feedback, the communication remains incomplete.

2 What are the eight parts of speech? Give one example of each.

Ans. According to their function in a sentence, words in English language are classified into the following eight parts of speech:

(i) **Noun** It is a word for a person, place, thing or idea. Nouns are sometimes used with an article (the, a, an). Nouns can be singular or plural, concrete or abstract. e.g. The young **girl** brought me a very long **letter** from the **teacher**.

(ii) **Pronoun** It is a word used in place of a noun. A pronoun is usually substituted for a specific noun, which is called its antecedent. The types of pronouns are personal, possessive, reflexive, relative and demonstrative. e.g. Rashmi was in a hurry, so **she** washed the car **herself**.

(iii) **Verb** In a sentence, the verb expresses an action or the state of the subject in the sentence. There is a main verb and sometimes one or more helping verbs in a sentence. Verbs also take different forms to express tense. e.g. She **was** driving the car.

(iv) **Adjective** It is a word used to modify or describe a noun or pronoun. It usually answers the question of which one, what kind or how many. e.g. Riya is a **beautiful** girl.

(v) **Adverb** It describes or modifies a verb, an adjective, or another adverb, but never a noun. It usually answers the questions of when, where, how, why, under what conditions or to what degree. e.g. She laughed **loudly**.

(vi) **Preposition** It is a word placed before a noun or pronoun to link it to another word in the sentence. e.g. The mouse jumped **off** the table.

(vii) **Conjunction** It joins words, phrases or clauses and indicates the relationship between them. e.g. You can have **either** chocolate **or** ice-cream.

(viii) **Interjection** It is a word used to express emotion. It is often followed by an exclaimation mark. e.g. **Well**, I don't know.

Self Assessment

Multiple Choice Questions

1. .... is an instance of visual communication.
   - (a) An e-mail
   - (b) A speech
   - (c) Eye contact
   - (d) Bar chart

2. Which of the following is not a factor causing a barrier in oral communication?
   - (a) Preconceived notions
   - (b) Physical hearing problem
   - (c) Emotions
   - (d) Semantics

Fill in the Blanks

3. Requesting clarification is part of a good .... phase of a communication cycle.

4. .... of a message implies that there are no grammatical, spelling or punctuation errors in the communication being sent.

True/False

5. Non-verbal communication does not occur without using any written or oral word.

6. Feedback is essential to complete the cycle of communication.

Very Short Answer (VSA) Type Questions

7. What is a semantic barrier to communication?

8. What is the function of an adjective in a sentence?

Short Answer (SA) Type Questions

9. Explain the difference between specific feedback and non-specific feedback by giving examples of each.

10. Write a typical paragraph containing five sentences on the topic 'The power of money' which fulfils all the requirements of a good paragraph.

Long Answer (LA) Type Questions

11. Explain the types of barriers to effective communication in detail.

12. Explain the principles of effective communication is detail.

Self Management Skills-II

Stress and Its Management

Stress is identified as a condition in which a person is tensed and worried. It can affect both our body and our mind. People having large amounts of stress can become tired, sick and unable to concentrate or think clearly. Sometimes they even suffer mental breakdown or what is called 'burn out'.

Stress is our body's way of responding to any kind of demand. Stress can cause symptoms such as cold hands or feet, tenseness, increased sweating, a nervous stomach, a dry mouth etc. These are all short-term symptoms of stress. It can be caused by both good and bad experiences.

When people feel stressed by something going on around them, their bodies react by releasing chemicals into the blood. These chemicals give more energy and strength, which can be a good thing if their stress is caused by physical danger but it can also be a bad thing, if the stress is in response to something emotional and there is no outlet for this extra energy and strength. The good stress is called 'eustress', whereas the bad stress is termed as 'distress'.

Types of Stress

Stress can result due to a stimulus from external factors such as the environment and social factors or internal factors such as fatigue, emotions or illness.

On the basis of the stimulus, stress may be classified into four different types:

1. Survival Stress

It is a common response to danger in all people and animals. When you are afraid that someone or something may physically hurt you, your body automatically responds with a burst of energy so that you will be better able to survive the dangerous situation (i.e. fight) or escape it altogether (i.e. flight). This is termed as the 'fight-or-flight response'.

2. Internal Stress

It generates within the human regarding the unreasonable matters. This internal stress is one of the most important kinds of stress to understand and manage because it keeps on building up as time passes. For example, some people become used to the kind of hurried, tense, lifestyle of persons living in large cities. They even look for stressful situations and feel stress about matters which may not be stressful at all. This stress affects our work performance adversely. Internal stress is a result of unexpressed worries.

3. Environmental Stress

It is a response to happenings around us that cause stress, such as noise, pollution, crowding, pressure of work, family tensions etc. Some of these may be under our control if we try to control them, whereas some may not be controllable by us. Identifying these environmental stresses and learning to avoid them or deal with them will help lower our stress level.

4. Fatigue Related Stress

This kind of stress builds up over a long time like by working too long or too hard at our job, school or home. It can also be caused by exercising too much or too long.

If you do not know how to manage your time well or how to take time out for rest and relaxation, you will become a victim of fatigue related stress. This can be one of the hardest kinds of stresses to avoid because many people feel that it is out of their control.

Identifying Stress

Stress management consists of a wide variety of techniques used for controlling or reducing a person's level of stress, especially chronic stress. It usually helps to improve everyday functioning. To manage stress successfully, we should first understand what causes stress in us and what its symptoms are.

Some ways to find out our stress level are:

- **The Alarm Response** The body responds to a stressful situation by pumping adrenalin so that the muscles become tense and the heart rate increases. Mostly, this causes distress, although we can also respond calmly to such situations. Everyone is different, with their unique reactions to events. There is no single level of stress that is optimal for all people. Some are more sensitive than others due to experiences in childhood, the influence of teachers, parents, religion etc.
- **Identifying Symptoms of Stress** Sometimes we fail to identify symptoms of stress in us because we have been adjusted to live with the stress for a long time. However, to manage stress effectively, we must be able to identify the various signs of stress in us when we observe them.

- **Causes of Stress** The type of personality determines to a large extent what causes stress in us. For example, if we are overambitious and set an unrealistically high goal for ourselves in any activity we undertake, we will definitely become likely to have a stress related physical problem. Other persons, who do not set such high goals, will achieve their goals. Thus, they will not have any stress related problems.
- **Personal Signs of Stress** We must understand our own personal signs of stress if we have to manage our stress. Some such signs may be too much sweating, shivering, biting your nails, lack of concentration, poor judgement, constant worrying etc.

Management of Stress

With proper planning and use of the right techniques, stress can be reduced or managed to remain within tolerable limits. These techniques have been well-known from quite some time and involve disciplined exercising as well as various relaxation techniques. They are shown in the diagram below:

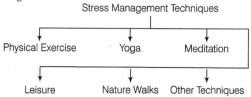

- **Physical Exercise** It is an activity done to achieve physical fitness and overall health. It improves blood circulation, lowers blood pressure, clears the mind of worrying thoughts, improves our self-image, makes us feel better about ourselves and increases social contact. It also has some direct stress-busting benefits which pumps up endorphins-chemicals in the brain that act as a natural pain killers. It also improves the ability to sleep which in trun reduces stress.
- **Yoga** Yoga is a mind-body practice that combines physical poses, controlled breathing and meditation or relaxation. It will help in stress management by relaxing the body and mind, develop a connection between the mind and the body, releasing emotional energy and helping to breathe more effectively.
- **Meditation** In meditation, we change from our normal activities to silence. We go beyond the noisy thoughts in the mind and enter a state of restful alertness. During meditation, although we are in a state of deep rest, our mind is fully alert and awake. At this time, the body experiences many healing effects which are the reverse of the 'fight-or-flight' response, such as decreased heart rate, normalisation of blood pressure, deeper breathing, reduced production of stress hormones, higher immunity, more efficient use of oxygen by the body and reduced inflammation.

- **Leisure** This means spending holidays with your family and friends, travelling to other areas in the country or outside and any other similar activities. Leisure gives you the benefits of enabling you to indulge in your interests or hobbies, gives you a 'break' from stress, provides an outlet for relief and also provides social contact.

- **Nature Walks** It means walking in the local park or similar such activity. These walks may be done more than once a day for short periods of time during which we indulge in 'thought-stopping', i.e. not to think about our day-to-day activities. Such an activity will help us to avoid 'burn out', promote adequate sleep, ease muscle tension and decrease mental worries.

- **Other Techniques** These include getting adequate sleep, which is a good stress reducer. When we wake refreshed after a night's sleep, we have adequate day time energy. Progressive relaxation and contraction of the body parts will effectively reduce tension, lower the blood pressure, combat fatigue, promote sleep, reduce pain, ease muscle tension, decrease mental worries and also increase productivity, concentration and clear thinking.

1. Worrying about matters we can do nothing about or worrying for no reason at all is a sign of .... stress.
   (a) survival   (b) internal
   (c) environmental   (d) fatigue related

2. Spending holidays with our family and friends to manage stress may be called as a .... activity.
   (a) nature walk   (b) relaxation
   (c) leisure   (d) None of these

3. Stress can be caused by both .... and .... experiences.

4. Too much sweating, shivering, biting your nails etc., are .... signs of stress.

Ability to Work Independently

One of the abilities that we require to develop in us is that of working independently. For doing this, we have to become a self-aware, self-motivated and self-regulating independent person.

A good way to start becoming independent is by carefully thinking about our own learning style. We should find out whether

- We prefer working independently or we need a more structured environment to work efficiently.
- We are self-motivated or we need regular feedback in order to make progress in our work.
- We work best at our own pace or we need to be prodded by others to work faster.
- We know what it means to be independent.

Necessary Skills for Independent Working

From the above, we can understand that some skills are required for developing an independent working style. These are:

- Becoming self-aware, self-monitoring and self-correcting.
- Knowing what we need to do.
- Taking the initiative rather than waiting to be told what to do.
- Doing what is asked to the best of our ability, without the need for external prodding and working until the job is completed.
- Learning to work at a pace that we can sustain for a long time.
- Taking ownership of our mistakes without looking for excuses.
- Refusing to let self-doubt or negative emotions due to negative past experiences take us away from the task.

Thus, the key to being independent is our self-awareness, self-motivation and self-regulation.

Self-awareness and Its Types

Self-awareness refers to our knowledge and understanding of ourselves. It includes our emotions, beliefs, assumptions, biases, knowledge base, abilities, motivations, interests etc., So, we should make a conscious effort to learn about ourselves, i.e. our abilities, beliefs, likes and dislikes. The feeling of self-awareness enhances our self-confidence.

There are four kinds of self-awareness. These are:

1. **About Your Strengths** To find out your strengths, find out what you like to do, what you are enthusiastic about doing and what work done by you is given good comments by others.

2. **About Your Weaknesses** If you know what you find difficult to do or cannot do, you can ask other people to help you in that task. Otherwise you can remove this weakness by learning that particular task.

3. **About Your Flaws** You should not hide your flaws but take other people's help in overcoming them.

4. **About Your Emotional Problems** A typical emotional problem is getting angry on small matters. Such emotional problems in your character should be kept under control when some incident triggers them.

Some useful questions to think about in this regard are:

- Do I enjoy working in the workshop/ laboratory or in an office?
- Do I enjoy explaining my work? How? Orally, in writing, or in both ways?
- Do I like working with others as a member of a team or do I prefer to work by myself?
- Am I a good listener?
- Can I handle disagreement with another person?
- Do I like to go into a problem deeply?
- Do I see the 'big picture' or the overall meaning of any matter?
- Do I prefer to work on short-term projects (lasting a few days) or long-term projects?
- Do I enjoy using tools and equipment? What kinds?
- Do I enjoy using computers and/or software?
- Do I enjoy travel? Can I speak one or more foreign languages conversationally? Can I read in another language?
- Am I self-motivated? Or do I require external prompts in order to meet deadlines and/or achieve results?

Our answers to these questions will help identify our skill sets, interests, career paths and what motivates us.

Self-motivation

Self-motivation refers to your ability to identify effective methods of making yourself move from thinking about something to taking action about it. Everyone is different. Some individuals are highly self-motivated while others require external deadlines or some type of reward or penalty in order to move from thought to action. Identifying your specific needs in this area is the first step.

A common barrier to action is often the perception that a task is too large or too complex to accomplish. If that is an issue for you, then a useful practice is to break down the job into several smaller and easier tasks, each of which can be accomplished in a set time period.

Self-regulation

Self-regulation focuses on your ability to influence personal and professional improvement based on your self-awareness and motivation. Useful questions you should ask yourself in an effort to self-regulate yourself are:

- Who will directly supervise or guide in my project? With what frequency (daily, weekly etc.)?
- What are the deadlines, if any, relevant to my project?
- What are the requirements, if any, for my project? These might include progress reports, oral presentations, a final written report or any other documents?
- What are the outcomes that I desire from my participation in this project? What, if anything, do I need to do in order to achieve these outcomes?

Check Point 02

1. Which one of the following is not a necessary skill for independent working?
   (a) Taking ownership of our mistakes
   (b) Becoming self-monitoring
   (c) Becoming self-aware
   (d) Need for supervision

2. Which one of the following is not a kind of self-awareness?
   (a) Knowing your weaknesses   (b) Knowing your relatives
   (c) Knowing your flaws   (d) Knowing your strengths

3. We should not hide our .... but take other people's .... in overcoming them.

4. What is the key to be able to work independently?

SUMMARY

- Stress is our body's way of responding to any kind of demand and can be caused by both good and bad experiences.
- Stress may be classified into four different types: survival, internal, environmental and fatigue related.
- We can identify our stress level by our alarm response, the symptoms, causes and personal signs.
- Stress can be managed by physical exercise, practices of yoga and meditation, leisure time, nature walks and other techniques.
- We need to cultivate in us the ability of working independently by becoming a self-aware, self-motivated and self-regulating person.
- Self-awareness means our knowledge and understanding of our strengths, weaknesses, flaws and emotions.
- Self-motivation is our ability to identify effective methods of making ourselves move from thinking about something to taking action about it.
- Self-regulation is our ability to influence personal and professional improvement based on our self-awareness and motivation.

Exam Practice

Multiple Choice Questions

1 Stress is identified as a condition in which a person is ....
(a) tensed
(b) worried
(c) relaxed
(d) Both (a) and (b)

Ans. (*d*) Both (a) and (b)

2 Which type of stress is termed as 'fight or flight response'?
(a) Environmental
(b) Survival
(c) Internal
(d) Fatigue related

Ans. (*b*) Survival

3 Internal stress is a result of
(a) pent-up worries
(b) laziness
(c) survival stress
(d) experiences

Ans. (*a*) pent-up worries

4 Physical exercise is used as a stress management technique because
(a) it improves blood circulation
(b) improves self-image
(c) makes us feel better
(d) All of the above

Ans. (*d*) All of the above

5 Self-awareness refers to
(a) our knowledge and understanding of ourselves
(b) systematic efforts to direct thoughts and actions
(c) ability to identify effective methods to move from thought to action.
(d) None of the above

Ans. (*a*) our knowledge and understanding of ourselves

6 Sonika gets up at 6 am and goes for her hobby classes. Then, she comes back home and finishes her homework before going to school. She does all work by herself. No one tells her to do so. This is called _____. **[CBSE SQP Term-I]**
(a) self-awareness
(b) self-motivation
(c) self-regulation
(d) discipline

Ans. (*b*) self-motivation

7 To perform well at work and life in general, you must be able to manage and improve yourself in various skills. Which of the following skills helps you to prioritise the things you have to do remove waste and redundancy from work? **[CBSE 2021 Term-I]**
(a) Responsibility
(b) Time management
(c) Self-awareness
(d) Adaptability

Ans. (*b*) Time management

8 Managing stress is about making a plan to be able to cope effectively with daily pressures. Always keep in mind the ABC of stress management. The acronym ABC stands for **[CBSE 2021 Term-I]**
(a) Ability, Burden, Concise
(b) Adore, Belief, Cause
(c) Adversity, Beliefs, Consequences
(d) Adapt, Balance, Cooperate

Ans. (*c*) Adversity, Beliefs, Consequences

9 Which one of the following is not a symptom of stress?
(a) Increased sweating
(b) Dry mouth
(c) Cold hands or feet
(d) None of these

Ans. (*d*) None of these

10 If we worry about matters we can do nothing about or we are worrying for no reason at all, we are having ....
(a) environmental stress
(b) eustress
(c) distress
(d) internal stress

Ans. (*d*) internal stress

11 We have the ability to work independently if we ....
(a) need regular feedback to make progress in our work
(b) work best at our own pace
(c) need a structured environment to work efficiently
(d) need to be prodded to work faster

Ans. (*b*) work best at our own pace

12 High expectations from self can leave one with chronic anxiety and stress, thus leading to _____ stress. **[CBSE SQP Term-I]**
(a) physical
(b) emotional
(c) mental
(d) financial

Ans. (*c*) mental

Fill in the Blanks

1 The .... responds to a stressful situation by pumping adrenalin so that the muscles become tense and the heart rate increases.

Ans. body

2 .... means that we do not think about our day-to-day activities during a nature walk.

Ans. 'Thought-stopping'

3 Self-awareness about our .... problems means that we know the drawbacks in our character which should be kept under control when some incident triggers them.

Ans. emotional

4 For improving our self-awareness, we may ourselves the question, "Do I like working with others as a member of a .... or do I prefer to work by .... ?"

Ans. team, myself

5 .... are chemicals in the brain that act as a pain killers.

Ans. Endorphins

6 With proper .... and use of right .... stress can be reduced or managed.

Ans. planning, techniques

True and False

1 Stress can effect both our mind and body.

Ans. True

2 Fatigue related stress builds up over a long time and can take a toll on our body.

Ans. True

3 Meditation is not helpful as a stress management technique.

Ans. False

4 We must not take ownership of our mistakes and look for excuses.

Ans. False

5 Self-regulation focuses on your ability to influence personal and professional improvement based on your self-awareness and motivation.

Ans. True

Very Short Answer (VSA) Type Questions

1 What happens when people have large amounts of stress?

Ans. People having large amounts of stress can become tired, sick and unable to concentrate clearly. Sometimes they even suffer from mental breakdown.

2 What is environmental stress?

Ans. It is a response to happenings around us that cause stress such as noise, pollution, crowding, pressure of work, family tensions etc.

3 What are the symptoms of stress?

Ans. Stress can cause symptoms such as cold hands or feet, tenseness, increased sweating, day mouth etc. These are all short-term symptoms of stress.

4 How leisure activities benefits in stress management?

Ans. Leisure gives the benefits by enabling a person to indulge in his/her interests, hobbies, gives them a break and provides an outlet for relief.

5 How can a person manage stress?

Ans. With proper planning and use of the right techniques, stress can be reduced or managed to remain within tolerable limits.

6 How human body responds to a stressful situation?

Ans. The human body responds to a stressful situation by pumping adrenalin so that the muscles become tense and the heart rate increases.

7 What are the personal signs of stress?

Ans. We must understand our own personal signs of stress and some signs may be too much sweating, shivering, biting nails, lack of concentration, poor judgement, constant worrying etc.

8 What is survival stress?

Ans. Survival stress is a common response to danger in all people and animals. When you are afraid that someone or something may physically hurt you, your body automatically responds with a burst of energy so that you will be better able to survive the dangerous situation or escape it altogether.

9 How does the practice of yoga help in stress management?

Ans. The practice of yoga helps in stress management by relaxing the body and mind, developing a connection between the mind and the body, releasing emotional energy and helping to breathe more effectively.

10 How can we become self-aware about our strengths?

Ans. We can become self-aware about our strengths by finding out what we like to do, what we are enthusiastic about doing and what work done by us is given good comments by others.

11 What should we do when we become aware of our flaws?

Ans. When we become aware of our flaws, we should not hide them, but take other people's help in overcoming them.

Short Answer (SA) Type Questions

1 How stress can be caused by both good and bad experiences?

Ans. Stress can be caused by both good and bad experiences like when people feel stressed by something going on around them, their bodies react by releasing chemicals into the blood. These chemicals give more energy and strength, which can be a good thing if their stress is caused by physical danger but it can also be a bad thing, if the stress is in response to something emotional and there is no outlet for this extra energy and strength. The good stress is called eustress, whereas the bad stress is termed as distress.

2 Why is self-regulation important in life?

Ans. Self-regulation is important in life due to following reasons:
  (i) Self-regulation allows you to keep a tab on your own emotions.
  (ii) Self-regulation enables to develop the idea about 'what is appropriate behaviour' and 'what is inappropriate behaviour' in a given social condition.
  (iii) It helps in controlling negative impulses and reciprocate emotions for actualising set goals.

3 What are the four kinds of self-awareness?

Ans. These are the four kinds of self-awareness are:
  (i) **Self-awareness about your Strengths** To find out your strenghts, find out what you like to do what you are enthusiastic about doing and what work done by you is given good comments by others.
  (ii) **Self-awareness about your Weaknesses** If you know what you find difficult to do or cannot do, you can take help from other people in that task. Otherwise you can remove this weakness by learning that particular task.

  (iii) **Self-awareness about your Flaws** you should not hide your flaws but take other people's help in overcoming them.
  (iv) **Self-awareness about your Erosional Problems** Emotional problems in your character should be kept under control when some incident triggers them.

4 What is fatigue related stress? Why is it difficult to avoid?

Ans. Fatigue related stress builds up over a long time and can take a heavy toll on our body. It is caused by working too long or too hard at our job, school or home. It can also be caused by exercising too much or too long. If you do not know how to manage your time well or how to take time out for rest and relaxation, you will become a victim of fatigue related stress. It is difficult to avoid because many people feel that it is out of their control.

5 What happens during meditation that makes it a useful technique for managing stress?

Ans. During meditation, we change from our normal activities to silence. We go beyond the noisy thoughts in the mind and enter a state of restful alertness, thus reducing stress. At this time, although we are in a state of deep rest, our mind is fully alert and awake. Thus, the body experiences many healing effects which are the reverse of the 'fight-or-flight' response, such as decreased heart rate, normalisation of blood pressure, deeper breathing, reduced production of stress hormones, higher immunity, more efficient use of oxygen by the body and reduced inflammation. All these changes in body function help in managing stress effectively.

6 What are the skills necessary for independent working? List any six.

Ans. The skills necessary for independent working are:
  (i) Becoming self-aware, self-monitoring and self-correcting.

(ii) Knowing what we need to do.

(iii) Taking the initiative rather than waiting to be told what to do.

(iv) Doing what is asked to the best of our ability, without the need for external prodding, and working until the job is completed.

(v) Learning to work at a pace that we can sustain for a long time.

(vi) Taking ownership of our mistakes without looking for excuses.

(vii) Refusing to let self-doubt or negative emotions due to negative past experiences take us away from the task. *(any six)*

7 How can we self-motivate ourselves for completing a task which appears to be too large or too complex to be done by us?

Ans. For completing a task which appears to be too large or too complex to be done by us, we can break down the job into several smaller and easier tasks, each of which can be accomplished in a set time period. This is possible only through self-motivating ourselves to find a workable solution to the task, as self-motivation is our ability to identify effective methods of thinking about something to taking action about it. Breaking down the job into smaller tasks comprises the thinking part, whereas accomplishing each small part of the task comprises the 'taking action' part.

Long Answer (LA) Type Questions

1 Explain the four types of stress in detail.

Ans. Stress can result due to stimulus from external factors such as environment and social factors or internal factors such as fatigue, emotions or illness.

On the basis of stimulus, stress may be classified into four types:

(i) **Survival Stress** When you are afraid that someone may physically hurt you, your body automatically responds with a burst of energy so that you will be better able to survive the dangerous situation or escape it altogether. This is known as Survival Stress.

(ii) **Internal Stress** It generates within the human regarding the unreasonable matters. This internal stress is one of the most important kind of stress to understand and manage because it keeps on building up as time passes.

(iii) **Environmental Stress** It is a response to happenings around us that cause stress such as noise, pollution, family tensions, etc. Some of these may be under our control if we try to control them, whereas some may not be controllable by us.

(iv) **Fatigue Related Stress** This kind of stress builds up over a long time. It can be caused by working too long or too hard at our job. It can also be caused by exercising too much or too long. If a person does not know how to manage his time well then he will become a victim of fatigue related stress.

2 What are the techniques that are used to manage stress?

Ans. Following are the techniques that are used to manage stress and they are as follows :

(i) **Physical Exercise** It is an activity done to achieve physical fitness to and overall health. It improves blood circulation, lowers the blood pressure, clears the mind of worrying thoughts, improves our self-image and makes us feel better about ourselves.

(ii) **Yoga** It helps in relaxing mind and body by developing a connection between the mind and body, releasing emotional energy and helping to breathe more effectively.

(iii) **Meditation** During meditation, although we are in a state of deep rest, our mind is fully alert and awake. At this time, body experiences many healing effects which are reverse of 'fight or flight' response, such as decreased heart rate, reduced production of stress hormones, higher immunity and reduced inflammation.

(iv) **Leisure** This means spending holidays with your family and friends. Leisure gives you benefits of enabling you to indulge in your interests or hobbies, gives you a break from stress, provides an outlet for relief and also provides social contact.

(v) **Nature Walks** It means walking in the park. These walks may be done more than once a day for a short period of time during which we do not think about our day-to-day activities during the nature walk. It promotes adequate sleep, ease muscle tension and decrease mental worries.

(vi) **Other Techniques** These include getting adequate sleep, which is a good stress reducer when we wake refreshed after a night's sleep, we have adequate daytime energy. Progressive relaxation and contraction of the body parts will effectively reduce tension, lower the blood pressure, combat fatigue, decrease mental worries etc.

Self Assessment

Multiple Choice Questions

1. Which one of the following is not a leisure activity?
   (a) Getting adequate sleep
   (b) Spending holidays with family and friends
   (c) Travelling to other areas
   (d) Indulging in your interests or hobbies

2. Which of the following skills are not required for developing an independent working style?
   (a) Taking ownership of our mistakes
   (b) Waiting to be told what to do
   (c) Knowing what we need to do
   (d) Learning to work at a sustainable pace

Fill in the Blanks

3. If done regularly, ... uses up excess energy released by the 'fight or flight' reaction and improves blood circulation.

4. Some individuals are highly .... while others require external deadlines or some type of reward or penalty.

True/False

5. People should hide their flaws to overcome any situation.

6. Environmental stress is a response to happenings around us.

Very Short Answer (VSA) Type Questions

7. What changes in the body does progressive relaxation and contraction of the body parts bring?

8. What is the first step in getting self-motivated?

Short Answer (SA) Type Questions

9. How is environmental stress different from internal stress? Explain two such differences.

10. What are the questions we should ask ourselves if we want to self-regulate ourselves? List three such questions.

Long Answer (LA) Type Questions

11. What are the necessary skills required for independent working?

12. How can we identify stress? Explain.

Basic ICT Skills-II

Word Processor

A word processor is a computer program used to create and print text documents. It is an application that allows to type in, edit, format, save and print text. The key advantage of a word processor is its ability to make changes easily such as correcting spelling, adding, deleting, formatting and relocating text.

The software packages that are helpful to learn about word processing are Microsoft Word, Open Office Writer, Corel WordPerfect, Apple Pages and Google Docs (Internet based).

These word processors are the ones most used by computer users. Out of these packages, **Open Office Writer** is open source and free distributed software. **Google Docs** is also free to use but is Internet based.

Opening and Exiting Word Processor

To open MS Word following steps must be followed:

- Click on **Start** button.
- Click on **All Programs** option.
- Click on **Microsoft Office**.
- Click on **Microsoft Office Word 2007**.

After these steps, the MS Word 2007 will be show on your computer.

To exit from MS Word, we can follow these steps:

Go to **Office** button
↓
Exit-Word
Or

Press **Close** button which is rightmost of title bar. If the open file is saved for its latest changes, the file will close immediately, thus closing word with it. Otherwise, the software will complain that the file is not saved for its latest changes.

Creating a Document

To create a new blank document following steps must be followed :

- Click on **Microsoft Office** button.
- Select **New**. The new document dialog box will appear.
- Select **Blank document** under the Blank and recent section. It will be highlighted by default.

- Click **Create**. A new blank document will appear in the word window.

Saving a Document

If you want to save the text being typed in, you may do so by just pressing **Ctrl + S** or you can follow the steps below:

- Click **Office** button in the top left-hand corner of the screen.
- From the menu, choose **Save**.
- Save the document with a suitable **File Name**.

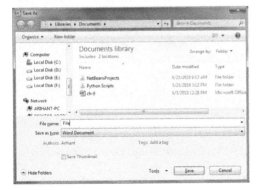

- Once you have typed in the name of a document, click **Save**.

The first time you save the file, you must give it some name, 'Save' or 'Save As' is capable of saving a file with a name. In the 'Save As' menu, you can save an existing document under another name. This is helpful if you have made changes to your document and then want to save the changes, but also keeps the original document in its original format and under its original name.

Features of Word Processor

Following are the features of word processor that are discussed below :

- **Creating a Table** To insert a table, following steps are followed :
  - Click on **Insert** tab.
  - Click on **Table** drop-down from **Tables** group.

  - Click on the cell corresponding to the dimensions of the table you want to add.
- **Text Editing** Word has ability to change text by adding, deleting and rearranging letters, words, sentences and paragraphs. Text editing is the main function or feature that users perform in word processor, which typically also handle graphics and multimedia files.
- **Word Wrap** Word wrap is a word processing feature that forces all text to be confined within defined margins.
- **Alignment** It is a term used to describe how text is placed on the screen in relation to the margins. There are four types of alignments possible in word that are :

  - **Left Align** The text is aligned with the left margin.
    - **Right Align** The text is aligned with the right margin.
    - **Center Align** The text is equally aligned on either side of the central vertical line.
    - **Justify** The text is aligned to both of left and right margins.

You may apply any alignment of the text using the **Home** tab → **Paragraph** group.

- **Font Size, Type and Face** The style with which letters will show up refers to a font. Text can be bold, italic or underlined in word. Follow these steps to make any kind of font change on the text :
  - Highlight the text that needs the font change to be effected.
  - Press the appropriate key from the **Home** tab → **Font** group.

  Other way to change around the font exists. It is :
  - Press the appropriate button for font change.
  - Type in the text which be all in the changed font.

- **Password Protection** It is possible to password protected the document, so the steps are:
  - Click on **Office** button.
  - Click on **Prepare** option.
  - Click on **Encrypt Document** button.
  - Encrypt Document dialog box will appear. Enter **Password** in password text box and press **OK** button.

  In order to remove the password from the file, follow these steps:
  - Click on **Office** button.
  - Click on **Info** option.
  - Click on **Protect Document** button.
  - Click on **Encrypt with Password**.
  - **Remove** the Password.

- **Printing the Document** In order to print the file follow these steps:
  - Click on **Office** button.
  - Click on **Print** option.
  - From the **Preview and Print** the document, choose option as required by you.
  - Click on **Print** button.

  The keyboard shortcut is **Ctrl+P** that will open up the Print window on the word screen.

- **Page Numbering** A page number can be affixed to every page of the document. This feature can be accessed through the **Insert** tab → **Header & Footer** group.

- **Header and Footer** A header is the top margin of each page and a footer is the bottom margin of each page. They are useful in large number of documents. To insert a header or footer, follow these steps :
- Select the **Insert** button.
- Click either **Header & Footer** command. A drop-down menu will appear.
- From the drop-down menu, select **Blank** to insert a blank header & footer, or choose one of the built-in options.
- The Design Tab will appear on the ribbon and the Header & Footer will appear in the document.

- **Autocorrect** It is an automatic data validation function commonly found in word processors and text editing interfaces. It is a useful tool in word for applying specific formatting or spelling for certain phrases often in your text. This feature will quickly fix the mis-spelling words and punctuation marks. To use Autocorrect, follow the below steps :
  - Click on **Review** tab → **Proofing** group.
  - Click on **Spelling & Grammar** option. Spelling and Grammar dialog box will appear.

- **Bullet and Numbering** Bullets and Numbering is a paragraph level attribute that applies a bullet character or a numeral to the start of the paragraph.

- **Find and Replace** Find and Replace helps you to find words or formats in a document and can let you replace all instances of a word or format. To use find and replace, use the shortcut **Ctrl +H** or navigate to editing in the Home tab of the ribbon, then choose Replace. The keyboard shortcut **Ctrl+F** can open up the find dialog box.

Note *You can know more about MS-Word in Chapter-2 Part B.*

Check Point 01

1 Which of the following software packages in word processing are Internet based?
  (a) Microsoft Word
  (b) Google Docs
  (c) Open Office Writer
  (d) Corel Word Perfect

2 In which type of alignment text is aligned to both of left and right margins?
  (a) Left   (b) Right
  (c) Justify   (d) Center

3 A word processor is a computer program used to .... and text documents.

4 Header is the .... margin of each page.

5 How can we insert Header or Footer in a word document?

Spreadsheet Application

Spreadsheet is a software application capable of organising, storing and analysing data in tabular form. It has multiple interacting sheets with data represented in text, numeric or in graphic form. Spreadsheet software is also known as a 'spreadsheet program' or 'spreadsheet application'.

Calculation and functionalities are easier to represent in spreadsheets than in word processors and thus, effective data handling is possible. Some of the applications apart from Excel are : OpenOffice Calc, Lotus 1-2-3, Gnumeric, WPS Office.

MS Excel

MS Excel can perform formula-based calculations and many other mathematical functions.

Creating a New Worksheet

To launch MS Excel 2007, click **Start** button → **All Programs** option → **Microsoft Office** → **Microsoft Office Excel 2007.**

After the given steps, a blank worksheet will open up.

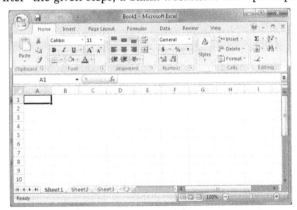

There are commands that can be used to add more worksheets to the workbook. Clicking on the **Insert worksheet** button to add a worksheet.

To open the workbook just double-click the file associated with the workbook and the workbook will be launched.

To enter the data into the worksheet, just click into any cell and start typing. If the active cell of the spreadsheet does not have the insertion pointer visible, just press F2 key.

Features of MS Excel

- **Resizing Fonts and Styles** To resize fonts and styles click on **Home** tab → **Font** group. Another method to change the font is :
  - Select all the cells or text you want to change.
  - Click on the required font buttons to change the attributes for the selected text.

    To resize the worksheet, you can use **Zoom** option as well.

- **Copying and Moving** Copying means to make a duplicate of a file. Moving means to remove the original text from its position and paste on another place. The shortcut key for copy is **Ctrl + C**, for cut is **Ctrl + X** and for paste is **Ctrl + V.**

- If you want to know how to copy or move without shortcuts, use the **Home tab** → **Clipboard** group. There are Copy, Cut and Paste commands in the group as mentioned.

- **Filter and Sorting** An important feature of Excel is to filter the data. The simplest filter of Excel is the **Filter** and other filter available is the **Advanced Filter**. In Advanced Filter, detailed rules are specified as a part of spreadsheet cells. Filters can be used in Excel to retain some particular records as visible on the Excel sheet.

  Sorting basically helps in arrangement of data in the correct order. The sort commands are part of the **Data** tab → **Sort and Filter** group of Excel.

  To sort the data you must select the entire data that you want to sort.

- **Formulas and Functions** Formula always start with an **equal to** sign (=).

  Functions on the other hand are pre-defined formulas in Excel. Both Formulas and Functions make the tasks easier. Like for instance, if you have entered numbers in adjacent cells as, 4, 5, 6, 7, 9, 11, 15, 21. You can easily calculate the sum of all these cells by

  = SUM (A1 : A8)

- **Password Protection** To set the password basically is to restrict access to particular workbook following steps are there:
  - Go to **Office** button → **Info** option.
  - Go to **Protect Document** button.
  - From drop-down menu, choose to click on **Encrypt with Password.**
  - A dialog box to enter the password will be opened.
  - Re-enter the password after the first time and click **OK.**

- **Printing a Spreadsheet** The steps of printing a spreadsheet are as follows :
  - Click on **Office button** Tab.
  - Click on **Print** option.
  - Print Interface opens up to choose Print settings.
  - Click on **Print** button. The spreadsheet gets printed.
- **Saving Spreadsheet in Various Formats** To save workbook, the steps are :
  - Click on **Office** button.
  - Click on **Save As** option.
  - From the **Save As** dialog box, click on **Save as type** and choose from one of many options to save the file.

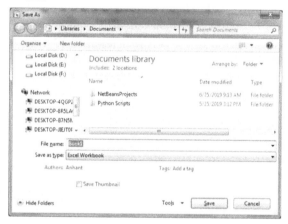

  - Choose the location for the file to be saved in from the left pane, if required.
  - Give some name to the file and click on **Save** button.

Note *You can know more about MS-Excel in Part B Chapter-3.*

Check Point 02

1 Which of the following shortcut key is used for pasting?
   (a) Ctrl + X   (b) Ctrl + V
   (c) Ctrl + C   (d) Ctrl + U
2 Which key is pressed if the active cell of the spreadsheet does not have the insertion pointer visible?
   (a) F1   (b) F3
   (c) F2   (d) F4
3 .... and .... are easier to represent in spreadsheets.
4 Formula always start with a/an .... sign.

Presentation Software

Presentation software is important for school, college or office purposes. It can animate all the elements that are part of a slide, like the text, pictures, figures, shapes, smart art etc. Apart from this, we may perform transition from slide to slide, with special effects as it is the part of the software.

There are some presentation softwares available and these include OpenOffice Impress, Keynote, Corel Presentations, SoftMaker Presentations.

We can create slides and display them as a part of slideshow in all these softwares. A new presentation can be created by launching **PowerPoint** or by pressing New from the Office button.

Features of Presentation Software

- **Entering and Editing Data** In MS PowerPoint software 2007 you have to insert text box in the slide to enter text. Inserting pictures do not need you to add text box and they provide the inserted picture with the placeholder. The File can be modified from slide to slide.
- **Adding a Slide** The shortcut key for adding a slide is **Ctrl + M** whereas another method of doing this is:
  - Click on **Home** tab, if not already on this tab.
  - Click on **New Slide** from slides group and choose the type of slide.
- **Deleting a Slide** Make the slide to be deleted the active slide and press **Delete** key from the keyboard. We may press **Ctrl + Z** to undo the action of deletion of slide.
- **Formatting Text**
  - **Select** the text you want to format.
  - Press any of the buttons from font group of **Home** tab.
    Or
  - **Home** tab → **Paragraph** group.
- **Inserting Clip Art and Images** For adding pictures in the presentation, we may use the Clip Art Gallery. We may also insert picture located on the computer into any slide.
  To insert the Clip Art the steps are:
  - Click on **Insert** tab.
  - Click on **Clip Art** command from **Illustrations** group.
  - Right pane of the screen opens in yours search criteria for image.
  - Click on **Go**.
  - Right-click on an image and click on **Insert** or **Copy**.

The steps to insert a picture from the computer into a slide are:

- Click on **Insert** tab → **Illustrations** group → **Picture** command.
- A dialog box will open. Navigate to the folder where the picture to be inserted resides.
- Select the picture and click on **Insert**.

- **Slide Layout** It is the arrangement of elements on the slide with which the slide is available. The slide is available in various layouts.
- **Slide Transition and Custom Animation** Slide transition is one of the effects of PowerPoint presentation. When one slide changes into other, a transition may show up if you have applied one. This effect is known as Slide Transition.

The Custom Animation command is a part of the Animations tab in PowerPoint 2007. Using the **Animations** tab → **Animations** group, various animation effects can be applied to the elements of a slide.

- **Saving and Printing a Presentation** The keyboard shortcut key is **Ctrl + S** to save the file while to save an existing file being worked on, click on **Save As** from **Office** button.
- The shortcut key for printing the presentation is **Ctrl + P**, it is capable of opening the **Print** Interface of MS PowerPoint 2007.

Note *You can know more about MS-PowerPoint in Part B Chapter-4.*

Check Point 03

1 By clicking inside the text part in a slide, you can prepare to:
  (a) edit text (b) insert clipart
  (c) insert image (d) None of these
2 The shortcut key for adding the slide is
  (a) Ctrl + M (b) Ctrl+Z
  (c) Ctrl+ X (d) Ctrl +V
3 .... is used to undo the action of deletion of file.
4 The slide layout is the .... on the slide.
5 What do you mean by Slide Transition?

SUMMARY

- A word processor is a computer program used to create and print text document.
- MS-Word, Open Office Writer, Corel WordPerfect, Apple Pages and Goole Docs ar the examples of Word Processor.
- Word Wrap is a word processing feature that forces all text to be confined within defined margins.
- A Header is the top margin of each page and a Footer is the bottom margin of each page.
- Spreadsheet software is a software application capable of organising, storing and analysing data in tabular form.
- MS-Excel, Open Office Calc, Lotus 1-2-3, Gnumeric and WPS Office are the examples of Spreadsheet software.
- MS-Excel can perform formula-base calculations and many other mathematical functions.
- Sorting basically helps in arrangement of data in the correct order.
- Presentation software can animate all the elements that are part of a slide, like the text, pictures, figures, shapes, smart art etc.
- MS-PowerPoint, Open Office Impress, Keynote, Corel Presentation, Softmaker Presentations are the examples of Presentation Softwares.
- Slide layout is the arrangement of elements on the slide with which the slide is available.

Exam Practice

$$\boxed{\textbf{Multiple Choice } \text{Questions}}$$

1 Which of the following software packages of word processing is not a part of it?
(a) Corel Word Perfect   (b) Open Office Writer
(c) Lotus 1-2-3   (d) Google Docs

Ans. (c) Lotus 1-2-3 is a Spreadsheet software

2 If a table has to be created which tab and group should be used?
(a) Insert tab → Tables group
(b) Home tab → Tables group
(c) Design tab → Tables group
(d) None of the above

Ans. (a) Insert tab → Tables group is used to create table in MS Word.

3 Text editing refers to
(a) word processing feature forces all text to be confined within defined margins.
(b) ability to change text by adding, deleting, rearranging the matter.
(c) the style with which letters will show up.
(d) used to describe how text is placed on the screen in relation to margins.

Ans. (b) Text editing refers to the ability to change text by adding, deleting, rearranging the matter.

4 How many types of alignment are possible in MS Word?
(a) 2   (b) 4   (c) 3   (d) 5

Ans. (b) 4 alignments are possible in MS Word as Left, Right, justify and center.

5 The shortcut key to replace the data is
(a) Ctrl + F   (b) Ctrl + H   (c) Ctrl+ V (d) Ctrl+ Z

Ans. (b) Ctrl + H

6 The keyboard shortcut to open up a find dialog box is
(a) Ctrl+V   (b) Ctrl+H   (c) Ctrl+F   (d) Ctrl+Z

Ans. (c) Ctrl + F

7 Lotus 1-2-3 and WPS Office are part of ....
(a) Word Processing
(b) Presentation Software
(c) Spreadsheet Software
(d) None of the above

Ans. (c) Lotus 1-2-3, Gnumeric, WPS Office etc., are a part of Spreadsheet Software.

8 Which of the following shortcut keys is used to cut?
(a) Ctrl+X   (b) Ctrl +Z   (c) Ctrl+V (d) Ctrl +C

Ans. (a) Ctrl + X

9 Which key is used to delete a slide in presentation?
(a) Backspace key   (b) Enter key
(c) Delete key   (d) Spacebar key

Ans. (c) Delete key

10 What is the shortcut to open the Print Interface for any Office tool?
(a) Ctrl+C   (b) Ctrl+P   (c) Ctrl+R (d) Ctrl+H

Ans. (b) Ctrl + P

11 A _____ operating system is a computing environment that reacts to input within a specific period of time. **[CBSE SQP Term-I]**
(a) single user   (b) multi-user
(c) real time   (d) distribute

Ans. (c) real time

12 Identify the measure to protect computer from threats and viruses. **[CBSE SQP Term-I]**
(a) Sharing password with friends
(b) Allow anyone to use your device
(c) Use Antivirus
(d) Leave computer without logging out

Ans. (c) Use Antivirus

13 Neha is receiving several mails from companies who are advertising a product or trying to attract her to their websites. Such type of mails are called ....
[CBSE 2021 Term-I]
(a) advertising mails   (b) bulk mails
(c) spam mails   (d) labelled mails

Ans. (c) spam mails

14 A computer automatically runs a basic program called .... as soon as it is switched ON or the power button is pushed ON.
[CBSE 2021 Term-I]
(a) BIOS (Basic Input/Output System)
(b) IOS (Input/Output System)
(c) BOSS (Basic On System Startup)
(d) POS (Power On System)

Ans. (a) BIOS (Basic Input/Output System)

Fill in the Blanks

1 .... is an open source and free distributed word processor.

Ans. Open Office Writer

2 The style with which letters will show up refers to a ....

Ans. font

3 Footer is the .... margin of each page.

Ans. bottom

4 Spreadsheet software is also knows as ....

Ans. spreadsheet program

5 Data handling is easier in ....

Ans. spreadsheets

6 MS Excel can perform .... calculations.

Ans. formula-based

7 The simplest filter of Excel is the ....

Ans. Filter

8 Password basically .... access to particular file.

Ans. restrict

9 Open Office Impress and Keynote are ....

Ans. presentation softwares

10 .... can be used for adding pictures in the presentation.

Ans. Clip Art Gallery

True and False

1 Google Docs is free to use but is Internet based.

Ans. True

2 Page number can be affixed to alternate page of the document.

Ans. False

3 Header & Footer command is available in Review tab.

Ans. False

4 In advanced filter, detailed rules are specified as a part of Spreadsheet cells.

Ans. True

5 Presentation software is important for school, college or office purposes.

Ans. True

6 Slide is not available in various layouts.

Ans. False

Very Short Answer (VSA) Type Questions

1 Define word wrap.

Ans. Word wrap is a word processing feature that forces all text to be confined within defined margins.

2 Define alignment.

Ans. Alignment is a term used to describe how text is placed on the screen in relation to the margins.

3 What do you mean by Autocorrect?

Ans. Autocorrect is an automatic data validation function commonly found in word processors and text editing interfaces.

4 Define copying.

Ans. Copying means to make a duplicate of a document or file.

5 Define moving.

Ans. Moving means to remove the original text from its position and paste an another place.

6 Why filters are used in MS Excel?

Ans. Filters can be used in Excel to retain some particular records as visible on the Excel sheet.

7 What do you mean by sorting?

Ans. Sorting basically helps in arrangement of data in the correct order.

8 How a new presentation can be created?

Ans. A new presentation can be created by launching PowerPoint or by pressing New from the Office button.

9 What do you understand by the term slide layout?

Ans. The slide layout is the arrangement of elements on the slide with which the slide is available.

Short Answer (SA) Type Questions

1 Explain the role of text editing in MS Word.

Ans. Text editing plays a significant role in MS Word as it has the ability to change the text by adding, deleting, rearranging letters, sentences and paragraphs. Text editing is the main feature that users perform in word processor which typically also handle graphics and multimedia files.

2 What are the alignments available in a word document?

Ans. In a word document, there are four types of alignments which are used to describe how text is placed on the screen in relation to the margins. These are the types of alignments :
- **Left Align** The text is aligned with the left margin.
- **Right Align** The text is aligned with the right margin.
- **Center Align** The text is equally aligned on either side of central vertical line.
- **Justify** The text is aligned to both of left and right margins.

3 Define formulas and functions.

Ans. Refer to text on Page no. 31.

4 What are the steps of saving spreadsheet in various formats?

Ans. The steps of saving spreadsheet in various formats are discussed below:
- First click on Office button.
- Click on Save As option.
- From the Save As dialog box, click on Save As type and choose from one of many options to save the file.
- Choose the location for the file to be saved in from the left pane, if required.
- Give same name to the file and click on Save.

5 What are the distinct features of presentation software?

Ans. The distinct features of presentation software are as follows:
- **Inserting Clip Art and Images** In the presentation software, we can add pictures with the help of Clip Art gallery. We may also insert picture located on the computer into any slide.
- **Slide Transition** It is one of the effects of PowerPoint Presentation. When one slide changes into other, a transition may show up if you have applied one.
- **Custom Animation** The custom animation command is a part of the Animations tab in PowerPoint 2007. Various animation effects can be applied to the elements of a slide.

Long Answer (LA) Type Questions

1 Explain the features of word processor in detail.

Ans. The features of word processor are discussed below:
- **Inserting Table** This feature is available across all the software part of the MS Office 2007. In MS Word, it is inserted on the document quite easily. A table of the chosen dimensions will be added to the document.
- **Text Editing** It is the main feature that users perform in word processor which typically also handle graphics and multimedia files.
- **Word Wrap** It is a word processing feature that forces all text to be confined within defined margins.
- **Header and Footer** A Header is the top margin of each page and a Footer is the bottom margin of each page. They are useful in large number of documents.
- **Autocorrect** It is an automatic data validation function commonly found in word processors and text editing interfaces.
- **Bullets and Numbering** Bullets and Numbering is a paragraph level attribute that applies as bullet character or a numeral to the start of a paragraph.
- **Find and Replace** It helps you to find words or formats in a document and can let you replace all instances of a word or format.

2 Explain the features of spreadsheet application or MS Excel in detail.

Ans. The features of spreadsheet application or MS Excel are as follows:
- **Filter and Sorting** An important feature of MS Excel is to filter the data. The simplest filter of Excel is the filter and other is Advanced Filter. In Advanced Filter, detailed rules are specified as a part of spreadsheet cells. Sorting helps in arrangement of data in the correct order. To sort the data we must select the entire data that we want to sort.
- **Formulas and Functions** Formula always starts with an equal to sign (=). It is one of the distinct feature of MS Excel. Functions on the other hand are pre-defined formulas in Excel. Both formula and functions make the tasks easier.
- **Resizing Fonts and Styles** To resize fonts and styles, click on Home Tab → Font Group. The method of modifying the font attributes is identical to that in word. Another way of resizing the worksheet is part of the status bar called Zoom option. Using this control, you may zoom the size of the cells in the worksheet.

Self Assessment

Multiple Choice Questions

1. Apple Pages is an example of
   (a) Word processor
   (b) Spreadsheet
   (c) Presentation
   (d) None of these

2. Which of the following is not a presentation software?
   (a) Key note
   (b) Impress
   (c) Corel presentation
   (d) Gnumeric

Fill in the Blanks

3. .... can be bold, italic or underlined in word.

4. To enter the data into the ...., just click into any cell and start typing.

True/False

5. Filters can be used in presentation.

6. A new presentation can be created by launching PowerPoint.

Very Short Answer (VSA) Type Questions

7. How to open MS Word?

8. Write the steps to print Spreadsheet.

Short Answer (SA) Type Questions

9. How can you Save and Print a presentation?

10. Define Find and Replace command in Word.

Long Answer (LA) Type Question

11. Explain the presentation software in detail.

Entrepreneurial Skills-II

Entrepreneur

- The word 'entrepreneur' is derived from the French word '*entrepreneur*' which means to undertake. An entrepreneur is an individual who creates a new business, bearing most of the risks and enjoying most of the rewards.
- According to Howard W. Johnson, "Entrepreneur is composite of these basic elements i.e. invention, innovation and adaptation".
- The term entrepreneurship refers to the functions performed by an entrepreneur. It is the process involving various actions to be undertaken by the entrepreneur in establishing a new enterprise.
- According to Joseph Schumpter, "Entrepreneurs as innovators, who use the process of entrepreneurship to shatter the status quo of the existing products and services, to set new products, new services."

Entrepreneurship and Society

Entrepreneurship is affected by economic opportunities and gains as the Entrepreneur lives in a society. Entrepreneurs promote investment, increase in production, bring competitiveness in business, reduce costs of products, and raise the standard of living in society :

Characteristics/Quality of Entrepreneur

For the successful enterprise, it is important to understand the characteristics/quality of successful entrepreneurs and it is described below :

- **Leadership** An entrepreneur must possess the characteristics of leadership and must lead a team for achievement of goals. The leader is able to clearly articulate their ideas and has a clear vision. An entrepreneurial leader realises the importance of initiative and reactiveness and they go out of their way to provide a support to the team.
- **Risk Taking** An entrepreneur with rational planning and firm decisions bear the risks. They have differentiated approach towards risks. Good entrepreneurs are always ready to invest their time and money but they always have a back up for every risk they take.

- **Innovativeness** With the changing needs and requirements of customers production should meet requirements with the help of innovative ideas. An entrepreneurial venture does not have to restrict itself to just one innovation or even one type of innovation. Success can be built on combination of innovation for example, a new product delivered in a new way with a new message.
- **Goal-oriented** Goal-oriented entrepreneurs achieve the maximum results from their efforts in business due to the fact they work towards clear and measurable targets.
- **Decision-Maker** An entrepreneur has to take many decisions to put his business idea into reality. He chooses the best suitable and profitable alternative.
- **Highly Optimistic** A successful entrepreneur is always optimistic and the present problems does not matter to them. He is always hopeful that the situation will became favourable for business in future.
- **Motivator** An entrepreneur has to create a spirit of team work and motivate them. So that he gets full cooperation from the employees.
- **Self-confident** An entrepreneur should have confidence to achieve his goals otherwise he won't be able to convince his team to achieve his goals.
- **Action-oriented** An entrepreneur should have an action oriented vision and ideology to plan things well.
- **Dynamic Agent** An entrepreneur creates new needs and new means to satisfy them. He has the ability to visualise new ventures and new plans.
- **High Achiever** An entrepreneurs are high achievers as they have a strong urge to achieve. The most important characteristic is his achievement motivation.
- **Trust in Self** An entrepreneur believes on their own decisions and actions as he has trust in his perseverance and creations. He does not believe in luck.

Functions of an Entrepreneur

The various functions of an entrepreneur are as follows :

- **Innovation** It includes introducing new products, opening new markets, new sources of raw material and new organisation structure.
- **Risk-Taking** An entrepreneur has to take risk by choosing one among various alternatives.
- **Decision-Making** It includes stabilising organisation's aims and objectives and changing them according to changing conditions, taking decisions on effective techniques, utilisation of financial resources etc. So, decision-making is an important function of an entrepreneur.

- **Organisation and Management** An entrepreneur organise and manage various economic and human factors through planning, coordination, control, supervision and direction.
- **Size and Scale of Business Unit** An entrepreneur has to decide about the size of business unit as he wants to establish one production unit or more dependent upon the demand of the product. Similarly, he has to decide about scale of production i.e. small scale, middle scale or large scale.
- **Appointment of Managerial and Other Work Force** It is the entrepreneur who appoints the management staff as well as other work force as per the requirement and needs of the enterprise.
- **Factors of Production** The factors of production i.e. land, labour, capital etc., should be in appropriate proportion and to maximise output of these factors is the responsibility of the entrepreneur.
- **Control and Direction** He must exercise control over all departments and direct them on a timely basis.
- **Finding Suitable Market** A proper research must be done to find a suitable market for selling the products. Other functions like advertisement and publicity, appointment of selling agents, providing incentives to various selling intermediaries to promote sales should be given priority.
- **New Inventions and Innovations** New inventions and innovations must be encouraged and introduced in production, sales, marketing, advertisement etc.
- **Establishing Relations with Government** An entrepreneur must establish good relations with government and its functionaries. His functions are to obtain licences, payment of taxes, selling the product to government, provision for export-import etc.
- **Establishing Contacts with Competitors** An entrepreneur must form contacts with the competitors to analyse the market. He must be in a position to make opportunities out of the given situation.

Role and Significance of Entrepreneurs

The role and significance of entrepreneurs are as follows :

- **Organiser of Society's Productive Resources** An entrepreneur is the organiser of society's productive resources. He is the person who assembles the unused natural, physical and human resources of the society, combines them as properly, establishes effective coordination between them and makes the economic activities dynamic.

- **Helpful in Capital Formation** An entrepreneur is helpful in capital formation as we know that increase in the rate of capital formation is quite essential for the economic development of any country. Those nations which are not able to increase the rate of capital formation or does it nominally remain backward from industrial development's point of view.

- **Increase in Employment Opportunities** An entrepreneur creates maximum employment opportunities in the society by way of establishing new industries, developing and expanding the existing industries and by undertaking innovative activities.

- **Development of New Production Techniques** An entrepreneur does not feel contended only with the existing techniques of production. Hence, he carries out various experiments for saving time, labour and capital in the production, as also to improve the variety and quality of the product and service.

- **Visionary Leader** An entrepreneur has a good vision towards the achievement of his goals. He is able to recognise profitable opportunities and conceptualise strategies.

- **Contribution of the Execution of Government Policies** An entrepreneur provide an important contribution in implementing government policies and achieving the national goals. An entrepreneurs cooperate with the government for implementations of development plans of the country.

- **Higher Productivity** Entrepreneur have the ability to produce more goods and services with less inputs. They play an important role in raising productivity.

- **Initiator** An entrepreneur is the one who initiates the process of creating an enterprise by coming up with the idea for the business and planning out how to turn that idea into reality.

- **Risk Taker** In an enterprise, an entrepreneur, being the owner, is the biggest risk taker. He is the one who finds the capital to back up his idea and also the person who is accountable in the face of the failure of that particular idea.

- **Backbone of Capitalist System** Capitalist economy is one in which there is a freedom to save and invest to compete and operate any business. An entrepreneur plays a vital and prominent role in the enterprise because he controls market by assuming the role of a competitor and a leader.

- **Ingredient of Modern Production System** An entrepreneur has become the 'balancing wheel' of modern global economy. They seek the unique product, change the technical frontiers and reshape public desires. Today, entrepreneurs act as an ingredient of modern production system as they create wealth and employment.

Myths of Entrepreneurship

Entrepreneurship is a set of activities performed by the entrepreneur. It is the process of identifying opportunities in the market place. It is the attempt to create value. Many entrepreneurs believe a set of myths about entrepreneurship and the most common are as follows :

- **Starting a Business is Easy** In reality, it is a very difficult and challenging process to start a successful business. The rate of failure of new ventures is very high but small entrepreneurships are comparatively easier to start.

- **Lot of Money to Finance New Business** Successful entrepreneurs design their business with little cash also.

- **Start up's cannot be Financed** Under the schemes like MUDRA, entrepreneurs can raise loans from banks.

- **Talent is More Important than Industry** This is not true as the nature of industry an entrepreneur chooses greatly effects the success and growth of the business.

- **Most Start up's are Successful** Mostly in the developing countries start up's fail as they could not manage to earn high profits.

Advantages of Entrepreneurship

The main advantages of adopting entrepreneurship as a career are discussed below :

- **Independence** An entrepreneur is himself a boss or owner and he can take all the decisions independently.

- **Exciting** Entrepreneurship can be very exciting with many entrepreneurs considering their ventures highly enjoyable. Everyday will be filled with new opportunities to challenge your determination, skills and abilities.

- **Wealth Creation** The principal focus of entrepreneurship is wealth creation and improved livelihood by means of making available goods and services. Entrepreneurial venture generates new wealth, new and improved products, services or technology form entrepreneurs, enable new markets to be developed and new wealth to be created.

- **Flexibility** As an entrepreneur you can schedule your work hours around other commitments, including quality time you would spend with your family.

- **Status** Success in entrepreneurship beings a considerable fame and prestige within the society.

- **Ambition-fulfilment** Through entrepreneurship one can fulfil his ambitions into original products or services.

Disadvantages of Entrepreneurship

Some of the disadvantages of entrepreneurship are as follows :

- **Huge Amount of Time** You have to dedicate a huge amount of time to your own business. Entrepreneurship is not easy and for it to be successful, you have to take a level of time commitment.
- **Risk** An entrepreneurship involves high risk of loss. If the business fails then it will wipe away all the personal savings.
- **Hard Work** An entrepreneur has to work very hard to make the new business very successful.
- **Uncertain Income** There is no regular or fixed income available to an entrepreneur. So, there is uncertain kind of income received by an entrepreneur.

- **Incompetent Staff** A new entrepreneur may not be able to hire qualified and experienced staff so there are chances of incompetency by the staff due to lack of experience and knowledge.

Check Point 01

1 Which of this is not a quality of successful entrepreneur?
(a) Leadership   (b) Motivator
(c) Goal-oriented   (d) Irrational

2 Which of the following is not the advantage of entrepreneurship?
(a) Status   (b) Independence
(c) Flexibility   (d) Huge amount of time

3 An entrepreneur should have an .... vision.

4 Entrepreneur must .... a team for achievement of goals.

SUMMARY

- Entrepreneurs are innovators who use the process of entrepreneurship to shatter the status quo of the existing products and services, to set new products, new services.
- Successful entrepreneurs are imbibed with certain characteristics such as leadership, innovativeness, goal-oriented, decision-maker, risk-taker, optimistic etc.
- An entrepreneur performs important functions which includes decision-making, risk taking, organisation, management, appointment of work force, control, direction etc.
- An entrepreneur plays a significant role as she/he is the organiser of society's productive resources, develops new production techniques, visionary leader, contributes to the execution of government policies, helpful in capital formation etc.
- Adoption of entrepreneurship as a career is beneficial as it provides independence, flexibility, promotes wealth creation, exciting, builds status and fulfil ambitions.
- Entrepreneurship is non-beneficial also due to huge amount of time, risk, hardwork, uncertain income and incompetent staff.

Exam Practice

Multiple Choice Questions

1 Innovation of an entrepreneur includes
(a) division of work
(b) opening new markets
(c) introducing new products
(d) Both (b) and (c)

Ans. (*d*) Both (b) and (c)

2 To find a suitable market an entrepreneur performs the functions of
(a) advertisement and publicity
(b) appointment of selling agents
(c) new organisation structure
(d) Both (a) and (b)

Ans. (*d*) Both (a) and (b)

3 Incompetent staff means
(a) experienced staff
(b) qualified staff
(c) not experienced and qualified
(d) None of the above

Ans. (*c*) not experienced and qualified

4 Which of the following is a disadvantage of entrepreneurship as a career?
(a) Uncertainty   (b) Independence
(c) Ambition fulfilment   (d) None of these

Ans. (*a*) Uncertainty

5 In which situation an entrepreneur will not be able to convince his fellow beings to achieve his goals?
(a) Low self-confidence
(b) Innovativeness
(c) Risk-taking
(d) None of these

Ans. (*a*) Low self-confidence

6 How can entrepreneur can get the work done from his/her team?
(a) By creating a spirit of teamwork
(b) By motivation
(c) Using harsh words and actions
(d) Both (a) and (b)

Ans. (*d*) Both (a) and (b)

Fill in the Blanks

1 New .... and .... must be encouraged and introduced in production.

Ans. invention, innovation

2 A proper .... must be done to find a suitable market for selling the products.

Ans. research

3 An entrepreneur is the .... of society's productive resources.

Ans. organiser

4 The entrepreneur creates maximum .... opportunities in the society.

Ans. employment

5 .... describes entrepreneurs as innovators.

Ans. Joseph Schumpter

6 An entrepreneur requires .... and .... to bear the market risk.

Ans. rational planning, firm decisions

7 Entrepreneurs create .... and .... in the society.

Ans. wealth, employment

8 An entrepreneur has to take many .... to put his business idea into ....

Ans. decisions, reality

True and False

1 Leadership qualities are not mandatory for a successful leader.

Ans. False

2 Innovation is necessary for entrepreneurship.

Ans. True

3 New development techniques will benefit the quality of the product.

Ans. True

4 Talent is more important than industry.

Ans. False

5 Leadership and goal oriented are the qualities of good entrepreneur.

Ans. True

Very Short Answer (VSA) Type Questions

1 Define an entrepreneur.

Ans. An entrepreneur is someone who perceives opportunity, organises resources needed for exploiting that opportunity and exploits it.

2 Give any one quality of a successful entrepreneur.

Ans. Leadership is one quality of an entrepreneur. An entrepreneur is essentially a leader. Entrepreneurs are people who exhibit qualities of leadership in solving problems. They have to lead a team for achievement of goals.

3 Name the term used for a false belief or opinion about something.

Ans. Myth is the term used for a false belief or opinion about something. There are many myths about entrepreneurship. It is a myth that 'it is easy to start a business', 'Startups cannot borrow from bank and many more'.

4 How decision-making is an important function of an entrepreneur?

Ans. Decision-making is an important function because it includes stabilising organisation's aims and objectives and changes them according to the changing conditions.

5 How an entrepreneur acts as a visionary leader?

Ans. Entrepreneur acts as a visionary leader as he is able to recognise profitable opportunities and successfully conceptualise strategies according to it.

6 What is the contribution of the entrepreneurs in the execution of Government policies?

Ans. The entrepreneurs provide an important contribution in implementing government policies and achieving the national goals. They cooperate with the government for implementations of development plans of the country.

Short Answer (SA) Type Questions

1 Explain any three characteristics or qualities of an entrepreneur.

Ans. The characteristics of successful entrepreneurs are as follows
  (i) **Leadership** An entrepreneur must posses the characteristics of leadership and must lead a team for achievement of goals. The leader is able to clearly articulate their ideas and has a clear vision.
  (ii) **Innovativeness** With the changing needs and requirements of customers production should meet requirements with the help in innovative ideas. An entrepreneur does not have to restrict itself to just one innovation rather he must use combination of innovation.
  (iii) **Decision Maker** An entrepreneur has to take many decisions to put his business idea into reality. He chooses the best suitable and profitable alternative.

2 What are the functions of an entrepreneur? Write any three.

Ans. The functions of an entrepreneur are as follows:
  (i) **Organisation and Management** An entrepreneur organises and manages various economic and human factors through planning, coordination, control, supervision and direction.
  (ii) **Size and Scale of Business Unit** An entrepreneur has to decide about the size of business unit as he wants to establish one production unit or more dependent upon the demand of the product. Similarly, he has to decide about scale of production i.e. Small Scale, Middle Scale or Large Scale.
  (iii) **Factors of Production** Another important function of an entrepreneur is the factors of production i.e. land, labour, capital etc., should be in right proportion and

to maximise output of these factors is the responsibility of the entrepreneur.

3 Explain the role and significance of entrepreneurs.

Ans. The role and significance of entrepreneurs are discussed below :

- **Organiser of Society's Productive Resources** An entrepreneur is the organises of society's productive resources. He is the person who assembles the unused natural, physical and human resources of the society, combines them properly, establishes effective coordination between them and makes the economic activities dynamic.
- **Helpful in Capital Formation** An entrepreneur is helpful in capital formation or we know that increase in the rate of capital formation is quite essential for the economic development of any country.
- **Increase in Employment Opportunities** An entrepreneur creates maximum employment opportunities in the society by way of establishing new industries, developing and expanding the existing industries and by undertaking innovative activities.

4 What are the myths of entrepreneurship? Explain.

Ans. The common set of myths of entrepreneurship are explained below :

- **Starting a Business is Easy** In reality it is a very difficult and challenging process to start a successful business. The rate of failure is high but small entrepreneurship are comparatively easier to start.
- **Lot of Money to Finance New Business** Successful entrepreneurs design their business with little cash also.
- **Start-up's can't be Financed** Under the scheme like MUDRA, entrepreneurs can raise loans from banks.
- **Talent is More Important than Industry** This is not true as the nature of industry an entrepreneur chooses greatly effects the success and growth of business.
- **Most Start up's are Successful** Mostly in the developing countries start-up's fail as they could not manage to earn high profits.

Long Answer (LA) Type Questions

1 Describe the advantages of entrepreneurship as a career.

Ans. The main advantages of adopting entrepreneurship as a career are discussed below :

- **Independence** An entrepreneur is himself a boss or owner and he can take all the decisions independently.
- **Exciting** Entrepreneurship can be very exciting with many entrepreneurs considering their ventures highly enjoyable. Every day will be filled with new opportunities to challenge your determination, skills and abilities.
- **Wealth Creation** The principal focus of entrepreneurship is wealth creation and improved livelihood by means of making available goods and services. Entrepreneurial ventures generates new wealth. New and improved products, services or technology from entrepreneurs, enable new markets to be developed and new wealth to be created.
- **Flexibility** As an entrepreneur you can schedule your work hours around other commitments, including quality time you would spend with your family.
- **Status** Success in entrepreneurship brings a considerable fame and prestige within the society.
- **Ambition-fulfilment** Through entrepreneurship one can fulfil his ambitions into original products or services.

2 Describe the disadvantages of entrepreneurship as a career.

Ans. Some of the common disadvantages of entrepreneurship as a career are as follows :

- **Huge Amount of Time** You have to dedicate a huge amount of time to your own business. entrepreneurship is not easy and for it to be successful, you have to take a level of time commitment.
- **Risk** Entrepreneurship involves high risk of loss. If the business fails then it will wipe away all the personal savings.
- **Hard Work** Entrepreneur has to work very hard to make the new business very successful.
- **Uncertain Amount** There is no regular or fixed income available to an entrepreneur. So, there is always uncertainty in terms of income.
- **Incompetent Staff** A new entrepreneur may not be able to hire qualified and experienced staff so there are chances of incompetency by the staff due to lack of experience and knowledge.

Self Assessment

Multiple Choice Questions

1. Decision-making function of entrepreneur includes
   (a) Hard work
   (b) Risk bearing
   (c) Utilisation of financial resources
   (d) All of these

2. Which system is being promoted by Entrepreneurs indirectly?
   (a) Capitalist
   (b) Socialist
   (c) Both (a) and (b)
   (d) None of these

Fill in the Blanks

3. Entrepreneurship involves high .... of loss.

4. No .... and .... income is available to an entrepreneur.

True/False

5. Raising the necessary funds is difficult for a first general entrepreneur.

6. An entrepreneur has no vision towards the achievement of his goal.

Very Short Answer (VSA) Type Questions

7. Describe the risk taking factor of an entrepreneurs.

8. Do you think an entrepreneur is innovative by nature. Explain?

Short Answer (SA) Type Questions

9. Explain the wealth creation factor of entrepreneurship.

10. Explain the risk taking quality of an entrepreneur.

Long Answer (LA) Type Question

11. Write a note on qualities of an entrepreneur.

Green Skills-II

Meaning and Definition of Sustainable Development

Sustainable development is a development that meets the needs of the present without compromising the ability of future generations to meet their own needs.

The important principles of sustainable development are:

- To carefully utilise all resources.
- To conserve resources so that they meet the demands and requirements of the future generations.
- To minimise the depletion of natural resources.

Sustainable development is the organising principle for meeting human development goals. It has its roots in ideas about sustainable forest management which were developed in Europe during the 17th and 18th centuries. The idea of sustainable development gained wide acceptance due to environmental concerns in the 20th century. The concept of sustainable development was popularised in 1987 by the United Nations World Commission on Environment and Development. In its **Our Common Future Report** or **Brundtland Report** it defined the idea as "Development that meets the needs of the present, without compromising the ability of future generations to meet their needs."

Importance of Sustainable Development

Sustainable development is necessary for the maintenance of the environment. The importance of sustainable development are as follows:

- **Proper Use of Means and Resources** Sustainable development teaches people to make use of means and resources for the maximum benefit without wastage. It helps to conserve and promote the environment.
- **Development of Positive Attitude** Sustainable development brings about changes in people's knowledge, attitude and skills. It awares the people the responsibility to use and preserve natural resources. It creates the feeling that natural resources are the common property of all and nobody can use the property according to his personal will. It helps to conserve natural and social environment.

- **Development Based on People's Participation** People's participation is to be given priority in development work in order to achieve the aim of sustainable development. It creates the interest of local people in development work and environment conservation with the feeling of ownership.
- **Limitation of Development** Limited but effective use of means and resources are enough for the people to satisfy their basic needs. Limited and non-renewable means and resources go on decreasing in globally due to over-use. Development works should be conducted as per carrying capacity.
- **Long Lasting Development** Sustainable development aims at achieving the goal of economic and social development without destroying the Earth's means and resources. It attempts to create the concept of maintaining the present work for the future and conserving the natural resources for future generation.

So, due to the realisation of importance of sustainable development, now there is a transcending concern for survival of the people and planet. We need to take a holistic view of the very basis of our existence. It is important to reconcile ambitious economic development and preserving the natural resources and ecosystem.

Check Point 01

1 Which of the following is not the principle of sustainable development?
(a) To carefully utilise all resources
(b) To conserve resources
(c) To minimise the depletion of natural resources
(d) None of the above
2 Sustainable development is necessary for the .... of the environment.
3 The idea of sustainable development gained wide acceptance due to environmental concerns in the ....
4 Define sustainability.

Problems Related to Sustainable Development

- Poor management of natural resources combined with growing economic activities will continue to pose serious challenges to environment.
- The most significant environmental problems are associated with resources that are renewable such as air and water. They have finite capacity to assimilate emissions and wastes but if pollution exceeds this capacity ecosystem can deteriorate rapidly.

- To assess the regenerative capacity of natural resources is difficult to determine. In the cases of soil erosion, atmospheric pollution etc., there is substantial uncertainity about the extent and outcomes of environmental degradation.
- The overall effects of economic activities on the environment are continuously changing.
- Due to rise in income, the demands for improvement in environmental quality will increase as well as the resources available for investment but it is not mandatory in some cases as problems are observed to get worse as income rise.
- Rise in population is another problem that would further lead to severe environmental degradation in the future.
- Another challenge is rise in demand for energy as it is estimated that the total manufacturing outputs in developing countries will increase to about six times the current levels by 2030.

Another challenge is rise in demand of food crops with the growth of population. To protect fragile soils and natural habitats, this will have to be achieved by raising yields on existing crop land.

Solutions for Sustainable Development

- Inspite of difficult circumstances sustainable development is achievable however, it would require a lots of concentrated and coordinated effort. The achievement of sustainable development requires the integration of economic, environmental and social components at all levels.
- The main principles of sustainable development are:
  - Respect and care for all forms of life.
  - People should learn to conserve the natural resoures in order to protect the living beings.
  - Conserving the Earth's vitality and diversity.
  - Improving the quality of human life.
  - Changing personal attitude and practices towards the environment.

Short-Term Solutions

- Illegal deforestation and smuggling of forest resources should be stopped.
- Proper balance ought to be maintained between deforestation and afforestation.
- Planning and building of industrial zones to manage and process are types of wastes.

- Proper treatment system, recycling of waste and their proper disposal should be undertaken.
- Adoption of Rainwater Harvesting Techniques, drip/Sprinkler irrigation and use of alternative sources of energy. Less chemical fertilizers should be used along with environment-friendly pesticides and weedicides.
- Polluting industries should be relocated outside the cities, far away from the populated areas.

Long-Term Solutions

- Government should make policies against illegal activities.
- Awareness campaigns should be launched for farmers and industrialists.
- Ecology must be protected through imposition of taxes and fines.
- Practice of sustainable agriculture must be promoted such as permaculture, agroforestry, mixed farming, multiple cropping and crop rotation.

United Nations Sustainable Development Summit (2015) sets global development goals. These goals are termed as Agenda 2030. The goals are:

1. End poverty in all forms everywhere.
2. End hunger, achieve food security and improved nutrition and promote sustainable agriculture.
3. Ensure healthy lives and well-being for all.
4. Ensure inclusive and quality education for all and promote lifelong learning.
5. Achieve gender equality and empower all women and girls.
6. Ensure access to water and sanitation for all.
7. Ensure access to affordable, reliable, sustainable and modern energy for all.
8. Promote inclusive and sustainable economic growth, employment and decent work for all.
9. Build resilient infrastructure, promote sustainable industrialisation and foster innovation.
10. Reduce inequality within and among countries.
11. Make cities inclusive, safe, resilient and production.
12. Ensure sustainable consumption and production.
13. Take urgent action to combat climate change and its impacts.
14. Conserve and sustainably use oceans, seas and marine resources.
15. Sustainably manage forests, halt and reverse land degradation, halt biodiversity loss.
16. Promote peaceful and inclusive societies.
17. Revitalise the global partnership for sustainable development.

Check Point 02

1 The most significant environmental problems are associated with resources like
  (a) air   (b) water
  (c) soil   (d) Both (a) and (b)

2 Awareness campaigns should be launched for
  (a) farmers   (b) industrialists
  (c) common people   (d) Both (a) and (b)

3 United Nations Sustainable Development Summit goals are termed as ....

4 The achievement of sustainable development requires the integration of economic, ... and .... components at all levels.

5 Write any one short-term solution related to sustainable development.

6 What are the main principles of sustainable development?

SUMMARY

- Sustainable development refers to the process of economic development where resources are used judiciously to satisfy needs of not only present generation but also to conserve them for the use of future generations.
- Sustainable development takes place without depleting the present natural resources. It is the organising principle for meeting human development goals.
- Sustainable development is necessary for proper use of means and resources, development of positive attitude, development based on people's participation, limitation of development and long lasting development.
- There are several problem related to sustainable development like poor management of resources, rise in population, rise in demand for energy etc.
- We can use short-term as well as long-term solutions to achieve the target of sustainable development through planning and coordinated effort.
- United Nations Sustainable Development Summit (2015) sets global development goals which are termed as Agenda 2030. It ensures healthy living and well-being for all.

Exam Practice

Multiple Choice Questions

1 Sustainable Forest Management which were development in Europe during the .... centuries.
(a) 16th and 18th
(b) 17th and 18th
(c) 18th and 19th
(d) 19th and 20th

Ans. (*b*) 17th and 18th

2 Sustainable development requires the judicious use of
(a) natural resources
(b) human resources
(c) man-made resources
(d) None of the above

Ans. (*a*) natural resources

3 Sustainable development is necessary because
(a) it helps to promote and conserve the environment
(b) it aware the people for effective use of natural resources
(c) it aims at achieving the goal of economic and social development
(d) All of the above

Ans. (*d*) All of the above

4 To save water as a resources which techniques must be adopted?
(a) Rainwater Harvesting
(b) Sprinkler Irrigation
(c) Recycling of Waste
(d) Both (a) and (b)

Ans. (*d*) Both (a) and (b)

5 Energy demand is developing countries will increase to .... times the current levels by 2030.
(a) four
(b) five
(c) six
(d) eight

Ans. (*c*) six

6 The biggest problem related to sustainable development is
(a) to safeguard forests
(b) to safeguard fisheries
(c) to safeguard croplands
(d) All of the above

Ans. (*d*) All of the above

7 If sustainable development is neglected then
(a) we shall have a safe and secure environment.
(b) it will destroy ecology and environment endangering the survival of future generation.
(c) mankind will continue to live and prosper.
(d) All of the above

Ans. (*b*) it will destroy ecology and environment endangering the survival of future generation.

Fill in the Blanks

1 .... of natural resources with growing economic activities will continue to pose serious challenges to environment.

Ans. Poor management

2 The overall effects of economic activities on the environment are continuously ....

Ans. changing

3 The ecology can be protected through imposition of .... and ....

Ans. deforestation, afforestation

4 Proper balance ought to be maintained between .... and .... for the achievement of sustainable goals.

Ans. taxes and fines

5 The government should make policies against .... activities.

Ans. illegal

True and False

1 Sustainable development is the organising Principle for meeting human development goals.

Ans. True

2 Sustainable development is not necessary for the maintenance of the environment.

Ans. False

3 Poor management of resources is a serious challenge to the environment.

Ans. True

4 Government should make policies against illegal activities.

Ans. True

5 Rainwater harvesting techniques are not useful at all.

Ans. False

Very Short Answer (VSA) Type Questions

1 Give the definition of sustainable development as suggested by Brundtland Report.

Ans. Development that meets the needs of the present, without compromising the ability of future generation to meet their needs.

2 Write any two challenges to sustainable development?

Ans. The two challenges to sustainable development are:
   (i) Rise in population level would lead to severe environmental degradation in the future.
   (ii) Poor management of natural resources combined with growing economic activities will continue to pose serious challenges to environment.

3 Give any one practice/sustainable process that is being used to help preserve the environment. **[CBSE SQP Term-II]**

Ans. One practice/sustainable process that is being used to help preserve the environment is organic farming. Organic farming is an agricultural system that uses fertilisers of organic origin such as compost manure, green manure and bone meal and places emphasis on techniques such as crop rotation and companion planting.

4 Give an example of large scale production of solar power in India. **[CBSE SQP Term-II]**

Ans. Charanka-Gujarat Solar Park is an example of large scale production of solar power in India.

5 The achievement of sustainable development requires what?

Ans. The achievement of sustainable development requires the integration of economic, environmental and social components at all levels.

6 'Reduced Inequalities' is one of the sustainable development goals set by the UN. Give any two ways to reduce inequalities. **[CBSE SQP Term-II]**

Ans. Two easy ways to reduce inequalities are as follows
   (i) **Helpful to one another** We should help everyone in spite of caste, religion, rich or poor, etc.
   (ii) **Be friendly with everyone** It doesn't matter, who they are or what they do, treat everyone the same way with kindness and respect.

Short Answer (SA) Type Questions

1 Why there is a need for sustainable development? Give reasons.

Ans. Sustainable development is necessary for the maintenance of the environment.

There is a need of sustainable development because of the following reasons:

(i) Sustainable development teaches people to make use of means and resources for the maximum benefit without wastage.

(ii) Sustainable development brings about changes in people's knowledge, attitude and skill.

(iii) Sustainable development aims at achieving the goal of economic and social development without destroying the Earth's means and resources.

2 The most significant environment problems are related to which type of resources?

Ans. The most significant environmental problems are associated with resources that are renewable such as air and water. They have a finite capacity to assimilate emissions and wastes but if pollution exceeds this capacity ecosystem will deteriorate rapidly at a huge pace.

3 Explain the short-term solutions related to sustainable development.

Ans. The short-term solutions to sustainable development are as follows:

(i) The practice of illegal deforestation and smuggling of forest resources should be stopped.

(ii) Proper balance ought to be maintained between deforestation and afforestation.

(iii) Planning and building of industrial zones to manage and process are types of wastes.

(iv) Proper treatment system, recycling of waste and their proper disposal should be undertaken.

(v) Adoption of rainwater harvesting techniques, drip/sprinkler irrigation and use of alternative sources of energy.

(vi) Less chemical fertilizers should be used along with environment friendly pesticides and weedicides.

Long Answer (LA) Type Question

1 Describe the meaning and importance of sustainable development.

Ans. Sustainable development refers to the process of economic development where resources are used judiciously to satisfy needs of not only present generation but also to conserve them for the use of future generations. Sustainable development takes place without depleting the present natural resources.

The importance of sustainable development is discussed below :

• It helps to conserve and make use of means and resources for the maximum benefit without wastage.

• It awares the people about the responsibility to use and preserve natural resources.

• It creates the feeling that natural resources are the common property of all and nobody can use the property according to his personal will. It helps to conserve natural and social environment.

• People's participation is to be given priority in development work in order to achieve the aim of sustainable development.

• It attempts to create the concept of maintaining the present work for the future and conserving natural resources for future generation.

Self Assessment

Multiple Choice Questions

1. The concept of sustainable development was popularised in
   (a) 1985
   (b) 1986
   (c) 1987
   (d) 1988

2. Sustainable development requires proper use of
   (a) natural resources
   (b) man-made resources
   (c) human resources
   (d) Both (a) and (b)

Fill in the Blanks

3. The most pressing environmental problems are associated with resources that are renewable, such as ....

4. Illegal .... and .... of forest resources and mineral should be stopped.

True/False

5. People should learn to conserve the natural resources.

6. Ecology must be protected through imposition of taxes and fines.

Very Short Answer (VSA) Type Questions

7. When did the idea of sustainable development become popular?

8. Mention any one serious problem relating to sustainable development.

Short Answer (SA) Type Questions

9. What are the main principle of sustainable development?

10. Explain the long-term solution related to sustainable development.

Long Answer (LA) Type Question

11. Write down the global development goals set up the United Nation Sustainable Development Summit (2015).

Information Technology

PART B

Subject Specific Skills

Digital Documentation (Advanced)

In earlier days, manual typewriters were used for typing a document, which was replaced by electronic typewriter and now a computer is used for this purpose.

Word processing, spreadsheet and presentation are most common activities performed in an office. Office Suite software is used to perform these activities effectively.

A document is a paper with written contents and the process of preparing a document is called documentation.

Documentation is required to preserve the contents for a long period or to be used as evidence. A document can be letters, reports, thesis, manuscripts, legal documents, books etc.

Word Processor

Word processing software is used for the creation of text-based documents. It is a GUI based software used in the windows environment. A word processor is a software package that processes textual matter and creates organised documents. In a precise manner, a word processor is a software application that, as directed by the user, performs word processing which includes the composition, editing, formatting and sometimes printing of any sort of material.

There are many software packages available to do the job of word processing. Some examples of word processing softwares are AppleWorks, Microsoft Word, StarOffice, TextMaker, WordPerfect, etc.

Features of Word Processor

Word processing packages have the following features:

1. Text editing
2. Auto formatting
3. Formatting text
4. OLE
5. GUI Interface
6. Language and grammar
7. Graphics
8. Mail merge
9. Security of files
10. Online help option, etc.

Getting Started with MS-Word 2007

To Start MS-Word 2007

Click Start button → All Programs → Microsoft Office → Microsoft Office Word 2007

It opens MS-Word with a blank document. By default, the name of the blank document is **Document1.docx**, where .docx or .doc is the extension of a MS-Word 2007 file.

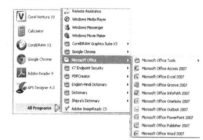

Start the MS-Word

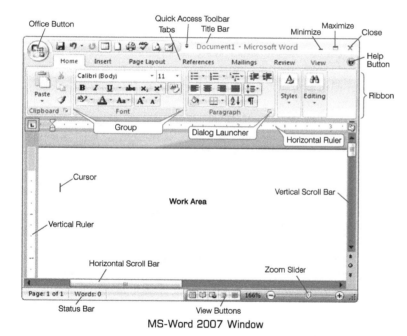

MS-Word 2007 Window

The major components of MS-Word 2007 are:

Office Button

It is found in the top-left corner of MS-Word window and loops like the pictures to the right. When the Office button is clicked, many of the options such as New, Open, Save, Save As, Prepare, Print, Send, Publish, Close, etc., can be found.

Title Bar

It is located at the top of the window and display the document name. The format of the name displayed on the title bar is **Document name-Microsoft Word.**

Quick Access Toolbar

It is placed to the right of the Office button. It contains shortcut for the commonly used tools, like save, undo, redo, etc. It can also be placed below the ribbon also.

Control Buttons

There are three types of control buttons as follows:

    (i) Minimize button

    (ii) Maximize or Restore down button

    (iii) Close button

Ribbon

In ribbon, there are many buttons/options that are grouped into categories according to tab such as Clipboard, Font, Paragraph, Styles, Editing, etc., which are the groups of Home tab.

Tabs

Tabs are similar to the menu system of MS-Word 2003. Instead of having drop down menus, MS-Word 2007 created a ribbon system, where buttons and commands are grouped under the tabs. Some groups include a dialog launcher button in their lower right corner to bring up additional options.

Different types of tabs are:

Home

Tab is used to change font, styles, setting of paragraph, alignment buttons etc.

Insert

Tab is used to insert page breaks, tables, illustrations, links, header and footer, text and symbols, object etc.

Page Layout

Tab is used to change themes, margins, orientation, insert a page border, column, format paragraph, etc.

References

Tab is used to insert table footnotes, citation and bibliography captions, index, etc.

Mailings

Tab is used to create envelopes, labels, start mail merge, write and insert fields and preview results, etc.

Review

Tab is used for proofing, comments, tracking, comparing the documents, etc.

View

Tab is used to change the outline or draft views, display the ruler or document map, zoom, switch windows, etc.

- After inserting a picture in MS-Word 2007, a new tab appears namely- Picture Tools Format. It includes adjust, picture styles, arrange and size groups in it. By using this tab, a user can edit pictures according to his/her need.

Ruler

It appears on the top and on the left side of the document window. Ruler is used to set tabs, indents and margins for a document. It allows to format the horizontal or vertical alignment of text in a document.

Scroll Bar

Scroll bar is used to view the whole active window. There are two types of scroll bars i.e. horizontal and vertical scroll bars.

Status Bar

It is displayed at the bottom of the window and used to view the information such as page number, current page, current template, column number, line number, etc.

Zoom Control

Lets you zoom in for a closer look at your text. The zoom control consists of a slider. You can slide it left or right to zoom in or out, to increase or decrease the zoom factor.

View Buttons

The group of five buttons located to the left of the zoom control lets you switch among word's various document views. Like

- Print Layout View
- Web Layout View
- Draft View
- Full Screen Reading View
- Outline View

Work Area/Work Space

It is the rectangular area of the document window, where you can type the text.

 Using Help Button

To open Help window, click the **Microsoft Office Help** button in the right corner of the ribbon or press the F1 key on your keyboard. Now, following Word Help dialog box appears.

Help option allows users to search and find any topic about that program. To use this feature ,write any topic name in text box and click on Search button or press Enter. It will then display the related information about that topic.

Word Help Dialog Box

Note MS–Word 2007 allows you to easily create a variety of professional looking documents using features such as Themes, Styles, Smart Art and More.

Creating a New Blank Document

Each time when you open MS-Word, a new blank document appears. However, you will also need to know how to create new documents while an existing document is open.

Steps to create a new blank document:

Step 1   Click the **Microsoft Office** button.

Step 2   Select **New**, the New Document dialog box will appear.

Step 3   Select **Blank Document** under the Blank and recent section. (It will be highlighted by default.)

Step 4   Click **Create**, a new blank document will be appear.

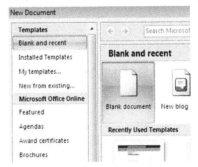

New Document Dialog Box

Saving a Document

To permanently store a document on hard disk, you must save the document and assign a name to it.

Use the Save As Command

Steps to save a document using Save As command:

Step 1	Click the **Microsoft Office** button.
Step 2	Then click **Save As → Word document** (or press Ctrl+S). The Save As dialog box will appear.

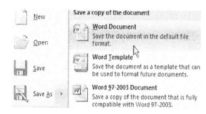

Step 3	Select the location, where you want to save the document using the drop down menu.
Step 4	Enter the name of the document in File name box.

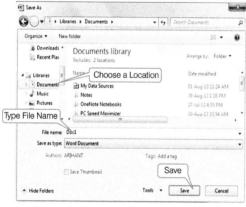

Save As dialog box

Step 5	Click the **Save** button.

Use the Save Command

Steps to save a document using Save command:

Step 1	Click the **Microsoft Office** button.
Step 2	Select **Save** from the menu.
Step 3	Save the document in its current location with the same file name.

 'Save' means the file gets saved under its current name, in whatever folder it was saved before or in the default folder of that computer whereas "Save As" gives you the opportunity to save the file under a different name and in another folder. "Save As" allows you to save the updated version with a new name while at the same time preserving the old version.

Closing a Document

Steps to close an active document:

Step 1	Click the **Microsoft Office** button.
Step 2	Click **Close**.

Modifying Layout of a Paragraph

When you format paragraphs within a document, you can change the look of the entire document. Formatting a paragraph allows you to change line spacing, indent lines and alter all of your paragraphs. Formatting is the general arrangement of text in the document. Many of the tools you can use to format your paragraphs will be located in the Page Layout tab of the Ribbon in the Paragraph group.

Paragraph Alignment

Paragraph alignment refers to how the left and right edges of a paragraph align on a page. You can left align, center, right align and justify a paragraph.

To set the alignment, follow the given steps:

Step 1	Click on **Page Layout** tab → click on the arrow right corner of the **Paragraph** group.
Step 2	Paragraph dialog box will appear. Click on **Indents and Spacing** tab.

Step 3 In General section, Alignment has various options as:

- **Left align** (Ctrl + L) A left aligned paragraph is considered normal. The left side of the paragraph is even and the right side is jagged.
- **Center align** (Ctrl + E) Centering a paragraph places each line in that paragraph in the middle of a page, with an equal amount of space to the line's right and left.
- **Right align** (Ctrl + R) A right aligned paragraph has its right margin even. The left margin, however, is jagged.
- **Justify** (Ctrl + J) Full justification occurs when both the left and right sides of a paragraph are lined up flush with the page margins.

Step 4 Select any given option and click OK.

Paragraph Indentations

An indentation is the distance between a margin and the text, not the edge of a page and the text.

We can indent a paragraph with three ways:

1. **Indent a full paragraph** To indent a full paragraph, follow the given steps:
   - Open the **Paragraph** dialog box.
   - In Indentation section, enter the value in **Left and Right** boxes.
   - Click **OK.**
2. **Indent first line of a paragraph** To have word automatically indent the first line of every paragraph, follow the given steps:
   - Click the **Page Layout** tab in the ribbon.
   - Open the **Paragraph** dialog box by clicking the Dialog Box Launcher button in the lower-right corner of the Paragraph group.
   - In Indentation area, select the **First line** option from the **Special** drop-down list.
   - Click **OK** button.

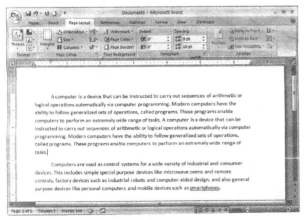

3. **Hanging indent of a paragraph** Hanging indent is the indent, the paragraph except first line. To hanging indent, follow the given points:
   - Open the **Paragraph** dialog box by dialog box launcher button.
   - In **Indentation** area, select the **Hanging** option from the Special drop-down list.
   - Click **OK** button.

Paragraph Spacing

Line spacing is measured in lines or points, which is referred to as leading. Changing the line spacing inserts extra space between all lines of text in a paragraph.

Extra spacing between paragraphs adds emphasis and make a document easier to read.

To format line spacing, follow the given steps:

Step 1 Select the text that you want to format.

Step 2 Open **Paragraph** dialog box by Paragraph group.

Step 3 In Spacing section, use the Line spacing drop-down menu to select a spacing option.

Step 4 Modify the **Before** and **After** points to adjust line spacing as needed.

Step 5 Click **OK** button.

Check Point 01

1 .... software is used for the creation of text based documents.

2 In how many ways, you can save a document?

3 Which alignment is used to align all the selected text equal from both the sides?

Header and Footer

You can make your documents professional and polished by utilising the header and footer sections. The header is a section of the document that appears at the top margin, while the footer is a section of the document that appears at the bottom margin.

Header and footer generally both contains information such as page number, date, document name, company logo, image etc., which are specified by page styles. Therefore, when inserted, all pages with the same page style will display same header and footer.

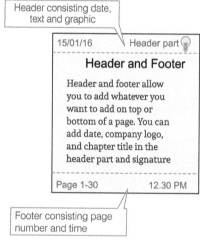

Header and Footer Areas

Insert Header or Footer

Steps to insert header or footer in a document are as follows:

Step 1   Click **Insert** tab.

Step 2   Select **Header** or **Footer** from **Header & Footer** group. A menu will appear with a list of **Built-In** options as shown below.

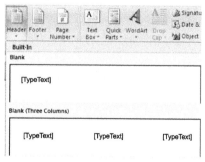

Step 3   Click one of the **Built-In** options as per your requirement and it will appear in the document.

Step 4   Then, **Header/Footer** workspace is activated on the page.

Step 5   Type information (number/text/date) or insert an image into the header or footer section.

Note   Once the Header/Footer workspace is activated, the **Header & Footer** Tools with **Design tab** is displayed similar to below figure:

Insert Date/Time into Header or Footer

Steps to insert date/time into header or footer are as follows:

Step 1   On the **Design** tab, in the **Insert** group, click the **Date & Time** option (after selecting Footer section).

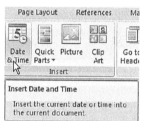

Clicking the Date & Time

Step 2   Select date and time format from the **Date and Time** dialog box.

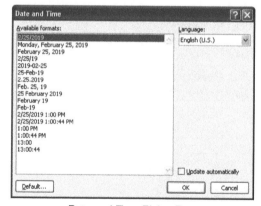

Date and Time Dialog Box

Step 3   Click **OK**.

Now, Date/Time will appear in the document.

Make the Header or Footer Different for Odd and Even Pages

Steps to make the header or footer different for odd and even pages are as follows:

Step 1   Choose **Page Layout** tab.

Step 2   Click the small icon at the bottom-right of the **Page Setup** group. A Page Setup dialog box will appear.

Page Setup dialog box

Step 3   Click **Layout** tab.

Step 4   Select **Different odd and even** check box.

Step 5   Click **OK**.

Edit the Content of Header or Footer

Steps to edit the content of header or footer are as follows:

Step 1   Click **Insert** tab.

Step 2   Select **Header** or **Footer** option from the Header & Footer group.

Step 3   Click **Edit Header** or **Edit Footer**.

or

Double click on **Header** or **Footer Workspace**. Now, you can edit the content of Header or Footer.

Remove Header or Footer

Steps to remove header or footer are as follows:

Step 1   Click **Insert** tab.

Step 2   Select **Header** or **Footer** option from the Header & Footer group.

Step 3   Click **Remove Header** or **Remove Footer**.

Now, header or footer gets removed from the document.

Check Point 02

1   It is a section of the document that appears at the top margin.
   (a) Header   (b) Footer
   (c) Superscript   (d) Subscript

2   Which information can be added to the header/footer?

3   Once the header and footer workspace is activated then which tab is displayed?

Managing Styles

A style is a set of formats consisting of such things as fonts, font colors, font sizes and paragraph formats.

Choose a Style

To choose a style, follow the given steps:

Step 1   Select the text which you want to format.

Step 2   On the **Home** tab, in the **Styles** group, hover over the each style and see the live preview on the text.

Step 3   If you want more styles then click on *arrow*. The drop-down list of styles will appear on the screen.

Step 4   Select the *style* which you want to apply on text.

Choose a Style Set

Word supplies you with predesigned style sets that contain styles for titles, subtitles, quotes, headings, lists and more.

To choose a style set, follow the given steps:

Step 1   Click on **Home** tab.

Step 2   Click **Change Styles** in the **Styles** group. A menu will appear.

Step 3   Select **Style Set** and a sub menu will appear.

Step 4   You can choose from any of the styles listed on the menu.

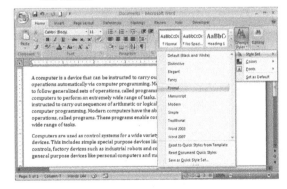

Modify a Style

To modify a style, follow the given steps:

Step 1   Click on **Home** tab.

Step 2   Click the **More list** arrow in the **Styles** group and right click the style that you want to modify and then click Modify.

Step 3   Modify Style dialog box will appear. Click the Type of Formatting.

Step 4   To add the style to the **Quick Style Gallery**, select the Add to Quick Style list check box.

Step 5   Click OK.

Create a New Style

To create a new style, follow the given steps:

Step 1   Select the **text** and then click **Home** tab.

Step 2   Click the **More list** arrow in the **Styles** group and then click on Save Selection as a New Quick Style.

Step 3   Type the name in Name text field and click on Modify.

Step 4   Create New Style from Formatting dialog box will appear.

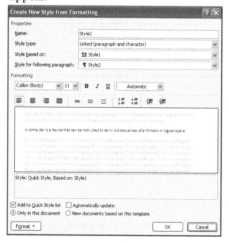

Step 5   Select the value of **Style type, Style based on** and **Style for following paragraph.**

Step 6   Select the **Formatting** option that you want.

Step 7   Click **OK** button.

Check Point 03

1   In which group, you can select Styles?
2   How can you display the Style Set menu?
3   To add the style to the Quick Style Gallery, which option is used?

Document Template

A template is a collection of styles that already has some formatting in place, such as fonts, logos, and line spacing and can be used as a starting point for almost anything that you want to create. Microsoft Word offers hundreds of free templates, including invoices, resumes, invitations and form letters, among others.

Create a Template

To create a template, follow the given steps:

Step 1   Click on **Microsoft Office** button.

Step 2   Select the **New** option from the menu that appears.

Step 3   **New Document** window will be appear.

Step 4   From the left side, select the **Installed Templates.**

Step 5   **Installed Templates** will open with different templates.

Step 6   Choose a **Built-In** template which you need. For example, Equity Letter.

Step 7   The preview of **Equity Letter** will appear on the right side of the window.

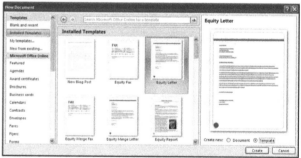

Step 8   In **Create new:**, select **Template** option and click **Create** button. The template will be created in your word document.

Save and Reuse Templates

You can save your template after some changes. Your templates are saved in My templates.

To save a template in My templates, follow the given steps:

Step 1   Click on **Microsoft Office** button.

Step 2   Select **Save As → Word Template.** The Save As dialog box will appear.

Step 3   Enter the name for the template in File name box.

Step 4 In **Save as type**, select **Word Template.**

Step 5 Click the **Save** button.

Your template will save in My templates folder.

Information about using Templates

Templates include placeholder text that is surrounded by brackets often, this placeholder text includes information regarding the content for specific area.

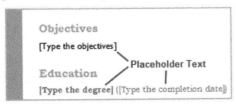

Additionally, some information is prefilled in the templates. You can modify your word options and change the prefilled information that appears.

To Insert Text into a Template

To insert text into a template, follow the given steps:

Step 1 Click near the text that you want to replace. The text will be highlighted, and a template tag will appear.

Step 2 Enter text. It will replace placeholder text with your entered text.

To Change Prefilled Information

To change the prefilled information, follow the given steps:

Step 1 Select the **Microsoft Office** button.

Step 2 Click the **Word Options** button. The **Word Options** dialog box will appear.

Step 3 Enter the User name and/or Initials in the **Personalise your copy of Microsoft Office** section from Popular.

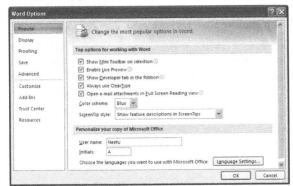

Step 4 Click **OK.**

Insert Page and Section Breaks

Sometimes, it will be necessary to create a document break, which will indicate to Word how the document is to be partitioned. There are two types of document breaks namely

(i) **Page Break** It partitions only the body text of the document. There are three kinds of page break:

- **Simple Page Break** It will force all the text behind the cursor onto the next page.

- **Column Break** If your document utilises columns, when inserting a column break, any text to the right of the cursor where the break is inserted is forced into the next column.

- **Text Wrapping Break** It moves any text to the right of the cursor to the next line. This kind of break may be particularly useful when your document contains images.

(ii) **Section Break** It partitions both the body text of the document as well as partition page margins, headers and footers, page numbers etc.

There are four kinds of section breaks:

- **Next Page Break** It forces the text to the right of the cursor to the following page, as well as partitions the document into sections, allowing for a change in margins, headers and footers as well as differently numbered pages and footnotes.

- **Continuous Break** It allows for the partition of a document, allowing the user to change headers and footers, page numbers, margins etc, yet without having to alter or otherwise move the body text of the document.

- **Even Page Break** It will shift all the text to the right of the cursor to the top of the next even page.

- **Odd Page Break** It will move the text to the right of the cursor to the top of the next odd page.

To Insert a Page Break

To insert a page break, follow the given steps:

Step 1 Where you want to break the page, place the insertion point.

Step 2 Click on **Page Layout** tab from ribbon.

Step 3 In the **Page Setup** group, select **Breaks** option. A sub menu will appear on the screen as follow :

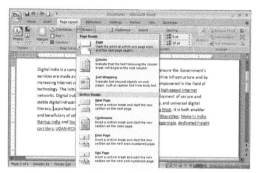

Step 4 In **Page Breaks** section, select the **Page** option. Now, page will break and content will be shown on next page.

Inserting Column Break

To insert a column break, first you need to insert columns in a document follow the given steps:

Step 1 Click where you want that page column to break.

Step 2 Click on **Page Layout** tab from the ribbon.

Step 3 Select **Page Setup** group → **Breaks**. A drop-down menu will appear.

Step 4 Select **Column** option.

To Insert Text Wrapping

To insert text wrapping, follow the given steps:

Step 1 Click where you want to text wrapping.

Step 2 Click **Page Layout** tab→**Page Setup** group→ **Breaks**. A drop-down menu will appear.

Step 3 Select **Text Wrapping** from **Page Breaks** section.

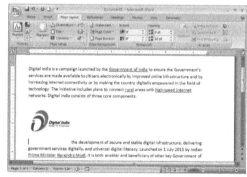

To Insert Section Breaks

To insert section break, follow the given steps:

Step 1 Click where you want to make a formatting change.

Step 2 On the **Page Layout** tab, in the **Page Setup** group, click **Breaks** option.

Step 3 In the **Section Breaks** group, click the **Section Break** Type that fits the type of formatting change that you want to make.

For example, If you are separating a document into chapters, you might want each chapter to start with an odd page. Click Odd Page in the Section Breaks group.

To Delete a Section Break

To delete a section break, follow the given steps:

Step 1 Scroll up or down the page until you locate the section break.

Step 2 Highlight the entire section break.

Step 3 Press **Delete.**

Check Point 04

1. .... is a collection of styles that already has some formatting in place.
2. How many types of document breaks?
3. In which break, text moves to the right of the cursor to the next line?
4. By which tab, you can insert column break in your document?

Formatting Text

To create and design effective documents, you need to know how to format text, in order to make your documents more appealing and formatted to draw the reader's attention.

Format Font Size

Steps to format the font size of text are as follows:

Step 1 Select the **text** that you want to modify.

Step 2 Click the **drop-down** arrow next to the Font Size box in the Font group on the **Home** tab. The **Font Size** drop-down menu will appear.

Step 3 Move your cursor over the various font sizes. A live preview of the font size will appear in the document.

Step 4 Choose the **Font Size** that you want to use.

Format Font Style

Steps to format the font style of text are as follows:

Step 1 Select the **text** that you want to modify.

Step 2 Click the **drop-down** arrow next to the **Font Style** box in the **Font** group on the **Home** tab. The Font Style drop-down menu will appear.

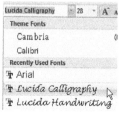

Step 3   Move your cursor over the various font styles. A live preview of the font will appear in the document.

Step 4   Choose the **Font Style** that you want to use.

Format Font Color

Steps to format the font color of text are as follows:

Step 1   Select the **text** that you want to modify.

Step 2   Click the **drop-down** arrow next to the **Font Color** box in the Font group on the **Home** tab. The Font Color menu will appear.

Step 3   Move your cursor over the various font colors. A live preview of the color will appear in the document.

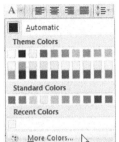

Step 4   Choose the **Font Color** that you want to use.

Note   Your color choices are not limited to the drop-down menu that appears. You can select **More Colors** ... option at the bottom of the list to access the Colors dialog box. Choose the color that you want and then, click **OK**.

Applying Character Formats

You can apply different formatting, such as bold and italic, to improve the look of your text in Word 2007. The Font group on the Home tab lists the most common character formats.

To apply character formats, follow the given steps:

Step 1   Select the text in which you want to apply character formatting. Click on Home tab, in the Font group various options are there, which are as follows

Symbol	Name	Description
B	Bold	To make text bold, press Ctrl+B or click the Bold button. Use bold to make text stand out on a page for titles and captions.
U	Underline	To make text underline, press Ctrl+U or click the Under Button.
I	Italic	To make text italic, press Ctrl+I or click the Italic button. It is useful for emphasizing text.
a̶b̶c̶	Strike through	It is common in legal stuff and when you mean to say something but then change your mind and think of something better to say.
x^2	Superscript	To make Superscript, pressing Ctrl+Shift+= or Superscript button. Superscript text appears above the line. e.g. $a^2 + b^2$
x_2	Subscript	To make subscript, pressing Ctrl + = or Subscript button. Subscript text appears below the line. e.g. H_2So_4

Shortcut Keys
Bold	–	Ctrl + B
Italic	–	Ctrl + I
Underline	–	Ctrl + U

Change the Text Case

Steps to change the text case, i.e. lowercase, uppercase are as follows:

Step 1   Select the **text** that you want to modify.

Step 2   Click the **Change Case** option from the **Font** group on the **Home** tab.

Text Case Options	Description
Sentence case	Changes the first letter of every sentence in uppercase.
lowercase	Changes the whole selected text in lowercase letters.
UPPERCASE	Changes the whole selected text in uppercase letters.
Capitalize Each Word	Changes first letter of every word in capital case.
tOGGLE cASE	It toggles whole selected text, i.e. changes each capital letter into lowercase and each small letter into uppercase.

Step 3   Select one of the **Text Case** options from the above list as per the requirement.

Insert Graphical Objects and Illustrations

You may want to insert various types of illustrations into your documents to make them more visually appealing illustrations include clipart, pictures etc.

Clip Art

It is a form of electronic graphic art that consists of simple illustrations as opposed to photographic images. Clip Art object includes effects such as shadows, outlines, colors, gradients and 3D effects.

To insert Clip Art, follow the given steps:

Step 1   Click the **Insert** tab on the ribbon.

Step 2   From the **Illustrations** group, click the **Clip Art** option. The Clip Art task pane will appear.

Step 3   In the **Search for:** box, type a description of what do you want and then click the **Go** button. e.g. computer.

After you click Go, the results are displayed in the task pane.

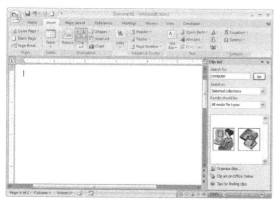

Step 4   Point the cursor at the image you want. A drop-down menu will appear on the side of Clip Art.

Step 5   Click the **Insert** option from drop-down menu. Selected picture will be show on word document.

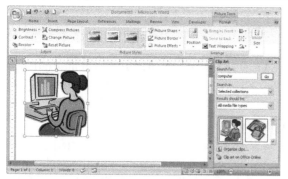

Step 6   Close the **Clip Art** task pane by clicking on 'x' sigh in its upper right corner.

Working with Pictures

Pictures can be added to Word documents and then, formatted in various ways. The picture tool in MS-Word make it easy to incorporate pictures into your documents and modify those images in an innovative ways.

Insert a Picture

Steps to insert a picture in a document are as follows:

Step 1   Place the insertion point, where you want to place the picture.

Step 2   Select the **Insert** tab.

Step 3   Click the **Picture** option in the Illustrations group. The **Insert Picture** dialog box will appear as shown below.

Step 4   Select the **picture**.

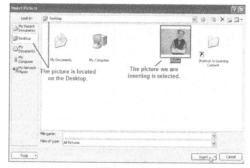

Insert Picture dialog box

Step 5   Click **Insert** button and then this picture will appear in your document.

Wrap Text Around a Picture

Steps to wrap text around a picture in a document are as follows:

Step 1   Select the picture.

Step 2   Select the **Picture Tools Format** tab. (This tab appears only after insertion of a picture).

Step 3   Click the **Text Wrapping** in the Arrange group.

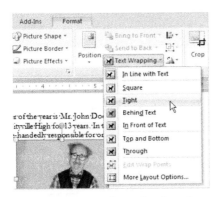

Step 4   Select any one option from the drop-down list. In this example, we will select **Tight.**

Step 5   Move the picture around to see how the text wraps for each setting.

Step 6   The Position button has pre-defined text wrapping settings. The Position button is placed to the left of the **Text Wrapping** button.

Step 7   Click the **Position** button and a drop-down list of **Text Wrapping** options will appear. Move your cursor over the various text wrapping styles. A live preview of text wrapping will appear in the document.

If you cannot get your text wrapped the way you wish, select **More Layout Options...** from the **Position** menu. You can make more precise changes from the Advanced Layout dialog box that appears.

Crop a Picture

Crop option allows a user to edit pictures.

Steps to crop a picture in a document are as follows:

Step 1   Select the picture.
Step 2   Click the **Picture Tools Format** tab.
Step 3   Click the **Crop** button from Size group. The black cropping handles appear around the picture.
Step 4   Click and move a handle to crop the picture.
Step 5   Corner handles will crop the picture proportionally.

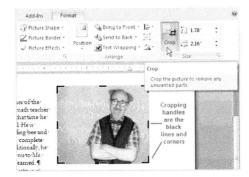

Compress a Picture

Steps to compress a picture in a document are as follows:

Step 1   Select the picture.
Step 2   Click the **Picture Tools Format** tab.
Step 3   Click the **Compress Pictures** in the Adjust group. A Compress Pictures dialog box will appear as shown below.

Step 4   Click the **Options...** button to access the **Compression Settings** dialog box as shown below.

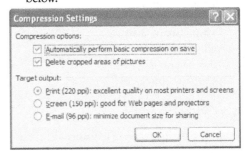

Step 5   Choose any of the **Target output:** as per the requirement.

Step 6   Click on the check box(s) under the **Compression options:** as per the requirement.

Step 7   Click **OK** in the **Compression Settings** dialog box.

Note   You need to monitor the file size of your picture and documents that include some graphics, especially if you send them *via* E-mail. Cropping and resizing the picture do not decrease the picture file size, but compression does.

Other Picture Tools

There are many other things that you can do to modify a picture. From the Picture Tools Format tab, some of the other useful features are as follows:

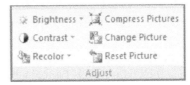

- **Brightness** Adjust the brightness of the picture.
- **Contrast** Adjust the contrast of the picture from light to dark.

- **Recolor** Modify the color in a variety of ways including black, white, sepia, pink, purple and many more.
- **Change Picture** Change to a different picture preserving the formatting and size of the current picture.
- **Reset Picture** Revert to original picture.

Change the Shape of a Picture

Word 2007 shapes menu is packed full of lines, arrows, squares and more.

Steps to change the shape of a picture in a document are as follows:

Step 1   Select the picture.

Step 2   Click the **Picture Tools Format** tab.

Step 3   Click the **Picture Shape** option from **Picture Styles** group. A Picture Shape menu will appear.

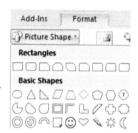

Step 4   Choose any **shape** as per the requirement.

Apply a Picture Style

Steps to apply a picture style in a document are as follows:

Step 1   Select the picture.

Step 2   Click the **Picture Tools Format** tab.

Step 3   Click More drop-down arrow in **Picture Styles** group to display all the Picture Styles.

Step 4   However, when a cursor moves over different picture styles, the live preview of the style will be displayed on the picture in a document.

Step 5   Choose any style as per the requirement.

Add a Border to a Picture Manually

Steps to add a border to a picture manually in a document are as follows:

Step 1   Select the picture.

Step 2   Click the **Picture Tools Format** tab.

Step 3   Click the **Picture Border** → select **Weight** → click any **point** for border.

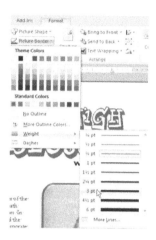

Check Point 05

1   What is the use of sentence case command?

2   Illustrations group is available on

   (a) Insert tab   (b) Review tab

   (c) Reference tab   (d) Page Layout tab

3   Which option of Picture Tools Format tab helps you to modify the color in a variety of ways?

Object Linking and Embedding (OLE)

It is a Microsoft technology that facilitates the sharing of applications data and objects written in different formats from multiple sources.

Linked Objects

When an object is linked, information can be updated if the source file is modified. Linked data is stored in the source file. Linking is also useful when you want to include information that is maintained independently such as data collected by a different department.

Embedded Objects

When you embed an Excel object, information in the Word file does not change if you modify the source Excel file. Embedded objects become part of the Word file and after they are inserted, they are no longer part of the source file.

To link or embed an object, follow the steps:

Step 1   Click on the **worksheet**, where you want to add the linked object.

Step 2   Select **Insert** tab from the ribbon.

Step 3   In the **Text** group, click on **Object** option. Object dialog box will appear as shown below.

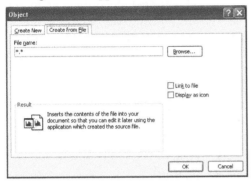

Step 4   In the Object dialog box, select the **Create from File** tab and then click **Browse** to find the file you want to insert.

Step 5   **Browse** dialog box will appear on the screen.

Step 6   To link to the source file, rather than embedding it into your Word document or email message, select **Link to file.**

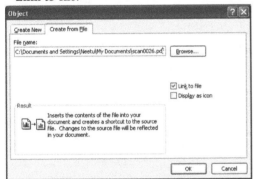

Step 7   If you want the inserted file to appear as a clickable icon, rather than the first page of the file, select **Display as icon.**

Step 8   If this check box is selected, you can choose a different icon by clicking **Change Icon.**

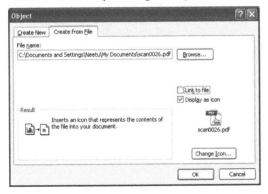

Inserting Shapes, Symbols and Special Characters

MS-Word allows creating of simple shapes and objects with its built-in Drawing Tools and also comes with a set of readymade shapes that can also be used in a Word document. Shape can also be combined with other shapes to make more complex shapes.

Now, we are going to study about inserting autoshapes, drawing custom shapes and editing custom shapes.

Note   When you insert any shape in your document, a new tab will appear at top named Drawing Tools Format.

Inserting Autoshapes

In the Insert tab from the Illustrations group, the Shapes option contains several categories of shapes, i.e. Lines, Basic Shapes, Block Arrows, Flowchart, Stars and Banners and Callouts that can be added very easily in the document.

To insert these shapes, follow the steps:

Step 1   On the ribbon, select the **Insert** tab. The Insert tab commands are visible.

Step 2   In the **Illustrations** group, click **Shapes** option → select the desired shape.

Step 3   Click and hold the mouse from where you want to start the shape.

Step 4   Drag the mouse to create the desired shape. An outline indicating the size of your shape appears.

Step 5   Release the mouse button. The shape will appear in your Word document.

OPTIONAL To create a frame for several shapes, in the **Illustrations** group, click **Shapes** → select **New Drawing Canvas** option from the drop-down menu.

A blank drawing will appear in your document, the Format commands are displayed as follows.

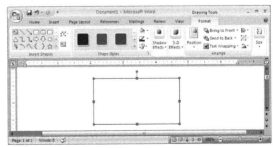

Drawing Custom Shapes

By using the three freehand drawing tools, i.e. Curve, Freeform and Scribble desired shapes can be created.

Curve lets you draw shapes that have different curves. Freeform lets you draw shapes that have both straight lines and curves. Scribble lets you draw shapes freehand with fine detail.

To draw custom shapes, from the **Insert** tab, in the **Illustrations** group, click **Shapes → Lines →** select the desired tool.

  (i) **To Create a Curve** Click and release the mouse button to begin your curve. As you draw, click and release the mouse button to anchor point which your curve will form around. To finish your drawing, double click.

  (ii) **To Create a Freeform** Click and release the mouse button to begin your freeform shape. As you draw, click and release the mouse button to anchor the endpoints of straight lines or click and drag the mouse to draw curves, you can do both in one drawing. To finish your drawing, double click.

  (iii) **To Create a Scribble** Click and drag the mouse to draw your scribble. To finish your drawing, release the mouse button.

Editing Custom Shapes

MS-Word provides a feature called **Edit Points**, to customise the look of custom shapes. This feature allows reshaping of small segments of a drawing.

For editing custom shapes follow the below steps:

Step 1   Click the **Custom Shape.**

Step 2   From the **Format** tab, in the **Insert Shapes** group, click **Edit Shape →** select **Edit Points.**

         Black dots, called Edit Points will appear at various places in the shape.

Step 3   To make the desired changes, click and drag an **Edit Points.**

Step 4   When you are finished editing of your object, to turn off **Edit Points**, click anywhere on the page outside of the shape.

Formatting Shapes

Once an object is created in a document, its appearance can be changed by moving, adjusting the size and changing the colour of the object. When selected, an object has 'handles' that can be used to stretch the object taller or shorter, wider or thinner, or proportionally larger or smaller.

You can also manipulate your objects in several other ways, such as shading them or adjusting them to contain text.

MS-Word 2007 allows you to preview any changes by temporarily changing the appearance of the selected shape, when your mouse hovers above a formatting option.

Working with Text in Shapes

MS-Word 2007 allows you to add text in shape without creating a text box within a shape. Working with text in shapes are done in many ways which are as follows:

Adding Text

For adding text in your document, follow the below steps:

Step 1   Right click on the shape → click on **Add Text** from the drop-down menu.

         Note If you have already added text to this object, the Add Text option changes to Edit Text.

Step 2   Type the text.

         Note To format the font, color and size of the text from the **Home** tab, use the various commands that are available in the **Font** group.

Step 3   When you are done entering and formatting the text, click anywhere outside of the shape.

Editing Text

You can always go back and edit text in an existing shape.

For editing text in your document, follow the below steps:

Step 1   Select the shape that contains the text which you want to edit.

Step 2   Click to begin working with the text.

         Note Depending on the chosen shape, the I-beam may appear below the shape instead of within the text.

Step 3   Make the desired changes.

Step 4   When finished, to deselect the text, click outside of the shape.

Text-Fitting Options

Several options are available to customise the text-fitting within the shape. For text-fitting in your document, follow the steps:

Step 1   Right click on the shape → select **Format AutoShape...** option from the drop-down menu.

Step 2   The **Format AutoShape** dialog box will appear.

Step 3   Select the **Text Box** tab.

Step 4   Select the desired option given below:

Options	Description
Internal margin	Specifies the distance between each edge of your shape and the text contained within it.
Vertical alignment	Changes the vertical placement of your text within the shape.
Word wrap text in AutoShape	Text appears on multiple lines to fit within your AutoShape optimally.
Resize AutoShape to fit text	Resizes the AutoShape to optimally fit your text.
Format Callout...	When working with callouts (e.g. word bubbles), provides options for changing formatting.
Convert to Frame...	Changes your shape to a plain text box.

Inserting WordArt Object

WordArt can be used to make displayed text more eye-catching. It is a text modifying feature in MS-Word.

It includes effects such as shadows, outlines, colors, gradients and 3D effects that can be added to a word or phrase. To insert a WordArt object in your document, follow the below steps:

Step 1   On the **Insert** tab, in the **Text** group, click **WordArt** option. The WordArt Gallery will appear.

Step 2   From the WordArt Gallery, select the desired style. The **Edit WordArt Text** dialog box will appear.

Step 3   In the **Text** box, type your text.

Step 4   To format your text, from the **Font** or **Size** pull-down list, make the desired selections.

Step 5   To change the font style, click **B**(Bold) or **I**(Italic).

Step 6   Click **OK** button.

Insert Mathematical Symbols

Microsoft Office Word 2007 allows insertion of mathematical symbols into equations.

To insert mathematical symbols, follow the below steps:

Step 1   On the **Insert** tab, in the **Symbols** group, click the arrow under **Equation** option and then, click **Insert New Equation**.

Step 2   Under **Design** tab, select **Equation** from **Tools** group and can add more symbols from **Symbols** group, click the **More** arrow.

Step 3   Click the arrow **next** to the name of the symbol set and then, click the name of the symbol set that you want to display. (As you can choose operators, scripts etc.)

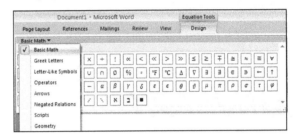

Step 4   Now, click the symbol that you want to insert.

Available Symbol Sets

There are 8 mathematical symbol sets available in MS-Word 2007 as follows:

Symbol Set	Subset	Definition
Basic Math	None	Commonly used mathematical symbols, such as > and <
Greek Letters	Lowercase	Lowercase letters from the Greek alphabet
	Uppercase	Uppercase letters from the Greek alphabet
Letter-Like Symbols	None	Symbols that resemble letters
Operators	Common Binary Operators	Symbols that act on two quantities, such as + and ÷
	Common Relational Operators	Symbols that express a relationship between two expressions, such as = and ~
	Basic N-ary Operators	Operators that act across a range of variables or terms
	Advanced Binary Operators	Additional symbols that act on two quantities
	Advanced Relational Operators	Additional symbols that express a relationship between two expressions
Arrows	None	Symbols that indicate direction
Negated Relations	None	Symbols that express a negated relationship

Symbol Set	Subset	Definition
Scripts	Scripts	The mathematical Script typeface
	Frakturs	The mathematical Fraktur typeface
	Double-Struck	The mathematical Double-Struck typeface
Geometry	None	Commonly used geometric symbols

Insert Special Symbol

To insert special symbol follow the given steps :

Step 1 Select **Insert** tab.

Step 2 Click **Symbol option** from **Symbols group**.

Step 3 Select **More Symbols...**

Step 4 The **Symbol dialog box** will appear and select the desired symbol.

Step 5 Click the **Insert** button.

Symbol will shown on your document.

Check Point 06

1 In MS-Word 2007, which tools are used to produce your own drawings or to improve the consistency?

2 How many options are contain by Shapes command in Insert tab?

3 Mr. Ajay wants to create a flowchart in Word document. Which features allow suitability to create flowchart in MS-Word?

4 Linked data is stored in the source file. State True or False?

SUMMARY

- A word processor is a package that processes textual matter and creates organised and faultless documents.
- Ruler is used to set tabs, indents and margins for a document.
- The scroll bar contains a slider that the user can drag to scroll through the window.
- Indent determines the distance of the paragraph from either the left or the right margin.
- A header or footer is a text or graphics that is usually printed at the top or at the bottom of every page in a document.
- A style is a set of text formatting characteristics such as font size, color and alignment.
- Template is a pre-established format for a document, stored in a computer.
- Text wrap is a feature supported by many Word processors that enable you to surround a picture or diagram with text.
- Formatting text in word involves tasks like bold the text, italic it, and change the font and size.
- Clip Art is a collection of pictures or images that can be imported into a document or another program.
- Object linking and ambedding enables you to create objects with one application and then link or embed them in a second application.
- Drawing tools are the tools which are used to produce own drawings or to improve the consistency.
- Drawing objects include shapes, diagrams, curves, lines and WordArt. These objects are part of your Word document.

Exam Practice

1 Which extension is given to a document by default in MS-Word?
(a) .odt   (b) .com
(c) .docx   (d) None of these

Ans. (c) .docx or .doc is the default extension of MS-Word 2007 document.

2 The Themes group is presented on .... tab.
(a) Home   (b) Page Layout
(c) References   (d) Picture Tools Format

Ans. (b) The Themes group is presented on Page Layout tab.

3 The status of your document like current page number and number of pages are given by ....
(a) Formatting toolbar   (b) Status bar
(c) Standard toolbar   (d) None of these

Ans. (b) Status bar gives the status of your document like current page number and number of pages.

4 A new text document can be created by
(a) File → Open
(b) File → New → Blank Document → Create
(c) Open → New → Create
(d) None of the above

Ans. (b) New text document can be created by File → New → Blank Document → Create

5 The documents can be saved by using
(a) Ctrl + S   (b) File → Save
(c) File → Save As   (d) All of these

Ans. (d) Documents can be saved by clicking File → Save As, File → Save or using Ctrl + S keys.

6 The general arrangement of the text in the document is ....
(a) margin   (b) text alignment
(c) clipboard   (d) formatting

Ans. (d) Formatting is the general arrangement of the text in the document.

7 Which of the following alignments are available in MS-Word 2007?
(a) Left   (b) Right
(c) Center   (d) All of these

Ans. (d) Alignment refers to how the left and right edges of a paragraph align on a page. These are left, right, center and justify.

8 The .... alignment makes sure that none of the edges of text appear ragged.
(a) left   (b) right
(c) center   (d) justify

Ans. (d) The justify alignment makes sure that none of the edges of text appear ragged.

9 Line or paragraph spacing is measured in terms of lines or points, which is referred as ....
(a) text wrapping   (b) PDF
(c) XPS   (d) leading

Ans. (d) Line or paragraph spacing is measured in lines or points, which is referred to as leading. When leading is reduced, it automatically brings the lines of text closer.

10 It is a section of the document that appears at the bottom margin of the page.
(a) Footer   (b) Header
(c) Head   (d) Tail

Ans. (a) Footer is a section of the document that appears at the bottom margin of the page.

11 Which of the following is a set of formats consisting of such things as fonts, colors etc?
(a) Style   (b) Margin
(c) Indent   (d) Leading

Ans. (a) A style is a set of formats consisting of such things as fonts, colors, font size and paragraph formats.

12 Template includes .... text that is surrounded by brackets.
(a) margin   (b) placeholder
(c) data source   (d) track changes

Ans. (b) Template is a collection of styles that includes placeholder text that is surrounded by brackets.

13 A_____ is a model that you use to create other documents.   [CBSE SQP Term-I]
(a) template   (b) document
(c) design   (d) copy paste

Ans. (a) template

14 Which shortcut key is used to make the selected text italic?
(a) Ctrl + I   (b) Shift + I
(c) F1 + I   (d) None of these

Ans. (a) Ctrl + I is the shortcut key to make the selected text italic.

15 In a document, ... is used to apply a style to many different areas quickly without having to go back to the Styles and Formatting window and double click every time. **[CBSE 2021 Term-I]**
(a) Fill format mode   (b) Formatting window
(c) Painter mode   (d) Text wrapping

Ans. (*a*) Fill format mode

16 In a document, _____ refers to the vertical or horizontal placement of a graphic in relation to the chosen anchor point. **[CBSE SQP Term-I]**
(a) arrangement   (b) anchoring
(c) alignment   (d) text wrapping

Ans. (*c*) alignment

17 We can underline the text by ....
(a) Ctrl + B   (b) Ctrl + I
(c) Ctrl+ U   (d) None of these

Ans. (*c*) Ctrl + U is the shortcut key for underlining the text.

18 Which of the following is not an Autoshape?
(a) Line   (b) Circle
(c) Curve   (d) ClipArt

Ans. (*d*) ClipArt is not an Autoshape, because it is not found under shapes.

19 _____ controls how graphics are stacked upon each other or relative to the text. **[CBSE SQP Term-I]**
(a) Arrangement   (b) Alignment
(c) Anchoring   (d) Wrapping

Ans. (*a*) Arrangement

20 Which tab of MS-Word contains the Shapes option?
(a) Home   (b) Review
(c) Insert   (d) Mailings

Ans. (*c*) Insert tab of MS-Word contains the Shapes option under Illustrations group.

21 _____ include fonts, alignment, borders, background, number formats (for example, currency, date, number) and cell protection in document. **[CBSE SQP Term-I]**
(a) Cell style   (b) Numbering style
(c) Paragraph style   (d) Character style

Ans. (*a*) Cell style

22 The Insert tab symbol option from Symbols group is used to
(a) insert the footer   (b) insert the header
(c) format document   (d) insert symbols

Ans. (*d*) Insert tab symbol option from Symbols group is used to insert symbols in a document.

23 .... splits text in columns at a specific point.
(a) Column break   (b) Page break
(c) Next page break   (d) Continuous break

Ans. (*a*) Column break splits text in columns at a specific point.

24 Tanu explained his class that to apply an existing style, except for .... , position the insertion point in the paragraph, frame or page and then double·click on the name of the style in one of these lists. **[CBSE 2021 Term-I]**
(a) Window style   (b) Character style
(c) Paragraph style   (d) Cell style

Ans. (*a*) Window style

25 Two other toolbars can be opened from Picture Toolbar are : the .... and .... **[CBSE 2021 Term-I]**
(a) Edit picture, Color picture
(b) Format, drawing
(c) Graphic Filter toolbar, Color toolbar
(d) Floating toolbar, Color toolbar

Ans. (*b*) Format, drawing

Fill in the Blanks

1 .... is a powerful tool that you can use to create effective documents.

Ans. MS-Word 2007

2 Alignment buttons are available on the ... tab.

Ans. Home

3 Under Insert tab, ... group contains the features like Shapes, ClipArt etc.

Ans. Illustrations

4 .... is the rectangular area of the document window, where user can type his/her content.

Ans. Work area or Work space

5 An indentation is the distance between a .... and ....

Ans. margin, text

6 .... can be used for inserting information at the top of each page automatically. **[CBSE Textbook]**

Ans. Header

7 .... and .... generally contain information such as page number, date, document name etc.

Ans. Header, Footer.

8 .... command is used to move the text to a new page.

Ans. Page break

9 .... breaks move any text to the right of the cursor to the next time.

Ans. Text wrapping

10 After selecting the text you need to click the .... in the font group to make the font size large than the current font size.
[CBSE Textbook]

Ans. Font size

11 MS-Word 2007 allows you to insert .... in your documents.

Ans. Pictures

12 Picture Shape option comes under .... tab.

Ans. Picture Tools Format

13 .... option allows a user to edit pictures.

Ans. Crop

14 Full form of OLE is ....

Ans. Object Linking and Embedding.

15 .... types of mathematical symbol sets are available in Word 2007.

Ans. 8

16 Symbol option is available under .... group in the Insert tab. **[CBSE Textbook]**

Ans. Symbols

True and False

1 MS-Word 2007 allows you to easily create a variety of professional looking documents using features such a Themes, Styles, SmartArt and more.

Ans. **True** MS-Word 2007 is a powerful tool that allows you to create a variety of professional looking documents because in Word 2007, all the things are replaced with a new navigation system.

2 Home tab of MS-Word contains the Object option.

Ans. **False** Insert tab of MS-Word contains the Object option.

3 After inserting a picture, a new tab appears.

Ans. **True** After inserting a picture in Word 2007 document, a new tab appears namely Picture Tools Format. This tab helps a user to edit his/her picture according to need.

4 The text layout within a paragraph with respect to document margins is called text alignment.

Ans. **True** Text layout within a paragraph with respect to document margins is called text alignment. Text alignment can be left, right, center or justify.

5 You cannot modify your Word options and change the defined information that appears.

Ans. **False** Word options and pre-filled information can be modified by using MS-Word 2007 new features.

6 Pictures can be added to Word documents and they cannot be formatted in various ways.

Ans. **False** Pictures can be formatted in various ways after adding it to the Word document like changing the shape, adding a border, modifying effects, applying a predefined style and more.

7 You can insert only text as a header.

Ans. **False** You can insert any text or graphic as a header at the top of every page in the document.

8 Section break partitions both the body text and partition page margin.

Ans. **True** Section break partitions both the body text of the document footers, page numbers etc.

9 ClipArt object includes effects such as shadows, outlines, colors, gradients and 3D effects.

Ans. **False** WordArt object includes effects such as shadows, outlines, colors, gradients and 3D effects that can be added to a word or phrase.

10 MS-Word 2007 tool menu is packed full of lines, arrows, squares and much more.

Ans. **False** Word 2007 tool menu is not packed full of lines, arrows, squares but Word 2007 shapes menu is packed full of all these features.

11 The Drawing Tools Format tab appears at the bottom of the Word document window.

Ans. **False** Drawing Tools Format tab appears at the top of the Word document window after inserting shapes.

12 You cannot insert Mathematical symbols into a Word document.

Ans. **False** Word 2007 allows insertion of Mathematical symbols.

13 To insert a symbol like © (copyright), you need to click on the Special Character option of the Insert tab.

Ans. **True** © is a special character which is added by Symbol option under Insert tab.

Very Short Answer (VSA) Type Questions

1 Define MS-Word 2007.

Ans. MS-Word 2007 is a Word processing software package, which allows you to easily create a variety of professional looking documents like letters, reports and other documents using features such as Themes, Styles, SmartArt and more. It is a powerful tool that you can use to create effective documents.

2 How do you indent a full paragraph?

Ans. To indent a full paragraph, follow the given steps:
 (i) Open the Paragraph dialog box.
 (ii) In Indentation section, enter the value in Left and Right boxes.
 (iii) Click OK button.

3 Explain Header and Footer.

Ans. The Header is a section of the document that appears on the top margin.

While the Footer is a section of the document that appears on the bottom margin.

Headers and Footers generally contain information such as page number, date, document name etc.

4 List any five items that can be added to the header area.　　**[CBSE Textbook]**

Ans. Five items that can be added to the header section of a document can be
 (i) The title of the document
 (ii) Name of the document
 (iii) Pic/logo for the document
 (iv) Menu (that contain home, about, services etc.)
 (v) Date and time

5 Write the steps to insert date/time into Header or Footer.

Ans. Steps to insert date/time into header or footer are as follows:
 (i) On the Design tab, in the Insert group, click the Date & Time option.
 (ii) Select date and time format from the Date and Time dialog box.
 (iii) Click OK button.
 Now, Date/Time will appear in the document.

6 What do you understand by template in MS-Word?

Ans. Templates are a special type of Word document that can hold text, styles, macros, keyboard shortcuts, custom toolbars, QAT and ribbon modifications and building blocks including AutoText entries.

7 Shivam wants to insert text into a template but he does not know how to do this? Help him to add text into a template.

Ans. To insert text into a template, he should follow given steps:
 ▪ Click near the text that he wants to replace. The text will be highlighted and a template tag will appear.
 ▪ Enter text. It will replace placeholder text with his entered text.

8 Distinguish between odd page break and even page break.

Ans. Difference between odd page break and even page break is that odd page break will insert a section break into your Word document that will break to the next odd page in the Word document while even page break will insert a section break into your Word document that happens on every even page of your Word document.

9 List any three word wrapping options available in a word processing software.　　**[CBSE Textbook]**

Ans. Three word wrapping options available in a word processing software are Square, Text and Through.

10 Riya is making her assignment on MS-Word document but while typing she typed some sentences in lower case. Now, she wants to change the text case of these sentences. Help her to achieve this.

Ans. She should change the text case by following steps:
 ▪ Select the text that she wants to modify.
 ▪ Click the Change Case option from the Font group on the Home tab.
 ▪ A menu will appear, select one of the text case option which she wants to apply.

11 List any two websites that offers free clip arts. **[CBSE Textbook]**

Ans. Websites that offer free clip arts are :
(i) openclipart
(ii) clker.com

12 What are objects in a word processing software? **[CBSE Textbook]**

Ans. The word processor object allows different formatting within the same object. However, word processor objects are printed as an image, so they require quite a bit more resources than a normal single or multiline text objects. Word processing objects includes text, graphical and embedded objects.

13 How can you define OLE?

Ans. OLE (Object Linking and Embedding) is a component document technology from Microsoft that allows you to dynamically link files and applications together. An object is a combination of data and the application needed to modify that data. You can thus embed objects in or link them to documents created with a different application.

For example, An excel spreadsheet can be embedded within a Microsoft Word document using OLE.

Short Answer (SA) Type Questions

1 What do you mean by ruler?

Ans. Ruler appears on the top and on the left side of the document window. It allows to format the horizontal or vertical alignment of text in a document.

Two types of ruler are available in MS-Word 2007 as follows
(i) Horizontal ruler indicates the width of the document.
(ii) Vertical ruler indicates the height of the document.

2 What is the difference between the Save and Save As options?

Ans. 'Save' means the file gets saved under its current name, in whatever folder it was saved before or in the default folder of that computer, whereas 'Save As' gives you the opportunity to save the file under a different name and in another folder. 'Save As' allows you to name the updated version with a new name and at the same time preserving the old version.

3 How can you modify a style in MS-Word?

Ans. To modify a style, follow the given steps:
- Click on Home tab.
- Click the More list arrow in the Styles group and right click the Style that you want to modify and then click Modify.
- Modify Style dialog box will appear. Click the type of Formatting.
- To add the style to the Quick Style Gallery, select the Add to Quick Style list check box.
- Click OK button.

4 How to insert column break in Word document?

Ans. To insert a column break, first you need to insert columns in a document, follow the given steps:
- Click where you want that page column to be break.
- Click on Page Layout tab from the ribbon.
- Select Page Setup group and then choose Breaks option. A drop-down menu will appear.
- Select Column option.

5 Define different types of text case options.

Ans. There are five text case options as follows:
(i) **Sentence case** It is used to change the first letter of every sentence in uppercase.
(ii) **Lowercase** It changes the whole selected text in lowercase letters.
(iii) **Uppercase** It changes the whole selected text in uppercase letters.
(iv) **Capitalise Each Word** It is used to change first letter of every word in capital case.
(v) **Togglecase** It toggles whole selected text, i.e., changes each capital letter into lowercase and each small letter into uppercase.

6 How can you change the shape of a picture?

Ans. Refer to text on Page no. 68.

7 Write the steps to insert autoshapes in Word document.

Ans. To insert autoshapes, follow the below steps:
- On the ribbon, select Insert tab → Illustrations group.
- Click Shapes option → select the desired shape.
- Click and hold the mouse from where you want to start the shape.
- Drag the mouse to create the desired shape. An outline indicating the size of your shape appears.
- Release the mouse button. The shape will appear in your Word document.

8 How will you insert Mathematical symbols in your Word document?

Ans. Refer to text on Page no. 71.

9 How to insert the copyright symbol into a Word document?

Ans. Steps to insert the copyright symbol into a Word document are as follows:
- Select **Insert** tab.
- Click **Symbol** option from **Symbols** group.
- Select **More Symbols** ... .
- The Symbol dialog box will appear and select the **copyright** symbol.
- Click the **Insert** button.

Long Answer (LA) Type Questions

1 Explain different types of tabs available in MS-Word 2007.

Ans. Refer to text on Page no. 56-57

2 Explain the different Paragraph alignments.

Ans. Refer to text on Page no. 58-59

3 What is the need to modify the spacing of the lines or paragraph of your text?

Ans. An important part of creating effective documents lies in the document design. Line spacing or paragraph spacing is measured in lines or points, which is referred to as leading.

As a part of designing, the document and making formatting decisions, you will need to know how to modify the spacing. Just as you can format spacing between lines in your document, you can also choose spacing options between each paragraph.

Typically, extra spaces are added between paragraphs, headings or subheadings. Extra spacing between paragraphs adds emphasis and makes a document easier to read. When you reduce the leading, you automatically bring the lines of text closer together. Increasing the leading will space the lines out, allowing for improved readability.

4 Write the steps to insert header or footer.

Ans. Refer to text on Page no. 60.

5 What is template? How to create it?

Ans. Refer to text on Page no. 62

6 Write the steps to compress a picture.

Ans. Refer to text on Page no. 67

7 What is OLE? How do you link or embed an object?

Ans. OLE stands for Object Linking and Embedding. It is a microsoft technology that facilitates the sharing of applications data and objects written in different formats from multiple sources.

To link or embed an object, follow the given steps:
- Click on the worksheet, where you want to add the linked object.
- Select Insert tab from the ribbon.
- In the Text group, click on Object option. Object dialog box will appear.
- In Object dialog box, select the Create from File tab and then click Browse to find the file you want to insert.
- Browse dialog box will appear.
- To link to the source fill, rather than embedding it into your Word document or e-mail message, select Link to file.
- If you want the inserted file to appear as a clickable icon, rather than the first page of the file, select Display as icon.

Application Oriented Questions

1 Previous versions of Word looked similar and operated in many of the same ways. They had menus, toolbars, task pane and a 'Familiar' feeling design. In MS-Word 2007, all these things are replaced with a new navigation system and many new features.
(i) What is MS-Word 2007?
(ii) List new features of MS-Word 2007.

Ans. (i) MS-Word 2007 is the word processing software in the Microsoft Office 2007 suite.
(ii) Some new features of MS-Word 2007 are as follows:
(a) The Ribbon System　　(b) Themes
(c) Quick Styles　　(d) Pictures
(e) Live Preview　　(f) Shapes
(g) ClipArt　　(h) Charts
(i) SmartArt

2 Following are some descriptors describing some terms. Identify the terms/features these refer to.
(i) It is a pre-designed document that you can use to create new documents with the same formatting.
(ii) It is a tool that you can use to produce professional looking documents.
(iii) It is a new feature of 2007 Office suite that allows you to see changes in your document before you actually select an item.

Ans. (i) Template　　(ii) Themes　　(iii) Live Preview

3 Sona wants to add her pictures in a Word document.
   (i) Which tab she should use?
   (ii) Which command she should use to open Insert Picture dialog box?
   (iii) Can she resize the image?
   (iv) Is it possible to wrap text around an image?

Ans. (i) Insert tab
   (ii) Picture command in the Illustrations group
   (iii) Yes
   (iv) Yes

4 A Tablet company sells Tablets and accessories. The head of the company's marketing department has created the following leaflet by using a Word processor. The leaflet will be distributed to all the retail shops, main markets and malls.

ABC Ltd. Special Offers

To celebrate the completion of our five years in business, we are offering these special deals:

▪ Purchase a new mobile in June and get 50% off on MRP.

▪ Purchase 4 handsets and get one free.

To get more details, please contact to Mr Naveen on 180010400.

Which of the following two options can improve the layout of the leaflet?
   (i) Line spacing
   (ii) Search facility
   (iii) Mail merging
   (iv) Center alignments
   (v) Hyperlink

Ans. Line spacing, Center alignments.

5 You can make your documents professional and polished by utilising the header and the footer sections.
   (i) What is a header?
   (ii) Can you insert date or time into a header?

Ans. (i) Header is a section of the document that appears at the top margin of every page.
   (ii) Yes, we can insert date or time into a header.

6 Rahul is using Word processor to create his chemistry coursework. He wants to insert his roll number and page numbers in the footer of a document.
   (i) Define footer.
   (ii) In the text coursework, Rahul wants to insert only page numbers.
      (a) Where should he insert page numbers?
         In the Header, In the Footer or In the text of every page.
      (b) Is it possible to insert a footer without inserting a header?

Ans. (i) Footer is a section that appears at the bottom of every page. You can insert text/numbers/graphics to the footer section.
   (ii) (a) In the Footer
      (b) Yes, it is possible to insert a footer without inserting a header.

Self Assessment

Multiple Choice Questions

1. In MS-Word 2007, the ruler helps
   - (a) to set tabs
   - (b) to set indents
   - (c) to change page margins
   - (d) All of these
2. Selecting text means selecting
   - (a) a word
   - (b) a complete line
   - (c) an entire sentence or whole document
   - (d) All of these
3. The page numbers can be added into a header or
   - (a) sections
   - (b) margins
   - (c) columns
   - (d) footer

Fill in the Blanks

4. Vertical and horizontal scroll bars are used to ....
5. The .... alignment makes sure that all the selected text is aligned to an equal distance from the both left and right margins.
6. Headers always appear at the .... and footers appear at the .... of every page.

True or False

7. Editing text in MS-Word 2007 only involves inserting text.
8. Header text is displayed at the bottom margin.
9. To insert a special symbol, select the Symbol option from the Insert menu.

Very Short Answer (VSA) Type Questions

10. What is the use of UPPERCASE text case option in MS-Word 2007?
11. What is the difference between header and footer?
12. How will you create a graphical looking arrow Symbol in Word document?

Short Answer (SA) Type Questions

13. Explain two ways to insert a picture.
14. Write down the steps to change line spacing.
15. Write steps to insert Mathematical symbols in a document.

Long Answer (LA) Type Questions

16. Define the following terms:
    - (i) Text alignment
    - (ii) Formatting
17. How can you link the object of the Word document?
18. What are the differences between Page break and Section break?

Electronic Spreadsheet (Advanced)

Microsoft Excel is a spreadsheet application program offered in the microsoft office software package that runs on a personal computer. An electronic spreadsheet is used for analysing, sharing and managing information for accounting purpose, performing mathematical calculations, budgeting, billing etc. A spreadsheet is a matrix of rows and columns similar to an accounting ledger.

The spreadsheet program also provides tools for creating graphs and inserting pictures etc. for analysing the data etc. Some examples of spreadsheet software are Lotus 1-2-3, Quattro-Pro, MS-Excel, VisiCalc etc. in which VisiCalc is the oldest spreadsheet package.

Elements of Electronic Spreadsheet

A spreadsheet which is also known as worksheet is an electronic document in which data is organised in the rows and columns of a grid and can be used in calculations. Each worksheet contains 1048576 rows and 16384 columns.

The intersection of each row and column is called **cell**. It may hold numbers, formulas, text, date and time etc.

A workbook is a document that contains one or more worksheets.

By default, every workbook contains 3 worksheets.

A **formula** is an equation that calculates the value to be displayed. A formula when used in a worksheet, must begin with an equal to (=) sign.

A **cell pointer** is a boundary that specifies which cell is active at particular moment.

A **cell address** is recognised by column label and row number. e.g. C2 where, C is a column label and 2 is a row number.

Opening of Spreadsheet

You may start MS-Excel by clicking the icon of MS-Excel or from Start button. To open the spreadsheet

Click at Start button → All Programs → Microsoft Office → Microsoft Office Excel 2007

By this, the main window of MS-Excel 2007 will open on your screen like the following figure.

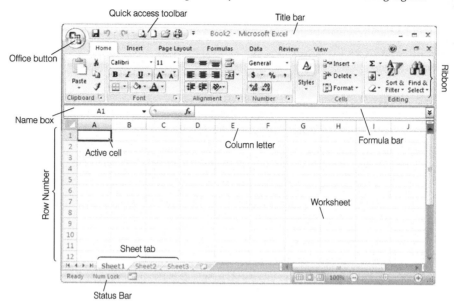

MS-Excel Window

The components of a spreadsheet window are as follows:

(i) **Office Button** It is found at the top-left corner of the window. It contains many options like New, Open, Save etc.

(ii) **Quick Access Toolbar** It is a customizable toolbar situated at the top-left corner of the window that contains a set of commands that are independent of the tab. These commands are those commands which are mostly used by the user.

(iii) **Title Bar** The bar located at the top of the application window is called title bar. It contains the name of the currently open document.

(iv) **Ribbon** It contains panel of commands which are organised into a set of tabs. Clicking a tab, displays several command groups. Each group has related command buttons.

Some Tabs and their Groups are as follows:

Tabs	Groups
Home	Clipboard, Font, Alignment, Number, Styles, Cells, Editing.
Insert	Tables, Ilustrations, Charts, Links, Text.
Page Layout	Themes, Page Setup, Scale to Fit, Sheet Options, Arrange.
Formulas	Function Library, Defined Names, Formula Auditing, Calculation.
Data	Get External Data, Connections, Sort & Filter, Data Tools, Outline.
Review	Proofing, Comments, Changes.
View	Workbook Views, Show/Hide, Zoom, Window, Macros.

(v) **Formula Bar** It displays the contents of the active cell. This could be a formula, data or just text.

(vi) **Name Box** It is located on left of the formula bar. It displays the cell reference or the name of the active cell.

(vii) **Worksheet** MS-Excel consists worksheets. Each worksheet contains columns and rows.

(viii) **Workbook** An Excel file is called a workbook. It contains several worksheets. By default, there are three worksheets in a workbook.

(ix) **Column Letter** Columns run vertically on a worksheet and each one is identified by a letter in the column header.

(x) **Row Number** Rows run horizontally in a worksheet and are identified by a number in the row header.

(xi) **Active Cell** The cell with the black outline. Data is always entered into the active cell.

(xii) **Sheet Tab** The tab at the bottom of a worksheet tells you the name of the worksheet such as Sheet 1, Sheet 2 etc. Switching between worksheets can be done by clicking on the tab of the sheet which you want to access.

(xiii) **Status Bar** It appears at the bottom of the workbook and provides such information like sum, average etc.

Note A workbook range refers to a group of cells.

Creating a New Workbook

Steps to create a new workbook are as follows:

Step 1   Click at **Microsoft Office** button.

Step 2   Select **New**. The **New Workbook** dialog box will appear and **Blank Workbook** is highlighted by default.

Step 3   Click **Create** button.

New Workbook Dialog Box

Opening an Existing Workbook

Steps to open an existing workbook are as follows:

Step 1   Click at **Microsoft Office** button.

Step 2   Select **Open**. The **Open** dialog box will appear.

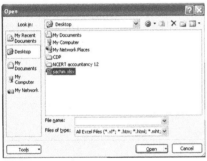

Open Dialog Box

Step 3   Choose the location and select the file which you want to open.

Step 4   Click **Open** button.

Use AutoSum in Cells

AutoSum is a function in Microsoft Excel and other spreadsheet programs that adds together a range of cells and displays the total in the cell below the selected range. It automatically enters the appropriate formula or function into your spreadsheet.

To use the AutoSum feature, follow the given steps:

Step 1   Select the cell where you want to get the result of values.

For example, enter the following details in the spreadsheet and select the cell B8 to get total Price of Product.

	A	B
1	Product	Price
2	Router	26.97
3	DDR 3	49.99
4	Memory DDR	52.99
5	Hard Drive	63.99
6	Video Card	117.99
7	Ultra ATA	119.95
8		

Step 2   Click the Σ (AutoSum) option available in the Home tab → Editing group.

Step 3   Clicking **AutoSum** button will automatically select the adjacent cells and add the
= Sum( ) function in selected cell B8.

	A	B	C	D
1	Product	Price		
2	Router	26.97		
3	DDR 3	49.99		
4	Memory DDR	52.99		
5	Hard Drive	63.99		
6	Video Card	117.99		
7	Ultra ATA	119.95		
8		=sum(B2:B7		
9		SUM(number1, [number2], ...)		

Step 4   To get total, press the **Enter** key on the keyboard.

	A	B
1	Product	Price
2	Router	26.97
3	DDR 3	49.99
4	Memory DDR	52.99
5	Hard Drive	63.99
6	Video Card	117.99
7	Ultra ATA	119.95
8		431.88

Conditional Formatting

Conditional formatting is a feature in Excel and other spreadsheet programs that allows to change the appearance (font, color, border, shading) of a cell, depending on certain conditions. When a conditional format is applied on a cell, it means the formatting of the cell is based on a condition.

Applying Conditional Formatting

The following spreadsheet contains marks of the students.

To highlight cells that are greater than 80, follow the given steps:

Step 1   Select a range of cells on which you want to apply conditional formatting.

Step 2   Click the **Conditional Formatting** option available in the **Styles** group of the **Home** tab. The conditional formatting drop-down menu will appear.

Step 3   In the drop-down menu click the **Highlight Cells Rules** option, a submenu will appear. Select the desired condition.

For example, To highlight the marks that are greater than 80, click the Greater Than option. Greater Than dialog box will appear.

Step 4   Greater Than dialog box enter the value **80** in the given text box and select a formatting style.

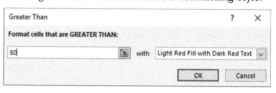

Step 5   Click **OK** to apply conditional formatting. The cell will be highlighted that are greater than 80.

Note   You can also highlight cells that are less than a value, between a low and high value etc.

Check Point 01

1   What is the intersection of a row and a column?

2   Which of the following option is located at the top of the active window?

    (a) Title bar   (b) Equation editor

    (c) Sheet tabs   (d) Office button

3   What is the icon of AutoSum?

4   Which option is used to add a range of cells and displays the total in the cell?

5   Name the method which is used to change the appearance of a cell.

Hide/Unhide/Freeze Rows and Columns

Hiding/Unhiding Rows and Columns

In Excel, you can hide rows and columns in several ways to change the view of the worksheet. When you finish your task, you can unhide the rows and columns to return the worksheet to its original state. This is useful as you may want the data to be included in the sheet, however you may not necessarily want all the data viewable.

Hide Rows/Columns

To hide rows/columns, follow the given steps:

Step 1 Select row or column, which is to be hidden.

Step 2 On the **Home** tab in the **Cells** group, click the **Format** option. The drop-down menu will appear.

Step 3 Select **Hide & Unhide** option, a submenu will appear. Select the Hide Rows or Hide Columns.

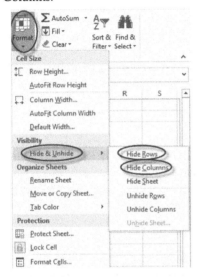

Step 4 The selected rows or columns will be hidden.

Unhide Rows/Columns

To unhide rows or columns, follow the given steps:

Step 1 In the spreadsheet, select the area where rows or columns are hidden.

Step 2 On the **Home** tab in the **Cells** group, click the **Format** option. The above drop-down menu will appear.

Step 3 Select **Hide & Unhide** option and then select Unhide Rows or Unhide Columns.

Freezing/Unfreezing Rows or Columns

When working with large datasets in Excel, you may often want to lock certain rows or columns so that you can view their contents while scrolling to another area of the worksheet. This can be done by using the freeze panes command.

Freezing Rows

To freeze rows, follow the given steps:

Step 1 Select the row above that which want to freeze.

⊿	A	B	C	D	E
1	Name	English	Hindi		
2	Neha		21	56	
3	Sonam	58	85		
4					

Step 2 Click the **Freeze Panes** option in the **Window** group of **View** tab. A drop-down menu will appear.

Step 3 In the drop-down menu, click the **Freeze Panes** option. All rows above of selection row will be frozen and a dark horizontal line will appear to indicate the freezing is done.

⊿	A	B	C	D	E
1	Name	English	Hindi		
2	Neha		21	56	
3	Sonam	58	85		
4					

Note Freeze Top Row → To lock the first row
Freeze First Column → To lock the first column
Freeze Panes → To lock several rows

Freezing Columns

To freeze the columns, follow the given steps:

Step 1 Select the column to the right of the last column you want to lock or freeze.

⊿	A	B	C	D
1	Name	English	Hindi	
2	Neha		21	56
3	Sonam	58	85	
4				
5				

Step 2 Click the **Freeze Panes** option in the **Window** group of **View** tab. A drop-down menu will appear.

Step 3 In the drop-down menu, click the **Freeze Panes** option. All the columns to the selected column will be frozen and a dark vertical line will appear to indicate freezing is done.

	A	B	C	D
1	Name	English	Hindi	
2	Neha	21	56	
3	Sonam	58	85	
4				
5				

Freezing Rows and Columns

To freeze both the rows and columns, follow the given steps:

Step 1 Select the Cell that is below the Row and to the right of Column that you want to freeze.

	A	B	C	D	E
1	Name	English	Hindi	Math	
2	Neha	21	56	75	
3	Sonam	58	85	65	
4	Shivani	75	65	81	
5	Deepa	67	32	71	
6					

Step 2 Click the **Freeze Panes** option in the **Window** group of **View** tab. A drop-down menu will appear.

Step 3 In the drop-down menu click the **Freeze Panes** option. All the columns left to the selected cell and above of the selected cell will be frozen and dark vertical and horizontal lines will appear to indicate the freezing is done.

	A	B	C	D	E
1	Name	English	Hindi	Math	
2	Neha	21	56	75	
3	Sonam	58	85	65	
4	Shivani	75	65	81	
5	Deepa	67	32	71	
6					

Unfreezing Row or Columns

To unlock frozen rows or columns, go to **View** tab, **Window** group and click Freeze Panes → Unfreeze Panes.

Set Page Breaks

Page breaks are dividers that break a worksheet into separate pages for printing. Microsoft Excel inserts automatic page breaks based on the paper size, margin setting, scale options and the positions of any manual page breaks that you insert. To print a worksheet with the exact number of pages that you want, you can adjust the page breaks in the worksheet before print it.

Inserting a Page Break

To insert page breaks, follow the given steps:

Step 1 Open Excel worksheet where you want to insert page breaks.

Step 2 Go to the **View** tab and click the **Page Break Preview** icon in the Workbook Views group.

> **Note** You can also see where page breaks will appear if you click Page Break Preview button image on the excel status bar.

Step 3 If you get the **Welcome to Page Break Preview** dialog box. Tick the 'Do not show this dialog again' check box to avoid seeing this message again.

Step 4 Now, you can easily view the location of page breaks in your worksheet.

Step 5 To add a horizontal page break, select the row above that you want to insert the page break.

	A	B	C	D
1	Name	Class	Address	Contact Number
2	Rekha	4th	Brahmpuri	9876321851
3	Neha	7th	Mohanpuri	4597315826
4	Sonam	2nd	Delhi road	9762481035
5	Prince	8th	Baghpat road	8625746814
6				

Step 6 Right click on this row and select the **Insert Page Break** option from the menu list.

Or Select the **Breaks** option in the **Page Setup** group of **Page Layout** tab. A horizontal line appears that indicates the page break.

	A	B	C	D	E
1	Name	Class	Address	Contact Number	
2	Rekha	4th	Brahmpuri	9876321851	
3	Neha	7th	Mohanpuri	4597315826	
4	Sonam	2nd	Delhi road 2	9762481035	
5	Prince	8th	Baghpat road	8625746814	
6					

Step 7 If you need to insert a vertical page break, select the column to the right of where you want to insert the page break.

	A	B	C	D	E
1	Name	Class	Address	Contact Number	
2	Rekha	4th	Brahmpuri	9876321851	
3	Neha	7th	Mohanpuri	4597315826	
4	Sonam	2nd	Delhi road	9762481035	
5	Prince	8th	Baghpat road	8625746814	
6					
7					
8					
9					
10					

Step 8 Right Click on this column and select the Insert Page Break option from the menu list or the **Breaks** option in the **Page Setup** group of **Page Layout** tab. A vertical line appears that indicates page break.

	A	B	C	D
1	**Name**	**Class**	**Address**	**Contact Number**
2	Rekha	4th	Brahmpuri	9876321851
3	Neha	7th	Mohanpuri	4597315826
4	Sonam	2nd	Delhi road	9762481035
5	Prince	8th	Baghpat road	8625746814
6				

Delete a Page Break

To delete a Page Break, follow the given steps :

Step 1 Select the worksheet that you want to modify.

Step 2 On the **View** tab, in the **Workbook Views** group, click the **Page Break Preview** or you can also click Page Break Preview button on the status bar.

Step 3 To delete a Horizontal Page Break, select the row below the Page Break that you want to delete.

Or

To delete a vertical page break, select the column to the right of the page break that you want to delete.

Step 4 On the **Page Layout** tab in the **Page Setup** group, click Breaks → **Remove Page Break**.

Step 5 The selected page will be removed.

Return to Normal View

To return to Normal View, after you finish working with the page breaks, on the **View** tab, in the **Workbook Views** group, click Normal.

Page Layout Setting

We can setup the page according to user's need from the Page Setup dialog box.

To open the Page Setup dialog box

Click Page Layout tab → Page Setup dialog box (⬊)

Page Setup Dialog Box

There are four tabs in Page Setup dialog box which are used to make different changes in page setup.

Tabs and their groups are as follows:

Tabs	Groups
Page	Orientation, Scaling, Paper size, Print quality etc.
Margins	Set margins from Left, Right, Bottom, Top and set Header or Footer margins etc.
Header/Footer	Header or footer settings etc.
Sheet	Print area, Print titles, Print, Page order.

1. Setting Page Margins

Page margins are the blank spaces between the worksheet data and the edges of the printed page.

To set page margins follow the given steps:

Step 1 On the **Page Layout** tab, click the **Custom Margins** command on the **Margins** drop-down menu in the Page Setup group or click the **Margins** tab of **Page Setup** dialog box.

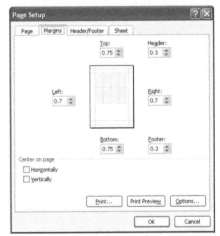

Margins Tab of Page Setup Dialog box

Step 2 Enter the new margin settings in the Top, Bottom, Left and Right text box and then click on **OK** button.

2. Setting Page Orientation

In excel, user select the Portrait or Landscape page orientation, which affects the layout of the printed page. The default page orientation is Portrait.

To set orientation of the page, follow the given steps:

Step 1 On the **Page Layout** tab, click the **Orientation** button in the **Page Setup** group.

Step 2 A drop-down menu appears, select either **Portrait** (to move vertically) or **Landscape** (to move horizontally).

3. Setting Size of Page

To change the paper size setting, click the **Size** button in the **Page Setup** group of the **Page Layout** tab and select the desired size from the resulting drop-down list.

4. Setting Print Area

On the worksheet, select the cells that you want to define as the print area. To set the print area, click Page Layout tab → Print Area in Page Setup group → Set Print Area

To clear the print area, click anywhere on the worksheet for which you want to clear the print area.

Or

Click Page Layout tab → Print Area in Page Setup → Clear Print Area

5. Setting Background

You can specify a background for the excel sheet using the following steps:

Step 1　Click the **Background** option under **Page Setup** group in the **Page Layout** tab. **Sheet Background** dialog box will appear.

Step 2　Select the background image that you want and click the **Insert** button.

Saving Workbook

Steps to save the workbook are as follows

Step 1　Click at Microsoft Office button.

Step 2　Do one of the following:
- Choose Save As, if you would like to save the file for the first time or save the file by different name.
- Choose Save, if the file has already been named.
- Press Ctrl+S from keyboard.

Step 3　Save As dialog box will appear.

Step 4　Type the file name in File name box and choose Excel Workbook from the Save as type list box.

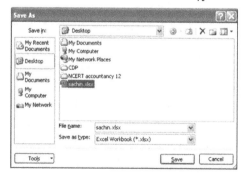

Save As Dialog Box

Step 5　Click at Save button.

The default extension of excel workbook is .xlsx.

Manage Workbook Views

The workbook views options allow user to view or see the spreadsheet differently. You can adjust the excel window to suit what you are currently working on by changing the view to match your current task.

There are five types of view available in the spreadsheet.

(i) **Normal** This is the default view of the spreadsheet application. Normal view is used for building and editing the worksheets.

(ii) **Page Layout** It displays worksheets as they would appear if you printed them out. Through this option, you can check from where the page begin and end as well as to see the header/footer on the page.

(iii) **Page Break Preview** You can use this option to see where the page breaks appear when you print the document. It displays the page breaks as blue line.

(iv) **Custom Views** You can use this option to save the current by display document and setting as a custom view which you can apply in future. It allows you to save specific display settings and print settings for a worksheet.

(v) **Full Screen** It displays only the worksheet, no formula bar, ribbon or status bar are visible. This allows you to maximise the amount of content you see in your worksheet.

Creating a Custom View

To create a custom view, follow the given steps:

Step 1　On a worksheet, change the display and print settings that you want to save in a custom view.

Step 2　On the **View** tab in the **Workbook Views** group, click the **Custom Views**.

Step 3　**Custom Views** dialog box will appear, click the **Add** button.

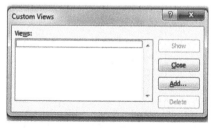

Step 4 The **Add View** dialog box will appear. In the Name text box, type a name for the view.

Step 5 Under include in view area, select the check boxes of the settings that you want to include. Click on the **OK** button.

Apply a Custom View

To apply a custom view, follow the given steps:

Step 1 On the **View** tab, in the **Workbook Views** group **Custom Views**.

Step 2 The **Custom Views** dialog box will appear, in the **Views** box, select the name of the View that you want to apply and then click **Show** button.

Note The worksheet that was active when you created the Custom View, is automatically displayed.

Delete a Custom View

To delete a custom view, follow the given steps:

Step 1 On the **View** tab, in the **Workbook Views** group click **Custom Views**.

Step 2 Custom views dialog box will appear. In the **Views** box click the name of the View that you want to delete and then click **Delete** button.

Check Point 02

1 Which tab is used to hide row or column?
2 When you freeze a row .... remains constant.
3 In which tab, Freeze Panes option is available?
4 What is used to break a worksheet into separate pages for printing?
5 .... is the blank space between the worksheet data and the edges of the printed page?

Apply Cell and Range Names

Assign a descriptive name to a cell or range in Excel to help make formulas in your worksheet much easier to understand and maintain. Assigning name is useful for quickly locating specific cells by entering the name in the Name box, while working with a large spreadsheet.

To assign name to a range of cells, follow the given steps:

Step 1 Select the cells or cell range that you want to apply the name.

	A	B	C
1	**Product Name**	Price	
2	Orange	45	
3	Mango	50	
4	Apple	80	
5	Banana	20	
6	Pineapple	50	
7	Grapes	60	
8	Cherry	45	
9	Tomato	25	
10	Potato	30	
11	Ginger	50	
12	Onion	20	
13	Total cost of fruits		
14			

Step 2 On the Formulas tab, click **Define Name** in the **Defined Names** group. The **New Name** dialog box will appear.

New Name Dialog Box

Step 3 In the **Name** text box, type a name for the range and click on the **OK** button.

Step 4 The name is assigned to the selected cells.

Step 5 If you would like to calculate the total cost of fruits then there is now no need to enter the formula as = Sum (B2 : B8). You can directly type it as = Sum (Fruits).

Step 6 The above mentioned formula will provide total cost of fruits.

	A	B	C
1	**Product Name**	Price	
2	Orange	45	
3	Mango	50	
4	Apple	80	
5	Banana	20	
6	Pineapple	50	
7	Grapes	60	
8	Cherry	45	
9	Tomato	25	
10	Potato	30	
11	Ginger	50	
12	Onion	20	
13	Total cost of fruits	350	

Working with Charts

A chart is a tool that is used in excel for representing data graphically.

Charts allow anyone to more easily see the meaning behind the numbers in the spreadsheet and to make showing comparisons and trends much easier. It is one of the most impressive features of MS-Excel.

Endless variations are available, allowing you to produce a chart, edit and format it, include titles and many more.

Types of Chart

Several different types of charts are available within excel. The type to choose will depending on the data involved and what information the chart is intended to convey or highlight. Different types of charts are as follows:

Column Charts

Values are display in the form of vertical columns in this chart. Many different data series and their values are displaying on x-axis and y-axis respectively.

Line Charts

These types of charts can be 2 or 3-dimensional. Line charts are used to compare trends over time. There are similarities with area charts but line chart tends to emphasise the rate of change rather than volume of change over time. 3-D lines appear as 'ribbons' which can be easier to see on the chart.

Pie Charts

These types of charts can be 2 or 3-dimensional. They are used to compare the size of the parts with the whole. Only one data series can be plotted, making up 100%. Pie charts within their own window can be made to 'explode' by dragging more pieces of pie away from the centre.

Bar Charts

These types of charts can be 2 or 3-dimensional. They are used to show individual figures at a specific time or to compare different items. Categories are listed vertically, so that bars appear on the horizontal, thus there is less emphasis on time flow. Bars extending to the right represent positive values while those extending left represent negative values.

Area Charts

These types of charts can be 2 or 3-dimensional. They are used to compare the changes in volume of a data series over time, emphasising the amount of change rather than the rate of change. Area charts show clearly, how individual data series contribute to make up the whole volume of information represented in the graph.

XY Scatter Charts

These types of charts are used to compare two different numeric data series and can be useful in determining whether one set of figures might be dependent on the other. They are also useful, if the data on the X-axis represents uneven intervals of time or increments of measurement.

Components of a Chart

Various components of chart are as follows:

(i) **X-axis** is a horizontal axis, which is also known as **category axis**.

(ii) **Y-axis** is a vertical axis, which is also known as **value axis**.

(iii) **Data series** is a set of values that you want to display in a chart.

(iv) **Chart area** is the total area that is enclosed by a chart.

(v) **Plot area** is the main region of the chart in which your data is plotted.

(vi) **Chart title** is the descriptive text aimed at helping user to identify the chart.

(vii) **Legends** is a unique color or pattern, which helps you to identify an individual data series.

(viii) **Gridlines** are the horizontal and vertical lines within the plot area in a chart.

(ix) **Data label** provides additional information about a value in the chart, that is coming from a worksheet cell.

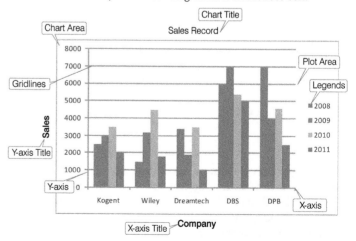

The chart shown in the above figure is based on the worksheet shown below:

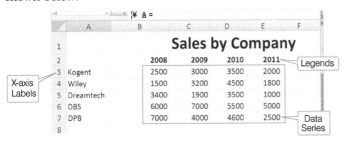

A Sales by Company worksheet

Creating a Chart

To create a chart, follow the given steps:

Step 1 Select the data that you want to show, including the column titles and the row labels.

Step 2 Click the **Insert** tab in the **Charts** group, click the type of chart that you want to create to have Excel display the available chart subtypes.

Step 3 Then, select anyone of them by clicking it.

Step 4 After selecting, click OK button.

Modifying and Formatting Charts

Once you insert a chart, a new set of **Chart Tools** arranged into three tabs, i.e. Design, Layout and Format will appear above the ribbon. These are only visible when the chart is selected.

1. Changing Type of the Chart

To change the chart type, follow the given steps:

Step 1 Select the chart and click on the **Design** tab.

Step 2 In the **Type** group, click on the **Change Chart Type** command.

Step 3 **Change Chart Type** dialog box will appear. Select the type of chart, you want to use.

Step 4 Click on the **OK** button.

2. Changing Layout of the Chart

To change layouts for the chart, follow the given steps:

Step 1 Select the chart and click on the **Design** tab.

Step 2 In the **Chart Layouts** group, select the required layout for the chart.

3. Changing Style of the Chart

For changing the chart style, follow the given steps:

Step 1 Select the chart and click on the **Design** tab.

Step 2 In the **Chart Styles** group, select the required style for the chart.

Step 3 Click the More arrow drop-down to view all the styles options.

Formatting the Chart

When formatting charts in excel, you must right click on the item to open the Formatting Window.

To format the chart, follow the given steps:

Step 1 Select the chart, that you want to format.

Step 2 If you need to change formatting options for the titles in the chart, you can use the command button on the Format tab of the **Chart Tools** contextual tab.

Step 3 To format the entire text box that contains the title, click one of the following buttons in **Shape Styles** group.

  (a) **Shape Fill** This button is used to select a new color for the text box containing the selected chart title.

  (b) **Shape Outline** This button is used to select a new color for the outline of the text box for the selected chart text.

  (c) **Shape Effects** This button is used to apply a new effect (shadow, reflection, glow, soft edge) to the text box containing the selected chart title.

Step 4 To apply predefined shape, click on the **Shape Styles** group in **Format** tab and select the style that you want to use.

Step 5 To change the format of chart text, click on **WordArt Styles** group in **Format** tab and select the WordArt that you want to apply.

Step 6 To format any object of **Chart Area**, right click on **Object**.

  For example, To format the axis of the chart then right click on the Axis of the chart and select the Format Axis. Format Axis dialog box will appear and select required option.

Sort and Filter Data

Sorting the Data

Sorting list is a common spreadsheet task that allows user to easily re-order the data. The most common type of sorting is alphabetical ordering which you can do in ascending or descending order.

Basic Sorts

To use ascending or descending sort which depends on one column, follow the given steps:

Step 1 Select those cells, which you want to sort.

Step 2 Click on **Sort & Filter** option from **Editing** group in **Home** tab. By this, you will get a drop-down menu.

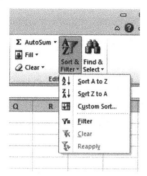

Step 3 From this menu, select **Sort Ascending** (A to Z) button or **Sort Descending** (Z to A) button.

Custom Sorts

To sorting more than one columns, follow the given steps

Step 1 Select those cells, which you want to sort.

Step 2 Click on **Sort & Filter** option from **Editing** group in **Home** tab. By this, you will get a drop-down menu.

Step 3 From this menu, select **Custom Sort** option and then **Sort** dialog box will appear.

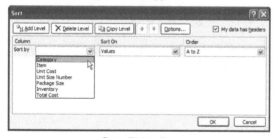

Sort Dialog Box

Step 4 Click on **Add Level** button and then select next column (which you want to sort).

Step 5 Click on **OK** button.

Filtering the Data

Filtering data is a quick and easy way to find and work with a subset of data in a range of cells or in a table column. Filtered data displays only the rows that meet criteria that you specify and hides rows that you do not want to display.

To filtering the data, follow the given steps:

Step 1 Select those column (which you want to filter).

Step 2 Click on **Sort & Filter** option from **Editing** group in **Home** tab. By this, you will get a drop-down menu.

Step 3 From this drop-down menu, select **Filter** option.

Step 4 Arrow sign will display the right side of first cell in selected columns.

Step 5 Click on arrow and select those words which you want to filter.

Step 6 Click on **Clear** option from **Sort & Filter** to clear.

Check Point 03

1 Which option is useful for quickly locating specific cells by entering the name in the name box, while working with a large spreadsheet?

2 Which chart is used to compare the size of the component with the whole?

(a) Bar chart   (b) Area chart

(c) Pie chart   (d) Line chart

3 Gridlines denotes the type of data plotted in a chart

(a) True   (b) False

4 Which option is used to easily reorder your worksheet data?

Cell Referencing

In excel, cell is referenced by a combination of row number and column letter. Cell referencing is a method by which a cell or series of cells in a formula is referred.

Referencing a cell is beneficial in formulas because it allows your formulas to update automatically, if the value in a particular cell changes and can also update formulas as cells are copied or moved.

Three types of cell referencing are as follows:

1. Relative Cell Referencing

When we want to copy a formula from one cell to another cell and also, we want to modify the cell references used in the formula according to the new cell, then it is called relative cell referencing. Consider the following example for understanding this concept.

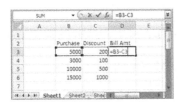

In the given screenshot, for calculating Bill Amt, we have entered formula (= B3 – C3) in cell D3.

Now, in case of relative cell referencing, if we will copy this formula in any other cell, the references used in formula B3 and C3 will change accordingly.

Let us copy this formula in cell D4. The formula will automatically become (= B4 – C4) in cell D4. Similarly, in cell D5 and D6 you can copy formula using relative referencing.

2. Absolute Cell Referencing

When we want to copy a formula from one cell to another cell, but we do not want to modify the cell references used in the formula according to the new cell, then it is called absolute cell referencing. For making the reference of a cell absolute, we need to use '$' (dollar) sign before row number and column letter. Consider the following example for understanding the concept.

In the above example in cell D3, we have written formula= B3 – C3. Now, when we will copy this formula in cell D4, it will be copied as it is, without any change.

3. Mixed Cell Referencing

When we use '$' sign either before row number or before column letter, then it is called mixed cell referencing. In other words, mixed referencing is a combination of both relative and absolute referencing. Consider the following example for understanding this concept:

In the above example in cell D3, we have written formula =B$3 – $C3. Now, when we will copy this formula in cell D4, it will be copied as = B$3 – $C4 because of mixed referencing.

Calculate Data Across Worksheets

Using multiple sheets in the same excel workbook helps organise data into distinct categories. Sometimes, in excel user need to perform calculations on multiple worksheets. Excel provides an easy way to calculate aggregate functions across a range of sheets.

In the below example, you will see how this can be performed against any range of sheets and sheet names. The data in the next three images (Data 1, Data 2 and Data 3) will be summed on the 'Summary' sheet.

(i)

Ist Sheet with Data

(ii)

2nd Sheet with Data

(iii)

3rd Sheet with Data

(iv) To add the data of all three sheets, click the Summary sheet and type formula in Cell A1 as = Sum (Data 1 : Data 3! A1)

After entering formula, press Enter key. Now, drag the AutoFill handle down to copy the formula in rest of cells. Excel changes cell references automatically and provides results accordingly.

Sum of all 3 Sheets

Using Multiple Workbooks and Linking Sheets

Spreadsheet also allows user to link the cells from various worksheets and from various workbook or spreadsheet. A link is a reference to a cell or a range of cells in another workbook. To link cells from different workbooks, follow the given steps:

Step 1 Open the workbook that will contain the external reference (the destination workbook) and the workbook that contains the data that you want to link to (the source workbook).

Step 2 In the source workbook, click on the **Save** option in the Quick Access Toolbar.

Step 3 Select the cell or cells in which you want to create the external reference.

Step 4 Type = if you want to perform calculations or functions on the external reference's value, type the operator or function that you want to precede the external reference.

Step 5 On the **View** tab, in the **Window** group, click **Switch Windows**, click the **Source Workbook** and then click the worksheet that contains the cells that you want to link to.

Step 6 Select the name that you want to link.

Sharing Worksheet Data

If you want several users to work in the same excel workbook simultaneously, you can save the workbook as a shared workbook. Users can enter data, insert rows and columns, add and changes formulas and change formatting.

To share the worksheet data, follow the given steps:

Step 1 Click the **Review** tab.

Step 2 Click **Share Workbook** in the **Changes** group.

Step 3 On the **Editing** tab, Select the **Allow changes by more than one user at the same time. This also allows workbook merging** check box and then click on **OK** button.

Step 4 In the **'Save As'** dialog box, save the shared workbook on a network location where other users can gain access to it.

Check Point 04

1 What is the combination of absolute and relative cell addressing?

2 Which tool allows you to copy formula or value from one cell to another?

3 Which tab is used to link the source workbook to the destination workbook?

4 Share Workbook option is available in which group?

Some Pointer Shapes in MS-Excel

Shape	Context	Action
⊹	The default pointer shape, appears in most excel workspace contexts	Moves cell pointer or selects a range of cells
↕ ↔	Appears, when the pointer is on the border of a window	Adjusts window size
↨ ⊹⊳	Appears, when the pointer is between a row or column divider	Adjusts height and width of rows and columns
I	Appears, when you are editing cell contents	Provides a text insertion point
⌐↓	Appears, when the pointer is on a column or row heading	Selects columns or rows
⤯	Appears, when the pointer is placed over a cell border, graphic or other object	Moves cells, graphics or objects
⌐+	Appears, when the pointer is on the 'fill corner' of a cell or cell range	AutoFills other cells with similar information
⇖	Appears, when mouse is placed over the Ribbon	The standard Microsoft Windows pointer, selects Ribbon and menu options

Keyboard Shortcuts for MS-Excel 2007

Ctrl Combination Shortcut Keys

Ctrl+Shift+(	Unhides any hidden row with the selection.
Ctrl+Shift+)	Unhides any hidden column with the selection.
Ctrl+Shift+~	Applies the General number format in Microsoft Excel.
Ctrl+Shift+$	Applies the Currency format with two decimal places.
Ctrl+Shift+%	Applies the Percentage format with no decimal places.
Ctrl+Shift+^	Applies the Exponential scientific number format with two decimal places.
Ctrl+Shift+#	Applies the Date format with the day, month and year.
Ctrl+Shift+@	Applies the Time format with the hour and minute and AM or PM.
Ctrl+Shift+!	Applies the Number format with two decimal places, thousands separator and minus sign(−) for negative values.
Ctrl+Shift+;	Enters the current time.
Ctrl+;	Enters the current date.
Ctrl+'	Copies a formula from the cell above the active cell into the cell or the Formula bar.
Ctrl+9	Hides the selected rows.
Ctrl+0	Hides the selected columns.
Ctrl+B	Applies or removes columns.
Ctrl+C	Copies the selected cells. Ctrl+C followed by another Ctrl+C displays the clipboard.
Ctrl+D	Uses the Fill Down command to copy the contents and format of the topmost cell a selected range into the cells below.
Ctrl+I	Applies or removes italic formatting.
Ctrl+N	Creates a new blank workbook.
Ctrl+O	Displays the Open dialog box to open or find a file. Ctrl+Shift+O selects all cells contain comments.
Ctrl+P	Displays the Print dialog box.
Ctrl+R	Uses the Fill Right command to copy the contents and format of the leftmost cell of a selected range into the cells to the right.

Ctrl+S	Saves the active file with its current file name location and file format.
Ctrl+U	Applies or removes underlining.
Ctrl+W	Closes the selected workbook window.
Ctrl+X	Cuts the selected cells.
Ctrl+Y	Repeats the last command or action, if possible.
Ctrl+Z	Uses the Undo command to reverse the last command or to delete the last entry that you typed.

Function Keys

F1	Displays the Help task pane.
F2	Edits the active cell and positions the insertion at the cell contents.
F6	Switches between the worksheet, ribbon, task pane and zoom controls.
F7	Displays the Spelling dialog box to check spelling in the active worksheet or selected range.
F11	Creates a chart of the data in the current range.
F12	Displays the Save As dialog box.

Other Useful Shortcuts Keys

Arrow Keys	Move one cell up, down, left or right in a worksheet.
Backspace	Deletes one character to the left in the formula bar.
Delete	Removes the cell contents (Data and formulas) from selected cells without affecting cell formats or contents.
Esc	Cancels an entry in the cell or formula bar.
Home	Moves to the beginning of a row in a worksheet.
Page Down	Moves one screen down in a worksheet.
Page Up	Moves one screen up in a worksheet.
Tab	Moves one cell to the right in a worksheet.

SUMMARY

- A spreadsheet is an interactive application for organisation, analysis and storage of data in tabular form.
- An excel workbook is a file that contains one or more worksheets that you can use to organise various kinds of related information.
- An excel worksheet is a single spreadsheet that contains cells organised by rows and columns.
- To quickly sum a row or a column of values in an excel worksheet, you can use the AutoSum button.
- Conditional formatting is a feature of Excel, which allows user to apply a format to a cell or a range of cells based on certain criteria.
- A page break is used to determine where the printed page ends and begins with the next one, so the content before the page break will be printed on one page and after the page break on another.
- Page margins are used to specify how much white space should be left around the information in the worksheet.
- The Workbook views allow user to view or see the spreadsheet differently.
- A range is a group or block of cells in a worksheet that have been selected or highlighted.
- A chart is a visual representation of data, in which the data are represented by symbols such as bars in a bar chart or lines in a line chart.
- Sorting is the process of arranging objects in a certain sequence or order according to specific rules.
- A cell reference refers to a cell or a range of cells on a worksheet and can be used in a formula so that Excel can find the values or data which you want that formula to calculate.
- AutoFill allows user to identify a series of data and automatically fill cells with the appropriate text.

Exam Practice

Multiple Choice Questions

1 Which of the following is a spreadsheet software?
(a) Lotus 1-2-3   (b) VisiCalc
(c) Both 'a' and 'b'   (d) None of these

Ans. (*c*) Some examples of spreadsheet software are Lotus 1-2-3, MS-Excel, VisiCalc etc., in which VisiCalc is the oldest spreadsheet package.

2 A worksheet is a
(a) collection of workbooks
(b) processing software
(c) combination of rows and columns
(d) None of the above

Ans. (*c*) A worksheet is a combination of rows and columns.

3 By default, a workbook in excel contains how many worksheets?
(a) 16   (b) 3
(c) 15   (d) 256

Ans. (*b*) By default, every workbook contains 3 worksheets in Excel.

4 AutoSum option is available in
(a) Home tab   (b) View tab
(c) Insert tab   (d) Layout tab

Ans. (*a*) AutoSum option is available in the Editing group of Home tab.

5 To access Freeze Panes, you will click the
(a) Format tab   (b) View tab
(c) Window tab   (d) Insert tab

Ans. (*b*) Click the Freeze Panes option in the Window group of View tab.

6 Which of the following option allows you to insert page breaks in spreadsheets?
(a) Manual pages   (b) Breaks
(c) Manual horizontal (d) None of these

Ans. (*b*) To insert page breaks in spreadsheet, click on the Breaks option in the Page Setup group of Page Layout tab.

7 Page margins are the
(a) cell
(b) horizontal space
(c) blank spaces
(d) vertical space

Ans. (*c*) Page margins are the blank spaces between the worksheet data and the edges of the printed page.

8 The default page orientation in spreadsheet is
(a) landscape   (b) horizontal
(c) portrait   (d) None of these

Ans. (*c*) The default page orientation in spreadsheet or excel is portrait.

9 How many types of views are available in the spreadsheet?
(a) 3   (b) 4
(c) 5   (d) 2

Ans. (*c*) There are five types of views available in the spreadsheet i.e. Normal, Page Layout, Page Break Preview, Custom Views and Full Screen.

10 If you want to locate a range of cells by its name, then you will enter its name in
(a) formula bar   (b) name box
(c) cell   (d) None of these

Ans. (*b*) In the name text box, type a name for the range and click on the OK button.

11 Arguments passed to a macro from Calc are always ....   **[CBSE 2021 Term-I]**
(a) strings   (b) references
(c) numbers   (d) values

Ans. (*d*) values

12 .... function takes data from a series of worksheets or workbooks and summaries it into a single worksheet that you can update easily.   **[CBSE 2021 Term-I]**
(a) Summation   (b) Data Consolidation
(c) Data Format   (d) Data Chart

Ans. (*b*) Data Consolidation

13 Which of the following charts selects only one range of data series?
(a) Line chart   (b) Pie chart
(c) Scatter chart (d) Bar chart

Ans. (*b*) Pie chart can select only one range of data series.

14 Which of the following component provides additional information in the chart?
(a) Legend   (b) Gridlines
(c) Data label   (d) Plot area

Ans. (*c*) Data label provides additional information about a value in the chart, that is coming from a worksheet cell.

15 In which group of Insert tab, various charts are available?
(a) Charts group   (b) Type group
(c) Shape Styles group   (d) None of these
Ans. (a) Various charts are available in Charts group of Insert tab.

16 Which allows you to reorder data?
(a) Sorting   (b) Filtering
(c) Scenario   (d) Custom sorting
Ans. (a) Sorting allows you to easily reorder your data.

17 Which function cannot be performed through Subtotal in a Spreadsheet?   **[CBSE SQP Term-I]**
(a) Sum   (b) Product
(c) Average   (d) Percentage
Ans. (d) Percentage

18 Find out the odd one.
(a) Absolute   (b) Relative
(c) Mixed   (d) AutoFill
Ans. (d) Absolute, relative and mixed are three types of cell referencing but AutoFill is not.

19 Cell address $B $3 in a formula means
(a) it is a mixed reference
(b) it is an absolute reference
(c) it is a relative reference
(d) None of the above
Ans. (b) $ sign in a formula need to add row number and column letter for absolute referencing.

20 While entering a formula, cell address B $ 5 represents
(a) absolute referencing   (b) mixed referencing
(c) relative referencing   (d) All of the above
Ans. (b) It represents mixed reference because we are using $ sign before row number 5 only. Hence, as we will drag this, only B will change but 5 will remain same.

21 To copy a formula from one cell to another.
(a) Drag the autofill handle
(b) Cut the cell
(c) Both 'a' and 'b'
(d) None of the above
Ans. (a) After entering formula, press Enter key. Now, drag the autofill handle down to copy the formula in rest of cells.

22 Scenarios are tool test for _____ questions.   **[CBSE SQP Term-I]**
(a) Auto   (b) Goal Seek
(c) What-if   (d) Drop Down
Ans. (c) What-if

23 For enter the current time in excel, you need to press
(a) Ctrl + Alt +;   (b) Shift + Alt +;
(c) Ctrl + Shift + ;   (d) None of these
Ans. (c) You need to press Ctrl + Shift + ; for enter the current time in excel.

24 Which of the following shortcut keys moves the cursor to the beginning of a row in a worksheet?
(a) End   (b) Home
(c) Page Up   (d) Up
Ans. (b) Home shortcut key is used to move the cursor to the beginning of a row in a worksheet.

25 Which allows you to display the specific data?
(a) Sorting   (b) Filtering
(c) Scenario   (d) Custom sorting
Ans. (b) Filtering allows the user to displays only the specific data that meet criteria.

26 Which tab is used to share the worksheet data?
(a) Home   (b) Review
(c) Insert   (d) Layout
Ans. (b) To share the worksheet data, click the Review tab.

27 It refers to a cell or a range of cells on a worksheet and can be used to find the values or data that you want formula to calculate.   **[CBSE SQP Term-I]**
(a) Row   (b) Column
(c) Autosum   (d) Cell reference
Ans. (d) Cell reference

28 Hema is a chartered accountant. She used to maintain the accounts in a spreadsheet on everyday basis. There are number of steps which she needs to follow every time. Can you suggest her a feature of spreadsheet through which she can perform these tasks quickly without repeating the steps every time?   **[CBSE SQP Term-I]**
(a) Record changes   (b) Track changes
(c) Goal seek   (d) Using macros
Ans. (d) Using macros

29 Raj has created a worksheet where he has added all the information of his employees. He wants every employee to go through the worksheet and update their address and phone number, if required. He also would like to know the changes done by his

employees. Which feature of spreadsheet he should enable to see the changes made by his employees? **[CBSE SQP Term-I]**
(a) Macro
(b) Link workbook
(c) Change worksheet
(d) Track changes

Ans. (*d*) Track changes

30 A chart is a tool that is used in
(a) mail merge　　　(b) database
(c) excel　　　　　　(d) document

Ans. (*c*) A chart is a tool that is used in excel for representing data graphically.

31 Which of the following charts is used for comparing the changes in data over a period of time?
(a) Bar chart　　　　(b) Area chart
(c) Scatter chart　　(d) Line chart

Ans. (*d*) Line chart is used for comparing the changes in data over a period of time.

32 If you are continually working with the same range, then you may give a name to the range using .... option under Data Menu.
[CBSE 2021 Term-I]
(a) Define data　　　(b) Define range
(c) Define reference　(d) Define addres

Ans. (*b*) Define range

33 In Calc, using the Subtotals dialog, you can select arrays and then choose a statistical function to apply to them. For efficiency, you can choose up to .... groups of array to which to apply a function. **[CBSE 2021 Term-I]**
(a) two　　　　　　(b) three
(c) four　　　　　　(d) five

Ans. (*b*) three

34 Solve option under Tools menu amounts to a more elaborate form of .... The difference is that the Solver deals with equations with multiple ....
[CBSE 2021 Term-I]
(a) Unknown variables, Goals Seek
(b) Variables, Equation
(c) Goal Seek, Unknown variables
(d) Subtotal, Goal Seek

Ans. (*c*) Goal Seek, Unknown variables

35 Rohan has ₹ 50,000 that he wants to invest in two mutual funds for one year. Fund A is a low risk fund with 18% interest rate and Fund B is a higher risk fund with 21% interest rate. Which feature of Spreadsheet (Calc) will be help him to decide? **[CBSE 2021 Term-I]**
(a) Solver　　　　　(b) Subtotal
(c) Linking sheets　　(d) Macros

Ans. (*a*) Solver

Fill in the Blanks

1 .... is used for analysing, sharing and managing information for accounting purpose.

Ans. Spreadsheet

2 Each worksheet contains .... rows and .... columns.

Ans. 1048576, 16384 (XFD)

3 .... is a function in excel that adds together a range of cells.

Ans. AutoSum

4 .... is used for adding the values given in cells automatically without writing the formula. **[CBSE Textbook Page no. 152]**

Ans. AutoSum

5 .... allows you to change the appearance of a cell.

Ans. Conditional formatting

6 Conditional formatting is available under .... styles group in Home tab.
[CBSE Textbook]

Ans. Conditional Formatting

7 Hide and Unhide option is available in .... tab.

Ans. Home

8 To insert a .... page break, select the row below where you want to insert the page break.

Ans. horizontal

9 To return to normal view after you finish working with the page breaks, you need to click .... in the .... group under the view tab. **[CBSE Textbook Page no. 161]**

Ans. Normal, Workbook views

10 Two types of page orientation are .... & .... **[CBSE Textbook Page no. 163]**

Ans. Portrait, Landscape

11 .... is the default view of the spreadsheet application.

Ans. Normal

12 Gridlines are the .... and .... lines within the plot area in a chart.

Ans. horizontal, vertical

13 In formatting the chart, ... button to select a new color for the text box containing the selected chart title.

Ans. Shape Fill

14 In .... referencing, the relative address of the cell gets adjusted with respect to the current cell.

Ans. relative

15 Spreadsheet allows to link the cells from various .... and from various ...

Ans. worksheet, workbook

16 Ctrl + N shortcut key is used to create a new blank ....

Ans. workbook

True and False

1 The spreadsheet program provides tools for creating graphs and inserting picture.

Ans. **True** The spreadsheet program also provides tools for creating graphs and inserting pictures for analysing the data.

2 A cell address is recognised by column number and row label.

Ans. **False** A cell address is recognised by column tabel and row number.

3 The title bar is located at the bottom of the application window.

Ans. **False** The bar located at the top of the application window is called title bar.

4 Freeze Top Row option is used to lock the first row.

Ans. **True** Freeze Top Row option is available under the Freeze Panes that is used to lock the first row.

5 Page breaks are dividers that insert a worksheet into separate pages for printing.

Ans. **False** Page breaks are used in excel to break a worksheet into separate pages for printing.

6 Four tabs are available in Page Setup dialog box.

Ans. **True** There are four tabs in Page Setup dialog box which are used to make different changes in Page Setup.

7 We cannot change the paper size in Page Setup group.

Ans. **False** Paper size can be changed in Page Setup group of the Page Layout tab.

8 Page Break Preview is used to see that where the page break appear when we print the document.

Ans. **True** Page Break Preview displays the page breaks as blue line when we print the document.

9 The title of the chart tells the type of the chart.

Ans. **False** The title of the chart tells the name of the chart.

10 The contents of a cell can be changed by pressing F2 key on keyboard.

Ans. **True** F2 is a shortcut for making cell editable.

Very Short Answer (VSA) Type Questions

1 Define the term formula.

Ans. A formula is an equation that calculates the value to be displayed. A formula when used in a worksheet, must begin with an equal to (=) sign.

2 How to open a spreadsheet in Excel?

Ans. To open the spreadsheet

Click at Start button→ All Programs →Microsoft Office →Microsoft Office Excel 2007

By this the main window of MS-Excel 2007 will open on your screen.

3 Define the term workbook.

Ans. A workbook is a collection of worksheets. By default, there are three worksheets in every workbook.

4 Reena is new to use an Excel. Her instructor asked her to open Excel and questioned about active cell. What is active cell?

Ans. An active cell is a cell with heavy black color boundary.

5 What will be the column names of the below statement?
(i) 26th column   (ii) 28th column

Ans. (i) Z   (ii) AB

6 How many ways are there for adding a new worksheet in an Excel workbook?

Ans. There are two methods of adding a new worksheet in an excel workbook; insert worksheet tab at the buttom and insert button on cells group under Home tab.

7 What is conditional formatting?

Ans. Conditional formatting allows user to format a cell based on the value in it. For example, if you want to highlight all the cells where the value is less than 30 with a red color, you can do that with conditional formatting.

8 List any five conditions/formates/items that can be used for conditional formatting.
[CBSE Textbook Page no. 155]

Ans. Five conditions/formats that can be used for conditional formatting are-
(i) Highlight Cells Rules   (ii) Top/Bottom Rules
(iii) Data Bars   (iv) Color Scales
(v) Icon Sets

9 What is freeze panes in MS-Excel?

Ans. To lock any row or column, Freeze Panes is used. The locked row or column will be visible on the screen even after we scroll the sheet vertically or horizontally.

10 What do you mean by Page Break?

Ans. A Page Break is used to determine where the printed page ends and begins the next one, so the content before the page break will be printed on one page and after the page break on another.

11 Name the tabs of spreadsheet which are available in Page Setup dialog box?

Ans. There are four tabs in Page Setup dialog box, which is used to make different changes in Page Setup. i.e. Page, Margins, Header/Footer and Sheet.

12 What is the use of workbook views in Excel?

Ans. Using the workbook views group of commands, you can view your Excel workbook in different layouts. Five types of views. i.e. Normal, Page Layout, Page Break Preview, Custom Views and Full Screen are available in spreadsheet.

13 How many cells would be there in the cell range [A1 : B2]?

Ans. There would be 4 cells in the given cell range.

14 Write down the formula for adding values of cells A1 to A5.

Ans. Formula for adding values of cells A1 to A5 would be = SUM(A1 : A5)

15 Write down the importance of legend in charts.

Ans. With the help of legend, each data series can be uniquely identified by assigning a unique color or pattern.

16 What do you mean by relative referencing?

Ans. Cell referencing in which the cells are referred by their relative position in the worksheet relative to a particular cell is called relative referencing.

17 In a spreadsheet software, the formula = A1 + A2 was entered in cell A3 and then copied into cell B3. What is the formula copied into B3?

Ans. = B1 + A2 will be copied into B3.

18 The cell A1 has value Monday. If you are asked to click and drag the Fill handle of A1 downside then what will be the contents of cell A2, A3, A4 and A5?

Ans. Cells A2 , A3 , A4 and A5 will contain Tuesday, Wednesday, Thursday and Friday respectively.

Short Answer (SA) Type Questions

1 Write down the significance of electronic spreadsheets.

Ans. Using electronic spreadsheets, large volume of data can be stored in worksheets. Worksheets can be managed, edited, viewed, retrieved and printed easily in desired format. Electronic spreadsheets support charts, which represent data pictorially.

2 Define the meaning of formula.

Ans. Formulas in Excel are used to perform calculations on data entered into the formula cell. Formulas begin with an equal (=) sign and are entered into the worksheet cell(s) where you want the results to appear.

3 What is the difference between a workbook and a worksheet?

Ans. Differences between workbook and worksheet are as follows:

Workbook	Worksheet
A workbook is an Excel file with one or more worksheets.	A worksheet is a single spreadsheet of data.
A workbook would be the entire binder, with everything in it.	A worksheet would be like one section in that binder.

4 Is it possible to remove a worksheet? State the process of doing it.

Ans. Yes, it is possible to remove a worksheet. To remove a worksheet right click on the Sheets tab of the sheet that you want to delete and choose Delete from pop-up menu, or choose Delete Sheet from the pop-up menu of Delete option on Cells group under Home tab.

5 What is the use of AutoSum in spreadsheet?

Ans. To quickly sum a row or a column of values in an Excel worksheet, you can use the AutoSum button in the Editing group of the Home tab. When you click this button, Excel inserts the built in sum function into the active cell and simultaneously selects what the program thinks is the most likely range of numbers that you want summed.

6 Why do you need to freeze rows and columns in a spreadsheet?

Ans. To keep an area of a worksheet visible while you scroll to another area of the worksheet, go to the View tab, where you can freeze panes to lock specific rows and columns in place, or you can split panes to create separate window of the same worksheet.

7 What are charts in MS-Excel?

Ans. To enable graphical representation of the data in Excel, charts are provided. A user can use any chart type, including column, bar, line, pie, scatter etc. by selecting an option from Insert tab's Charts group.

8 For what purpose pie charts are useful?

Ans. Pie charts are useful for the following purposes:
   (i) They convey approximate propositional relationship at a point in time.
   (ii) They compare part of a whole at a given point in time.
   (iii) Exploded portion of a pie chart emphasise a small proportion of part.

9 List seven chart elements.
                                    [CBSE Texbook Page no. 171]

Ans. The chart elements are as follows :
   (i) **X-axis** is a horizontal axis known as category axis.
   (ii) **Y-axis** is a vertical axis known as value axis.
   (iii) **Data Series** is the set of values you want to plot in the chart.
   (iv) **Chart Area** is the total area of the chart.
   (v) **Chart Title** is the descriptive text aimed at helping user to identify the chart.
   (vi) **Gridlines** are horizontal and vertical lines which are inserted in the chart.
   (vii) **Data Label** provides additional information about a data marker.

10 How cell reference is useful in the calculation?

Ans. In order to avoid writing the data again and again for calculating purpose, cell reference is used. When you write any formula, for specific function, you need to direct Excel the specific location of that data. This location is referred as, cell reference. So, everytime a new value added to the cell, the cell will calculate according to the reference cell formula.

Long Answer (LA) Type Questions

1 How can conditional formatting be used to identify duplicates in excel? Write the steps.

Ans. Conditional formatting is one of the most simple powerful feature in excel spreadsheets. You can use conditional formatting when you want to highlight cells that meet a specified condition. Conditional formatting in excel can be used to identify duplicates in a datasheet.

   1. Select the dataset in which you want to highlight duplicates.

   2. Go to Home tab → Conditional Formatting → Highlight Cells Rules → Duplicate Values.

   3. Duplicate values dialog box will appear in the Duplicate Values dialog box, make sure duplicate is selected in the left drop-down. You can specify the format to be applied by using the right drop-down. There are some existing formats that you can use, or specify your own format using the Custom Format option.

   4. Click OK button.

2 Explain the steps to hide rows and columns.

Ans. Refer to text on Page no. 85.

3 Explain the concept of workbook views alongwith its various types.

Ans. Refer to text on Page no. 88.

4 List five chart types available in spreadsheet.
[CBSE Textbook Page no. 171]

Ans. The five types of charts in Excel are given below:

Line Chart Data that is arranged in columns or rows on a worksheet can be plotted in a Line chart. Line chart's can display continuous data over time, set against a common scale and are therefore ideal for showing trends in data at equal intervals. In a Line chart, category data is distributed evenly along the horizontal axis and all value data is distributed evenly along the vertical axis.

Pie Chart Data that is arranged in one column or row only on a worksheet can be plotted in a Pie chart. Pie charts show the size of items in one data series, proportional to the sum of the items. The data points in a Pie chart are displayed as a percentage of the whole pie.

Scatter Chart Data that is arranged in columns and rows on a worksheet can be plotted in an XY (Scatter) chart. Scatter charts show the relationships among the numeric values in several data series, or plots two groups of numbers as one series of XY coordinates.

Bar Chart Data that is arranged in columns or rows on a worksheet can be plotted in a Bar chart. Bar charts illustrate comparisons among individual items.

Area Chart Data that is arranged in columns or rows on a worksheet can be plotted in an Area chart. Area charts emphasise the magnitude of change over time and can be used to draw attention to the total value across a trend. For example, Data that represents profit over time can be plotted in an Area chart to emphasise the total profit.

5 What is excel sort and filter?

Ans. Refer to text on Page no. 91-92.

6 Explain the concept of cell referencing alongwith its various types.

Ans. Excel supports three types of cell referencing which are as follows:

(i) **Relative** Every relative cell reference in formula automatically changes when the formula is copied down a column or across a row. As the example illustrated here shows, when the formula is entered (= B4 − C4) is cell D4 then this formula copied in D5 then it will change into (= B5 − C5) related to cell.

(ii) **Absolute** An absolute cell reference is fixed. Absolute references do not change if you copy a formula from one cell to another. Absolute reference have dollar sign ($) like S9. When the formula = C4*D9 is copied into another cell, the absolute cell reference remains as D9.

(iii) **Mixed** A mixed cell reference has either an absolute column and a relative row, or a absolute row and a relative column. e.g. $A1 is an absolute reference to column A and a relative reference to row 1. As a mixed reference is copied from one cell to another, the absolute reference stays the same but the relative reference changes.

Application Oriented Questions

1 Open Excel on your computer and create the following half year report of salary of employees.

A	B	C	D	E	F	G	H
1				Half Year Report			
2 Name	April	May	June	July	August	September	Total
3 Neha	20000	20001	20002	20003	20004	20005	
4 Pooja	15000	14000	13000	20000	22000	34000	
5 Kavita	10000	11000	16000	50000	26000	27000	
6							

Use the AutoSum and AutoFill features to get the total of six months salary of each employees.

Ans. Select the cell (B3 : G3) and click the Σ AutoSum option available in the Home tab → Editing group. After that AutoSum button will automatically add the range in cell H3. Now, drag the AutoFill handle down to copy the formula in Cells H4 and H5.

A	B	C	D	E	F	G	H
1				Half Year Report			
2 Name	April	May	June	July	August	September	Total
3 Neha	20000	20001	20002	20003	20004	20005	120015
4 Pooja	15000	14000	13000	20000	22000	34000	118000
5 Kavita	10000	11000	16000	50000	26000	27000	140000
6							

2 Describe, how the owner of the restaurant could use the spreadsheet for financial modeling?

Ans. (i) Decide on a total purchasing need for next week/month/year.

(ii) Change figures in spreadsheet.

(iii) Raise/lower/add/delete any value.

(iv) Compare results with predicted/total needed/target results.

(v) To general use for budgeting like to calculate profit.

3 Enter the following details in sheet and perform the given tasks.

	A	B	C	D	E
1			**Employee Records**		
2	Emp_Code	Name	Dept	City	Salary
3	101	Rohan	HR	Delhi	50000
4	102	Anuj	Account	Punjab	60000
5	103	Rahul	Sales	Noida	45000
6	104	Pooja	Admin	Mumbai	60000
7	105	Neha	HR	Pune	70000
8					

(i) Hide the column D and row 3

(ii) Freeze the row 3.

Ans. (i) Select the row 3, on the Home tab in the Cells group, click the Format option. Select Hide & Unhide and then Hide Rows. The row 3 will be hidden. Similarly, select the column D, on the Home tab in the cells group, click the Format option. Select Hide & Unhide and then Hide Columns. The column D will be hidden.

(ii) Select the row 3, click the Freeze Panes option in the Window group of View tab. Click on the Freeze Panes option. All rows above the row 3 will be frozen and a horizontal line will appear to indicate the freezing is done.

4 Arihant stationery keeps stock of various stationeries in his shop. The proprietor wants to maintain a stock value and reorder level for following items as given in a spreadsheet. Write formulas for the operations (i) to (iii) and answer the questions (iv) and (v) based on the spreadsheet given below alongwith the relevant cell address.

	A	B	C	D	E	F	G	H
1	Item Code	Item Name	Minimum Stock Quantity	Quantity in Stock (Unit)	Rate (₹)	Stock Value (₹)	Quantity to Order (Unit)	Order Value
2	101	P. Holder	200	500	35			
3	123	Whitner	450	150	25			
4	113	Steppler Pin	250	450	5			
5	156	Paper cutter	300	600	10			

Sheet1 / Sheet2 / Sheet3 /

(i) To calculate the Stock Value as product of 'Quantity in Stock' and 'Rate' for each item present in the spreadsheet.

(ii) To calculate the 'Quantity to Order' as 'Minimum Stock-Quantity'-'Quantity in Stock' for each item.

(iii) To calculate the 'Order Value' as product of 'Quantity to Order' and 'Rate' for the items if 'Quantity to Order' > = 0, else assign the value as 0.

(iv) Proprietor wants to graphically represent his stationery stock. Suggest him the most appropriate feature of MS-Excel.

(v) If Quantity in Stock's value changes, will have to redo all the calculations for that particular column. Explain.

Ans. (i) At cell F2, type = D2*E2 and then copy this formula using Fill handle in range F3 : F5.

(ii) At cell G2, type = C2-D2 and then copy this formula using fill handle in range G3 : G5.

(iii) At cell H2, type = IF (G2 > = 0, G2*E2, 0) and copy this formula using Fill handle in the range H3 : H5.

(iv) He should create chart of any type to graphically represent his data.

(v) No, the recalculation is not again required because the formula and functions that are given changes according to the values in the cells.

5 Neha Mittal wants to store data of her monthly expenditure for a period of two year and also wants to perform some calculation and analysis. Which microsoft application, will you suggest Neha should use for this purpose and why?

Ans. Microsoft Excel should be used because it cannot only be used for storing data, but also be used to perform calculations and analysis of the data.

Self Assessment

Multiple Choice Questions

1. AutoSum automatically selects the value around
   (a) adjacent cells   (b) non-adjacent cells   (c) Both 'a' and 'b'   (d) None of these

2. In which group of Page Layout tab, 'Breaks' option is available?
   (a) Page Setup   (b) Workbook Views   (c) Arrange   (d) None of these

3. Which of the following is a view of Excel?
   (a) Normal   (b) Page Layout   (c) Full Screen   (d) All of these

Fill in the blanks

4. To insert a .... page break, select the column to the right of where you want to insert the page break.

5. Sort helps you to arrange the selected data either in an .... or .... order.

6. Assigning names to cells in a worksheet help you to .... specific cells.

True or False

7. There is only one type of chart in Excel.

8. Page Setup option is not available under the Page Layout tab.

9. Sorting allows you to easily reorder your data.

Very Short Answer (VSA) Type Questions

10. What are the total number of rows and columns in a worksheet?

11. What is the maximum number of worksheets can insert in Excel workbook?

12. What is the shortcut key to close the selected workbook window?

Short Answer (SA) Type Questions

13. How to perform addition to get total of values by using AutoSum feature?

14. How will you delete a page break from the worksheet?

15. How will you modify the default size of page into letter size?

Long Answer (LA) Type Questions

16. Explain the concept of electronic spreadsheet alongwith its various elements.

17. Write down the steps to insert a Page Break.

18. What do you mean by chart in MS-Excel? Why is it important to have an appropriate chart?

Application Oriented Type Questions

19. Create a student marks list of 10 students and five subjects. Highlight the marks of the students according to the following conditions.

Condition	Formatting
Marks > 60	Fill Green Color
Marks < 60	Fill Yellow Color

20. Modify the chart layout by converting it into bar chart.

Database Management System

Database Concept

A database is a collection of logically related information/data, which is available for one or more users organised in a way, so that it can be easily accessed, managed and updated. It is actually a place, where related piece of information is stored and various operations can be performed on it by the user.

A database is basically a computer based record/data/information keeping system. Data is raw, unorganised facts and entities relevant to the user need to be processed such as a digital representation of text, numbers, graphical images or sound. The data are stored in such a way that they are independent of the programs used by the people for accessing the data.

e.g. Consider the names, telephone numbers and addresses of the relatives etc. You may have recorded this data in an indexed address book or you may have stored it on a hard drive, using application software such as **Microsoft Access** or **OpenOffice.org BASE**.

Database can be created with the help of following structure:

Character → Field → Record → File → Database

Database Structure

Information When data is processed, organised, structured or presented in a given context so as to make it useful is called information.

Character The values of data are in the form of letter, number or special character.

File It is a collection of related record.

Need for a Database

The need for a database arose in the early 1960s in response to the traditional file processing system. In the file processing system, the data is stored in the form of files and a number of application programs are written by programmers to add, modify, delete and retrieve data to and from appropriate files.

However, the file processing system has a number of problems, which are as follows:

- Some information may be duplicate in several files.
- The file processing system lacks the insulation between program and data.
- Handling new queries is difficult, since it requires change in the existing application programs or requires a new application program.
- Unable to maintain data standards and does not provide data sharing.
- In this system, all the integrity rules need to be explicitly programmed in all application programs, which are using that particular data item.
- This system also lacks security features.

To overcome these problems, database system was designed.

Components of a Database

A database consists of several components. Each component plays an important role in the database system environment.

The major components of database are as follows:

Data

It is raw numbers, characters or facts represented by value. Most of the organisations generate, store and process large amount of data. The data acts as a bridge between the hardware and the software. Data may be of different types such as User data, Metadata and Application Metadata.

Software

It is a set of programs that lies between the stored data and the users of database. It is used to control and manage the overall computerised database. It uses different types of software such as MySQL, Oracle etc.

Hardware

It is the physical aspect of computer, telecommunication and database, which consists of the secondary storage devices such as magnetic disks, optical discs etc., on which data is stored.

Users

It is the person, who needs information from the database to carry out its primary business responsibilities. The various types of users which can access the database system are as follows:

(i) **Database Administrator (DBA)** A person, who is responsible for managing or establishing policies for the maintenance and handling the overall database management system is called DBA.

(ii) **Application Programmer** A people, who writes application programs in programming languages to interact and manipulate the database are called *application programmer*.

(iii) **End-user** A person, who interacts with the database system to perform different operations on the database like inserting, deleting etc., through menus or forms is called end-user.

Features of a Database

Features of a database to let you manage your data are as follows:

Tables

It is the building block of any relational database model, where all the actual data is defined and entered. A database consists of many tables. Tables (relations) consist of cells at the intersection of records (rows) and fields (columns). Different types of operations are done on the tables such as sorting, filtering, retrieving and editing of data. It is also known as a **file**.

(i) **Fields or Columns (Data item)** It is an area (within the record), reserved for a specific piece of data. It is the individual sub-component of one record. It contains set of characters. e.g. Customer number, customer name, street address, city, state, phone number, current address, date of birth, etc. Field in a table is also known as **column** or **attribute**.

(ii) **Records or Rows or Tuples** It is the collection of data items of all the fields (information) pertaining to one entity or a complete unit of information, i.e. a person, company, transition etc. Record of a table is also known as **row, entity** or **tuple**.

Queries

It is an inquiry into the database using the SELECT statement. These statements give you filtered data according to your conditions and specifications indicating the fields, records and summaries which a user wants to fetch from a database.

It allows you to extract information from the database based on the conditions that you define in query. MS-Access 2007 supports the database object query.

Forms

In a database, a form is a window or a screen that contains numerous fields or spaces to enter data. Forms can be used to view and edit your data. It is an interface in user specified layout.

e.g. A user can create a data entry form that looks exactly like a paper form. People generally prefer to enter data into a well-designed form, rather than a table.

Reports

When you want to print those records which are fetched from your database, design a report. It is an effective way to present data in a printed format. It allows you to represent data retrieved from one or more tables, so that it can be analysed.

Database Server

The term database server may refer to both hardware and software used to run a database, according to the context. As software, a database server is the back end portion of a database application, following the traditional client server model.

Check Point 01

1 What is the name given to a collection of logically related data?
2 Name the components of a database.
3 What is the use of software in database?
4 Which of the following is used to present data in a printed format?
   (a) Reports   (b) Forms
   (c) Queries   (d) Tables

Database Management System (DBMS)

It is a collection of programs that enables users to create, maintain database and control all the access to the database. It is a computer based record keeping system.

The primary goal of the DBMS is to provide an environment that is convenient and efficient for user to retrieve and store information. It acts as an interface between the application program and the data stored in the database.

DBMS is a software package that manages database. e.g. MySQL, INGRES, MS-ACCESS etc.

DBMS is actually a tool that is used to perform any kind of operation on data in database. It also maintains data consistency in case of multiple users. The purpose of a DBMS is to bridge the gap between information and data.

Some basic processes that are supported by a DBMS are as follows:

- Specification of data types, structures and constraints to be considered in an application.
- Storing the data itself into persistent storage.
- Manipulation of the database.
- Querying the database to retrieve desired information.
- Updating the content of the database.

A short list of database applications would include:

- Inventory
- Membership
- Shipping
- Invoicing
- Security
- Mailing
- Payroll
- Orders
- Reservation
- Accounting
- Catalogues
- Medical records

Relational Database Management System (RDBMS)

RDBMS is a type of DBMS that stores data in the form of relations (tables). Relational databases are powerful, so they require few assumptions about how data is related or how it will be extracted from the databases.

An important feature of relational database system is that a single database can be spread across several tables. Base, Oracle, DB2, SAP, Sybase, ASE, Informix, Access etc. are the examples of RDBMS.

Working of a Database

Database is created to operate large quantities of information by input, store, retrieve and manage the information. It is a centralised location which provides an easy way to access the data by several users. It does not keep the separate copies of a particular data file still a number of users can access the same data at the same time.

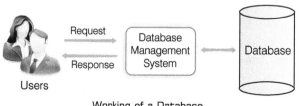

Working of a Database

As the diagram shows, DBMS works as an interface between the user and the centralised database. First, a request or a query is forwarded to a DBMS which works (i.e. a searching process is started on the centralised database) on the received query with the available data and if the result is obtained, it is forwarded to the user.

If the output does not completely fulfill the requirements of the user then a rollback (again search) is done and again search process is performed until the desired output is obtained.

Advantages of a Database/DBMS

The centralised nature of database system provides several advantages, which overcome the limitations of the conventional file processing system. These advantages are as follows:

(i) **Reduce Data Redundancy** Redundancy means 'duplication of data'. This eliminates the replication of data item in different files, extra processing required to face the data item from a large database. This also ensures data consistency and saves the storage space.

(ii) **Enforcing Data Integrity** It means that the data contained in the database is accurate and consistent. Integrity constraints or consistency rules can be applied to database, so that the correct data can be entered into the database.

(iii) **Data Sharing** The data stored in the database can be shared among multiple users or application programs.

(iv) **Data Security** The DBMS ensures that the access of database is done only through an authorised user.

(v) **Ease of Application Development** The application programmer needs to develop the application programs according to the user's needs.

(vi) **Backup and Recovery** The DBMS provides backup and recovery sub-system that is responsible to recover data from hardware and software failures.

(vii) **Multiple Views of Data** A view may be the subset of database. Various users may have different views of the database itself.

(viii) **Enforced Standards** It can ensure that all the data follow the applicable standards.

(ix) **Data Independence** System data descriptions are independent from the application programs.

Disadvantages of a Database/DBMS

There are many advantages of database, but database also have some minor disadvantages. These disadvantages are as follows:

(i) **Cost of Hardware and Software** Through the use of a database system, new costs are generated due to additional hardware and software requirements.

(ii) **Complexity** A database system creates additional complexity and requirements.

(iii) **Database Failures** If database is corrupted due to power failure or it is corrupted on the storage media, then our valuable data may be lost or the system will stop working.

(iv) **Lower Efficiency** A database system is a multi-user software, which is less efficient.

- **Data sharing** refers to the process of sharing single piece of data among different users.
- Multiple mismatching copies of the same data is known as **data inconsistency**. If a field value is stored in two places in the database, then storage space is wasted and changing the data in one place will not cause data inconsistency.
- **Data redundancy** leads to data inconsistency.

Data Integrity

Data Integrity ensures the accuracy, reliability and consistency of the data during any operation.

Each type of data integrity are as follows:

(i) **Entity Integrity** It defines the primary key of a table. Entity integrity rule on a column does not allow duplicate and null values.

(ii) **Domain Integrity** It defines the type, range and format of data allowed in a column. Domain integrity states that all values in a column must be of same type.

(iii) **Referential Integrity** It defines the foreign key concepts. Referential integrity ensures that data in related tables remains accurate and consistent before and after changes.

(iv) **User Defined Integrity** If there is some business requirements which do not fit any above data integrity then user can create own integrity, which is called user defined integrity.

Key Fields

The key is defined as the *column* or the set of columns of the database table which is used to identify each record uniquely in a relation. If a table has id, name and address as the column names then each one is known as the *key* for that table. The key field is a unique identifier for each record.

e.g. In Student table, you could use a combination of the lastname and firstname (or perhaps lastname, firstname to ensure you to identify each student uniquely) as a key field.

Relationship Between Keys

Types of Key Fields

The following are the types of key fields available in the DBMS system:

Primary Key

A field or a set of fields that uniquely identify each record in a table is known as a *primary key*. Each relation has atleast one column for which each row that must have a unique value. Only one column attribute can be defined as a primary key for each table.

A primary key must possess the following properties:

- It does not allow null values.
- It has a unique index.
- It allows numbers and text both.

e.g. In the student's table, studentId works as a primary key because it contains Ids which are unique for each student.

Note Data cannot be primary key.

Candidate Key

The set of all attributes which can uniquely identify each tuple of a relation are known as *candidate keys*. Each table may have one or more candidate keys and one of them will become the primary key. The candidate key of a relation is always a minimal key. e.g. Column studentId and the combination of firstname and lastname work as the candidate keys for the student table.

A candidate key must possess the following properties:

- For each row, the value of the key must uniquely identify that row.
- No attribute in the key can be discarded without destroying the property of unique identification.

Alternate Key

From the set of candidate keys after selecting one of the keys as a primary key, all other remaining keys are known as *alternate keys*.

e.g. From the candidate keys (studentId, combination of firstname and lastname), if studentId is chosen as a primary key, then the combination of firstname and lastname columns work as alternate keys.

Foreign Key

A field of a table (relation) that references the primary key of another table is referred to as *foreign key*. The relationship between two tables is established with the help of foreign key. A table may have multiple foreign keys and each foreign key can have a different referenced table. Foreign keys play an essential role in **database design**, when tables are broken apart, then foreign keys make it possible for them to be reconstructed.

e.g. CourseId column of student table (reference table) works as a foreign key as well as a primary key for course table (referenced table).

Data Storage

A data type is a data storage format that can contain a specific type or range of values. The fields within a database often require a specific type of data to be input.

e.g. A school's record for a table student may use a character data type for the students first name and last name. The student's date of admission and date of birth would be stored in a date format, while his or her marks in each subject may be stored as a numeric.

In MS-Access, data types can be categorised into the following types:

Data Types	Description
Text	Allows to store text or combination of text and numbers, as well as numbers that don't require calculations such as phone numbers. Also, it is a default data type.
Memo	Allows to store long blocks of text that use text formatting.
Number	Holds numeric values which are used for calculations and zip code. It includes various types such as Byte, Integer, Long Integer, (Single, Double) Replication ID and Decimal.

Data Types	Description
Date/Time	Allows to store date and time value for the year 100 to 9999.
Currency	Allows to store monetary values that can be used in calculations. Accurate upto 15 digits on L.H.S. and 4 digits on R.H.S. of decimal point.
AutoNumber	Allows to store numbers that are automatically generated for each record. It increases the number automatically when you add records.
Yes/No	Allows boolean value. (i.e. one of two possible values)
OLE Object	OLE is an acronym for Object Linking and Embedding. It can store objects such as a video clip, a picture, word document or any other binary data.
Hyperlink	Allows to store hyperlinks such as E-mail addresses.
Attachment	Allows to store files such as digital photos. Multiple files can be attached per record.
Lookup Wizard...	Lets you type a list of options, which can be chosen from a drop down list.

Field Length (Field Size)

It refers to the maximum number of characters that a field can contain. Each character requires one byte for its storage.

Field length is of two types which are as follows:

1. **Fixed Length Field** It is a type of field length in which the number of characters you enter in a field is fixed. These are present in **Format** option in **Data Type Formatting** group (in Datasheet tab) such as Currency, Euro, Percent etc.
2. **Variable Length Field** In this type of field length, the number of characters is not fixed. Actually, the number of characters of the data entered in the field decide the field length.

The field length or field size of each data type are as follows:

Data Type	Field Length or Field Size	Data Type	Field Length or Field Size
Text	0-255 characters	Memo	0-65,536 characters
Number	1, 2, 4, 8 or 16 bytes	Date/Time	8 bytes
Currency	8 bytes	AutoNumber	4 or 16 bytes
Yes/No	1 bit (0 or 1)	OLE Object	Upto 2 GB
Hyperlink	Each part contains upto 2048 characters	Lookup Wizard...	4 bytes

Numeric Data Types

It allows the database server to store numbers such as integers and real numbers in a column.

e.g. Age of the students, numbers obtained in subjects, etc.

Types	Length in Bytes	Minimum Value (Signed)	Maximum Value (Signed)	Minimum Value (Unsigned)	Maximum Value (Unsigned)
TINYINT	1	-128	127	0	255
SMALLINT	2	-32768	32767	0	65535
MEDIUMINT	3	-8388608	8388607	0	16777215
INT	4	-2147483648	2147483647	0	4294967295
BIGINT	8	-9223372036854775808	9223372036854775807	0	18446744073709551615

FLOAT (N, D) A small number with floating decimal point. It cannot be unsigned. Its size is 4 bytes. Here, N represents the total number of digits (including decimals) and 'D' represents the number of decimals.

DOUBLE (N, D) A large number with floating decimal point. It cannot be unsigned. Its size is 8 bytes.

DECIMAL (N, D) It cannot be unsigned. The maximum number of digits may be specified in the N parameter. The maximum number of digits to the right of the decimal point is specified in the D parameter.

String/Text Data Types

It allows the database server to store string values such as name of the students, Address, etc.

Types	Description	Display Format	Range in Characters
CHAR	Contains non-binary strings. Length is fixed as you declare while creating a table. When stored, they are right-padded with spaces to the specified length.	Trailing spaces are removed	The length can be any value from 0 to 255.
VARCHAR	Contains non-binary strings. Columns are variable length strings. It contains alphanumeric value.	As stored	A value from 0 to 255 before MySQL 5.0.3.
BLOB or TEXT	BLOB are 'Binary Large Objects' and are used to store large amount of binary data.	As stored	0 to 65535 characters.

Date and Time Data Types

It allows the database server to store a date using the fields YEAR, MONTH and DAY in the format YYYY-MM-DD. e.g. Date of admission, Date of birth, etc.

Types	Description	Display Format	Range
DATETIME	Use when you need values containing both date and time information.	YYYY-MM-DD HH:MM:SS	'1000-01-01 00:00:00' to '9999-12-31 23:59:59'
DATE	Use when you need only date information.	YYYY-MM-DD	'1000-01-01' to '9999-12-31'.
TIMESTAMP	Values are converted from the current time zone to UTC (Co-ordinated Universal Time) while storing and converted back from UTC to the current time zone when retrieved.	YYYY-MM-DD HH:MM:SS	'1970-01-01 00:00:01' UTC to '2038-01-19 03:14:07' UTC

Check Point 02

1 RDBMS is a type of .... that stores data in the form of tables.
2 What do you mean by 'Data redundancy'?
3 The candidate key of a relation is always a minimal key. State True or False.
4 Which used to store files such as video clip, picture etc?

Manipulating Data

In a database, structure and manipulation of data are done by some commands. For this, we can use SQL commands. SQL (Structured Query Language) commands are the instructions used to communicate with the database to perform specific task that work with data.

SQL commands can be used not only for searching the database but also to perform various other functions like, create tables, add data to tables, modify data, drop the tables, set permissions for users and many more.

Data Definition Language (DDL)

DDL is used to define the structure of your tables and other objects in the database. In DBMS, it is used to specify a database schema as a set of definitions (expressed in DDL). In SQL, the Data Definition Language allows you to create, alter and destroy database objects.

Basically, a data definition language is a computer language used to create and modify the structure of database objects in a database. These database objects include views, schemes, tables, indexes, etc.

This term is also known as **data description language** in some contexts, as it describes the fields and records in a database table.

Data definition language consists of various commands that lets you to perform some specified tasks as follows :

(i) CREATE Uses to create objects in the database.

(ii) ALTER Uses to alter the structure of the database table. This command can add up additional columns, drop existing columns and even change the data type of columns involved in a database table.

(iii) DROP Uses to delete objects from the database.

(iv) TRUNCATE Uses to remove all records from a table.

(v) RENAME Uses to rename an object.

Data Manipulation Language (DML)

DML provides various commands used to access and manipulate data in existing database. This manipulation involves inserting data into database tables, retrieving existing data, deleting data from existing tables and modifying existing data.

DML is mostly incorporated in SQL database. The basic goal of DML is to provide efficient human interaction with the system.

The DMLs are of two types :

Procedural DMLs These require a user to specify what data is needed and how to get it.

Non-Procedural DMLs These require a user to specify what data is needed without specifying how to get it.

Various data manipulation language commands are as follows :

(i) SELECT Used to retrieve data from a database.

(ii) INSERT Used to insert data into a table.

(iii) UPDATE Used to update existing data within a table.

(iv) DELETE Used to delete all records from a table, the space of the records remains.

(v) LOCK TABLE Used to control concurrency.

A query language is a portion of a DML involving information retrieval only. The terms DML and query language are often used synonymously.

Differences between DDL and DML

DDL	DML
DDL is the abbreviation of Data Definition Language.	DML is the abbreviation of Data Manipulation Language.
It is used to create and modify the structure of database objects in database.	It is used to retrieve, store, modify, delete, insert and update data in database.
DDL commands allow us to perform tasks related to data definition.	DML commands are used to manipulate data.
For example, CREATE, ALTER, and DROP commands.	For example, SELECT, UPDATE, and INSERT commands.

Transaction Control Language (TCL)

TCL is playing an important role in SQL. TCL commands are used to manage transactions in database. These are also used to manage the changes made by DML statements. It allows statements to be grouped together into logical transactions. A transaction is a single unit of work.

Each individual statement is a transaction. If a transaction is successful, all of the data modifications made during the transaction are committed and became a permanent part of the database. If a transaction encounters an error and must be cancelled or rolled back, then all of the data modifications are erased. To manage all these operations, transaction control language commands are used.

Various transaction control commands are as follows :

(i) COMMIT Used to save the work done.

(ii) SAVEPOINT Used to identify a point in a transaction to which you can later rollback.

(iii) ROLLBACK Used to restore database to original since the last COMMIT.

(iv) SET TRANSACTION It establishes properties for the current transactions.

Data Control Language (DCL)

DCL commands are used to assign security levels in database which involves multiple user setups. They are used to grant defined role and access privileges to the users.

There are two kinds of user in the schema

- **Users** They work with the data, but cannot change the structure of the schema. They write data manipulation language.

- **Admin** They can change the structure of the schema and control access to the schema objects. They write data definition language.

Basically, the DCL component of the SQL language is used to create privileges that allow to users access and manipulation of the database.

Two types of DCL commands are :

(i) GRANT Used to give user's access privileges to database.

(ii) REVOKE Used to withdraw access privileges given with the GRANT command.

Creating a Database Object

MS-Access provides two ways to create a database, which are as follows:

1. Creating a Blank Database

To create a new blank database, you need to perform the steps which are as follows:

Step 1 Start **Microsoft Access 2007,** then getting started with Microsoft Office Access page will appear.

Step 2 Click on **Blank Database** icon, the Blank Database pane will appear at the right hand side as shown in the below figure:

Blank Database

Create a Microsoft Office Access database that does not contain any existing data or objects.

File Name:

| Database 13.accdb |

C: Users\Arihant\My Documents\

[Create] [Cancel]

Step 3 Type a name for the database in the **File Name:** box. *If you do not give a file name extension, Access automatically adds the default extension .accdb.*

To change the location of the file from the default, click on **Browse** ( ) icon for changing the location.

Step 4 Click **Create** button.

Access creates the database with an empty table named **Table1,** which will open in **Datasheet View.**

The cursor is placed in the first empty cell in the **Add New Field** column as shown in following figure :

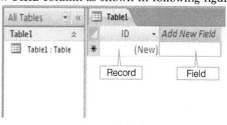

Empty Table1

2. Creating a Database using Templates

Template is a complete tracking application with predefined tables, forms, reports, queries, macros and relationships. Each template creates a complete end-to-end solution that you can use either with no modification or customise to suit your business needs. Steps to create a database using templates are as follows:

Step 1 Start **Microsoft Access 2007,** then getting started with Microsoft Office Access page will appear.

Step 2 Several featured templates are displayed in the middle of the page, click the **template** that you want to use.

You can also download additional templates from the Office Online Website.

Step 3 Type a name for your database in the **File Name:** box.

Step 4 Click **Create** (or **Download,** for an Office Online template).

Check Point 03

1 Which command is used to define the structure of your tables?
   (a) DDL   (b) DCL   (c) DML   (d) TCL
2 Rollbacks are used to restore database to original since the last COMMIT. True or False.
3 What is template?

Creating a Table

In MS-Access 2007, two types of views are available to create a table as follows:

Datasheet View It provides a visual way to create a table. It is a simple view which arranges the data in rows and columns and allows to edit the data, but not allow to change the format of the database, other than minor changes (such as insert or delete columns).

Design View It allows you to create or change the table. You can set or change every available properties for each field and can open existing tables in Design View, add, remove or change fields.

1. To Create a Table Using Datasheet View

Steps to create a table using the Datasheet View are as follows:

Step 1   Open the **database**.

Step 2   Go to **Create** tab in the ribbon and select the **Table** command in Tables group.

Step 3   After clicking at the **Table** command, a **Datasheet** tab will appear as shown below:

Step 4   In the above figure, the field ID is automatically generated that is of datatype AutoNumber. Due to which, its values are automatically generated for each record and field ID uniquely identifies the record in a table.

Steps to add a new field are as follows:

Step 1   Double click the **Add New Field** column label.

or

Right click the **Add New Field** column label. A menu will appear, click on **Rename Column** option.

Step 2   Type the **Field name**.

Step 3   Press **Enter**.

Step 4   Type the next field name. Continue, until you have created all of the fields in your table.

Steps to explicitly assign a data type to a field areas are as follows:

Step 1   Click the **Field label** for the field which you want to assign a data type.

Step 2   Activate the **Datasheet** tab.

Step 3   Click dropdown arrow next to the **Data Type** field from **Data Type & Formatting** group and then, choose a data type.

Note   By default data type consists as a Text.

Make Changes in a Datasheet View

Some of the changes made in a table from a Datasheet View window are as follows:

Insert a Field

Steps to add a field into a table are as follows:

Step 1   Right click on the **table** and click **Datasheet View**.

Step 2   To insert a new column, click the **Insert** in **Datasheet** tab or right click the **header** (Field Name) of the field that follows the new field.

Step 3   Click at **Insert Column** from the menu.

Delete a Field

Steps to delete a field from a table are as follows:

Step 1   To delete the column, click **Delete** in **Datasheet** tab or right click the **Field Name** of the field, you want to delete.

Step 2   Click at **Delete Column** from the menu.

Step 3   Now, MS-Access will display a prompt message to confirm that you want to delete the field(s) or not?

Step 4   Click on **Yes** button to permanently delete the field(s).

Rename a Field

Steps to rename a field into a table are as follows:

Step 1   Just double click the **Field Name** to highlight it.

or

Right click the **Field Name** that you want to change and click at **Rename Column** from the menu.

or

Select on **Datasheet** tab and click on **Rename** option from **Fields & Column** group.

Step 2   Click the **Field Name** if you want to edit or just start typing to replace the name completely.

Hide a Column

You can temporarily hide a column in a Datasheet View such that you can view other columns in a large datasheet.

Steps to hide a column into a table are as follows:

Step 1   Right click at the **Field Name** of the field that you want to hide.

Step 2   Click **Hide Columns** from the menu.

Freeze Columns

Freezing a field means that no matter how far you scroll in a datasheet, you will always see the frozen field on the left side pane.

Steps for freezing column(s) in a table are as follows:

Step 1   Right click at the **Field Name** of the field that you want to freeze.

Step 2   Click **Freeze Columns** from the menu.

Unfreeze All Columns

Steps to unfreeze all columns in a table are as follows:

Step 1 Right click at the **Field Name** of any field.

Step 2 Click **Unfreeze All Columns** from the menu.

2. To Create a Table Using Design View

Steps to create a table using the Design View are as follows:

Step 1 Open the **Database**.

Step 2 Go to **Create** tab in the ribbon and select the **Table Design** command from Tables group.

Step 3 After clicking at the **Table Design** command, a **Design** tab and a field entry area at middle with field property area will appear at bottom as shown in the following figure :

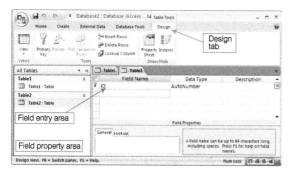

Note The field entry area is used for entering field's name, data type and description. This description is optional and the field properties pane is used for entering more details for each field, i.e. field size, validation rule etc. The table needs to be opened in Design View to access the field properties.

Steps to add a new field are as follows:

Step 1 Click on the first cell in the **Field Name** column and type the field name.

Step 2 Press **Enter**. The neighbouring cell in the **Data Type** column is selected. To select the data type, click the drop-down arrow to the right of the **Data Type** field and select an alternative data type.

Step 3 Press **Enter**. A cell in the **Description** column will be selected. Enter a description, if required.

Step 4 Press **Enter** and repeat the above process for other fields.

Steps to set the field properties are as follows:

Step 1 Click once on a **Field Name** for which you want to set the field property.

Step 2 The Field Properties will appear at the bottom of the screen as shown in the following figure:

Field Properties	
General Lookup	
Field Size	Long Integer
New Values	Increment
Format	
Caption	
Indexed	Yes (No Duplicates)
Smart Tags	
Text Align	General

Step 3 Click the **General** tab.

Step 4 Choose the **property** and click on the **drop-down** list next to it.

Step 5 The application of a property depends on its type. You may need to type a value, click a button and choose from a list of options or click a button and use a wizard to develop the property.

Make Changes in a Design View

The Design View of a table can be modified by the following changes:

Insert a Field

Steps to insert a field in a table are as follows:

Step 1 Select the **field**, before which you want to insert a new field.

Step 2 To insert a new field, click at the **Insert Rows** in the **Design** tab.

or

Right click at the **selected field** and click at the **Insert Rows** option from the context menu.

Step 3 A new field is added to the table design thus, you can enter field name, data type and description.

Delete a Field

Steps to delete a field from a table are as follows:

Step 1 Select the **field** that you want to delete.

Step 2 Click at the **Delete Rows** command in the **Design** tab.

or

Right click at the **selected field** and choose the option **Delete Rows** from context menu.

Step 3 Now, MS-Access will display a prompt message to confirm that you want to delete the field(s) or not.

Step 4 Click on **Yes** button to permanently delete the field(s).

Rename a Field

You can change a field name by placing the cursor on the field, double click on it and type the new name.

Naming and Saving of a Table

Steps to save a table are as follows:

Step 1   To save the table, click the **Save** button at the top of the screen or click the **Office** button and select **Save**. The **Save As** dialog box will appear as shown in following figure:

Save As dialog box

Step 2   Type the name that you want to give to your table in **Table Name:** text box.

Step 3   Click **OK.**

Step 4   The table will be listed in the **Tables** window on the left hand side.

Note   To save changes, you can also use keyboard shortcut Ctrl + S key.

Entering/Removing Record into/from a Table

Once a table has been created, the field and its properties are defined, you can start to enter the records. This is done in a **Datasheet View**. If you create table in **Design View**, you need to switch to the **Datasheet View** to enter records.

Insert a Record

Steps to insert a record in a Datasheet View are as follows:

Step 1   When you create a table, a new blank record automatically appears in the second row of the table

or

If you enter data in the last record, a new blank record will automatically appear at the end of the table.

Step 2   **Type data** into the fields.

Step 3   When you have finished adding records in the datasheet, **save** it and **close** it.

Delete an Existing Record

Steps to delete an existing record are as follows:

Step 1   **Select** the row which you want to delete.

Step 2   Right click on the row and select the **Delete Record** from context menu.

Step 3   Now, MS-Access will display a prompt message to confirm that you want to delete the record(s) or not.

Step 4   Click on **Yes** button to permanently delete the record(s).

Opening an Existing Table

Existing table can be opened by two ways which are as follows:

1.   **In Datasheet View**   To open a table in a **Datasheet View**, follow these steps:

Step 1   Find a table in the **All Access Objects** list (the left hand window).

Step 2   Right click on a table and select **Datasheet View**. Datasheet View represents the data in a table.

or

Select **Home** tab and click the **View** drop-down arrow from Views and select the **Datasheet View**.

2.   **In Design View**   To open a table in a **Design View**, follow these steps:

Step 1   Find a table in the **All Access Objects** list (the left hand window).

Step 2   Right click on the table and select **Design View**. Design View represents the structure of the table.

or

Select the **Home** tab and click the **View** drop-down arrow from Views group and select the **Design View**.

Renaming and Deleting a Table

Steps to rename a table are as follows:

Step 1   Find a table in the **All Access Objects** list (the left hand window).

Step 2   Right click on a **table** and select **Rename** from context menu that appears.

Note   If you are working on this table, then it will display a prompt message that you can't rename the database object, 'Table1' while it's open. So, firstly close this table.

Step 3   Now, type a new name for the table.

Step 4   Press **Enter** from the keyboard.

Steps to delete a table are as follows:

Step 1   Find a table in the **All Access Objects** list.

Step 2   Right click on a **table** and select **Delete**.

Step 3   Now, MS-Access will display the prompt message to confirm that you want to delete the table or not.

Step 4   Click on **Yes** button to delete a table with its contents.

Building Forms

Forms are used for entering, modifying and viewing records you likely have had to fill out forms on many occasions, like when visiting a doctor's clinic, applying for a job or registering for school. When you enter information in a form in Access, the data goes exactly where the database designer wants it to go: in one or more related tables.

There are three ways to create forms in Access :

1. Use of Form Command

To create a form using a Form command, follow the given steps:

Step 1   First, select the table for which you want to create form.

Step 2   In ribbon, click on Create tab.

Step 3   Select Form option in the Forms group.

Form will look like as shown below :

2. Use of Split Form

To create a form using a Split Form command, follow the given steps:

Step 1   First, select the table for which you want to create a form.

Step 2   Click the Create tab in the ribbon.

Step 3   Select Split Form option from the Forms group.

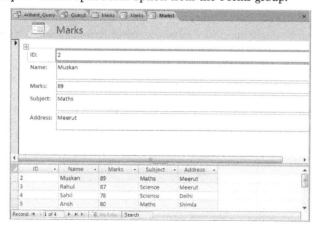

After this, form will be shown in the upper part and lower part will show the datasheet view.

3. Use of Form Wizard

To create a form using Form Wizard command, follow the given steps:

Step 1   Click on create tab. In the Forms group, select the More Forms option.

Step 2   A drop down menu will appear. Select the Form Wizard option.

Step 3   Form Wizard dialog box will appear as shown below:

Step 4   In the Form Wizard, select the fields by > symbol from the Available Fields. Click on Next button.

Step 5   Next window will appear.

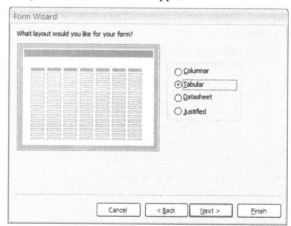

Step 6   Choose any option out of Columnar, Tabular, Datasheet and Justified. For example, we choose Tabular.

Now, click on Next button. The next window will appear. Here, enter the name of your form and click on Finish button.

Check Point 04

1 Design View provides a visual way to create a table. State True or False.
2 What do you mean by freezing?
3 Why are forms used in database?

Create and Manage Queries

Queries are the basis of power in a database. It is a way to get specific information from the database. They give us the ability to ask questions, record the questions for later and to take actions on the answers. There are two methods for creating a query in MS-Access 2007. These are

1. Query Design Method

MS-Office Access 2007 provides you the functionality to create a query by using a Design View.

Steps to create a query through a Design View are as follows :

Step 1 Open the **Create** tab from the ribbon and select the **Query Design** command from **Other** group.

Step 2 The **Show Table** dialog box will appear as shown in the following figure:

Show Table Dialog Box

Step 3 Select a table in the **Tables** tab and click the **Add** button to add a table.

Step 4 The selected table is being displayed as shown in the following figure. You can click the **Close** button to close the **Show Table** dialog box.

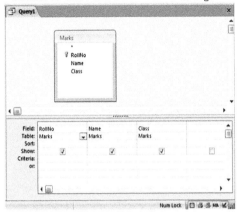

Step 5 Edit the **Field row** and other rows.

Step 6 Save the query by using shortcut **Ctrl+ S** key. The **Save** As dialog box will appear, enter the name of your query in Query Name text field and then, click **OK** button.

Save As Dialog Box

Step 7 Select the **Design** tab, click **Run** from **Results** group

Step 8 The query will display the output in a tabular form.

2. Query Wizard Method

To create query using Query Wizard method, follow the given steps :

Step 1 In the ribbon, click on Create tab.

Step 2 In the Other group, click on Query Wizard option.

Step 3 A New Query dialog box will appear as shown below :

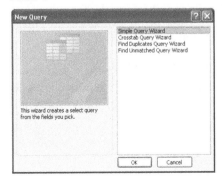

Step 4   Click the Simple Query Wizard and press OK button.

Step 5   Simple Query Wizard dialog box will appear.

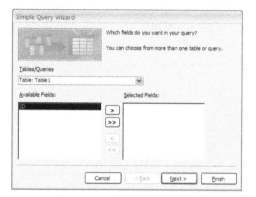

Step 6   In this dialog box, select fields from Available Fields by > Symbol. Click on Next button.

Step 7   The next screen will appear. Enter the title for your query and click the Finish button.

MySQL Command Basics

MySQL database is a way of organising a group of tables and table stores the data in the form of rows and columns. To create a bunch of different tables that share a common theme, you would group them into one database to make the management process easier. So, for manipulating data, we need to know about MySQL commands, which are described below:

Create Command

Create a database Creating database is an easier task. You need to just type the name of the database in a CREATE DATABASE command.

Syntax
```
CREATE DATABASE [IF NOT EXISTS]<database_name>;
```

CREATE DATABASE command will create an empty database with the specified name and would not contain any table.

IF NOT EXISTS is an optional part of this statement which prevents you from an error if there exists a database with the given name in the database catalogue.

For example, `mysql>CREATE DATABASE BOOK;`

Output `Query OK, 1 row affected <0.01 sec>`

Tables are created using CREATE TABLE command.

Syntax
```
CREATE TABLE table_name
(
    column_name1 data_type(size),
    column_name2 data_type(size),
    ------
);
```

Here,

CREATE TABLE defines a new table.

table_name defines the name of a table.

column_name defines the name of a column.

data_type specifies that which type of data can be contained in a particular column.

For example,
```
mysql > CREATE TABLE STUDENT (Student_Code
integer, Student_Name char(20), Sex char(1),
Grade char(2), Total_Marks decimal);
```

Output
```
Query OK, 0 row affected <0.06 sec>
```

Some Rules for Creating Tables

Some rules for creating tables are as follows:

(*i*) The table and column names must start with a letter and can be followed by letters, numbers, or underscores.

(*ii*) Table or column names not to exceed a total of 30 characters in length and not use any SQL reserved keywords as names for tables or column names (such as 'select', 'create', 'insert', etc).

(*iii*) It is important to make sure that you are using an open parenthesis before the beginning of a table definition and a closing parenthesis after the end of the last column definition.

(*iv*) Separate each column definition with a comma (,).

(*v*) All SQL statements should end with a semi-colon (;).

Insert Command

The INSERT command is used to add a single record or multiple records into a table.

Syntax

```
INSERT INTO <table_name>(col_1, col_2,
col_3,.., col_n) VALUES(value_1,
value_2,... value_n);
```

Here,

`table_name` defines the name of a table where data will be inserted.

`col_1`, `col_2`, `col_3,...`, `col_n` are the columns of the current table.

`value_1`, `value_2,...` `value_n` are the data values against each column.

For example, The following information exists in the table STUDENT

Roll_No	Name	Subject
101	Rahul	Art
102	Vikas	Science
103	Puneet	Science
104	Sachin	Art
105	Uday	Commerce

To add a new row into the STUDENT table use the INSERT command as follow :

```
mysql>INSERT INTO STUDENT(Roll_No, Name,
Subject) VALUES(106, 'Ajay', 'Science');
```

Now, the table STUDENT will look like as follows :

Roll_No	Name	Subject
101	Rahul	Art
102	Vikas	Science
103	Puneet	Science
104	Sachin	Art
105	Uday	Commerce
106	Ajay	Science

Select Command

The most commonly used SQL command is SELECT statement. The SQL SELECT statement is used to query or retrieve data from a table in the database. A query may retrieve information from specified columns or from all of the columns in the table.

Syntax

```
SELECT column_list
FROM table_name;
```

Selecting Specific Columns

To select any specific column or information from the table, we use the following command:

Syntax

```
SELECT<column_name1>,[<column_name2>,…,<column_nameN>
]
 FROM <table_name>;
```

Example *To display the column Emp_Code and Emp_Salary from table COMPANY*

Table: COMPANY

Emp_Code	Emp_Name	Emp_Salary	Emp_Dep	Joining_Date
101	Ravi	28000	D02	2010-10-10
102	Neeru	70000	D03	2013-06-04
103	Shrey	60000	D05	2011-03-02
104	Puneet	15000	D07	2009-05-01
105	Sneha	12000	D08	2008-04-03

```
mysql>SELECT Emp_Code, Emp_Salary FROM COMPANY;
```

Output

Emp_Code	Emp_Salary
101	28000
102	70000
103	60000
104	15000
105	12000

Selecting All Columns

To select all the columns of a table or entire table, we can use an asterisk (*) symbol in place of column_name list.

Syntax

```
SELECT * FROM <table_name>;
```

Example *To display all the columns of table COMPANY.*

```
mysql>SELECT * FROM COMPANY;
```

Output

It will display the complete table COMPANY.

UPDATE Command

The UPDATE command is used to update a single record or multiple record in a table. The UPDATE command is used to modify the existing rows in a table.

Syntax

```
UPDATE<table_name > SET <column1> = <value1>,
<column2> = <value2> ,.....
WHERE <condition>;
```

Example *To update Emp_Salary with 28000 of those employees whose Emp_Code is 100.*

```
mysql> UPDATE COMPANY SET Emp_Salary=28000
            WHERE Emp_Code=100;
```

The above query will update the Emp_Salary by 28000 whose Emp_Code is 100.

DELETE Command

To discard unwanted data from a database, the DELETE command is used. The DELETE command uses a WHERE clause.

If you don't use a WHERE clause, all rows in the table will be deleted.

Syntax
```
DELETE FROM <table_name> WHERE <condition>;
```

Example *To delete the record of employee Puneet from the table COMPANY.*

```
mysql>DELETE FROM COMPANY
            WHERE Emp_Name ='Puneet';
```

The above query will delete the record of Puneet from table COMPANY

Delete All Rows To delete all rows in a table without deleting the table structure, the following command is used.

Syntax   DELETE FROM<table–name>;

Example *To delete all rows from table COMPANY.*

```
mysql>DELETE FROM COMPANY;
```

The above query will delete all data of table COMPANY.

Design Report

Report offers you the ability to present your data in print. Reports are useful because they allow you to present components of your database in easy to read format. There are two methods to design a report in MS-Access. These are:

1. Use of Report Command

To design a report using Report command, follow the given steps:

Step 1 First select the table for which you want to design report

Step 2 In the ribbon, click on Create tab.

Step 3 Select the Report command from the Reports group. Report will show on the screen.

After design a report, there are three new tabs will be appear under the Report Layout Tools as Arrange, Format and Page Setup.

2. Use of Report Wizard

To design a report using Report Wizard, follow the given steps:

- First select the table for which you want to design reports.
- Click on Create tab from ribbon.
- In the Reports group, select Report Wizard option. Report Wizard dialog box will appear on the screen.

- Choose fields from here which are exist in Available Fields and click on Next button.
- After this, next screen will appear, click on Next button. The next screen will appear as shown below :

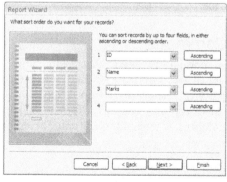

- Here, you can sort your fields as ascending or descending order and click on Next button.

- Next screen will appear with Layout and Orientation options.

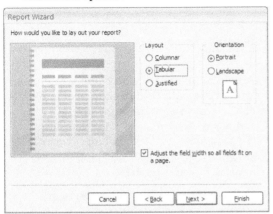

- You can select any layout from Layout section and Portrait or Landscape from Orientation section. Click on Next button.
- Next screen will appear where you can give the title for your report. Click on Finish.

Printing a Report

To print a report, follow the given steps:

- You can print the report by clicking on Print command in the Print Preview tab. Print dialog box will appear on the screen.
- Here, you can set your printer and click on OK button.

Check Point 05

1. Table or column names not to exceed a total of .... characters in length.
2. What is the meaning of selecting specific columns?
3. Name the methods to design a report in MS-Access.

SUMMARY

- Data is a collection of raw facts.
- The processed form of data is known as information.
- A database is defined as an organised collection of data/information.
- A database contains several components such as data, software, hardware and user.
- User is that person who needs the information from the database. These are Database Administrator, Application programmer etc.
- A table organises the information in the form of rows and columns.
- In database, fields are used to maintain relationship between tables.
- Records are composed of fields, each of which contains one item of information.
- DBMS is a software system that handles large amount of a data and is used to manage database.
- A Relational Database Management System (RDBMS) is a DBMS that is based on the relational model.
- A field that holds unique data, identifies the file or a database are known as key fields.
- DBMS provides various key fields as Primary key, candidate key, alternate key and foreign key.
- A data type is a data storage format that can contain a specific type or range of values.
- SQL commands are a set of instructions that used to interact with the database like Sql, Server, Mysql, Oracle etc.
- A form is a database element that is used to view, enter and edit records in a table.
- A query refers to the action of retrieving data from your database.
- A report allows you to present data retrieved from one or more tables so that, it can be analysed and printed, if required.

Exam Practice

Multiple Choice Questions

1 Facilities offered by databases are
  (a) the ability to store a large amount of data in a structured format, easy update, sort query, production of reports.
  (b) easy edition, spell check, perform calculations, library of mathematical functions, replication.
  (c) the ability to rotate images, copy and paste, fill scale.
  (d) None of the above

Ans. (*a*) Databases have ability to store a large amount of data in structured format, easy update, sort query, production of reports.

2 Which of the following is not an example of database?
  (a) Cross knot game
  (b) Employee payroll management
  (c) Numeric calculator
  (d) Customer management system

Ans. (*c*) Numeric calculator because it is used to calculate the numeric numbers only as it is unable to store data.

3 Which one of the following is an example of RDBMS ? **[CBSE 2021 Term-I]**
  (a) MongoDB (b) Windows registry
  (c) Publisher (d) Oracle

Ans. (*d*) Oracle

4 Which of the following best describes a form?
  (a) Form enables people to enter or view data in a database easily.
  (b) Form summarises and prints data.
  (c) A form filters data from a database based on a criteria
  (d) All of the above

Ans. (*a*) Form enables people to enter or view data in a database easily.

5 Database servers are referred to as _____. **[CBSE SQP Term-I]**
  (a) front-ends (b) back-ends
  (c) clients (d) model

Ans. (*b*) back-ends

6 A table is a set of data elements that is organised using a model of vertical _____ and horizontal _____.
  (a) rows, tables (b) columns, rows
  (c) rows, columns (d) forms, reports

Ans. (*b*) columns, rows

7 Out of the following, which one is the most appropriate data field in context of employee table, if only one of these is required?
  (a) Age in years (b) Data of birth
  (c) Age in days (d) Age in months

Ans. (*b*) Date of birth is the most appropriate data field in context of employee table.

8 Which of the following is not the main building block of a database?
  (a) Lists (b) Queries
  (c) Reports (d) Forms

Ans. (*a*) The main building blocks of database are tables, queries, forms and reports.

9 The .... has evolved since the 1960s to ease increasing difficulties in designing, building and maintaining complex information systems. **[CBSE 2021 Term-I]**
  (a) Knowledge concept (b) Formula concept
  (c) Database concept (d) Forms concept

Ans. (*c*) Database concept

10 Malini wants to store a huge amount of information about her zone in a database. Should not be repeated in her file. Her friend Gargi explained her various benefits or storing data in RDBMS. It helps in preventing/controlling duplication of data. Which of the following terms is used to refer to duplication data? **[CBSE 2021 Term-I]**
  (a) Data sharing
  (b) Data privacy
  (c) Data redundancy
  (d) Data integrity

Ans. (*c*) Data redundancy

11 Computer based record keeping system known as
  (a) Data Manipulation System
  (b) Computerised Data System
  (c) Computerised Record Keeping System
  (d) DBMS

Ans. (*d*) DBMS is a collection of programs that enable to create and maintain database. Also , it is a computer based record keeping system.

12 RDBMS provides relational operators to manipulate the data. Here, RDBMS refers to
(a) Record Database Management System
(b) Relational Database Management System
(c) Reference Database Management System
(d) None of the above

Ans. (b) RDBMS stands for Relational Database Management System which provides operator to manipulate the data stored into the database table.

13 A database that contains tables linked by common fields is called a
(a) Centralised database
(b) Flat file database
(c) Relational database
(d) None of the above

Ans. (c) Relational database stores data in the form of tables which are linked by common fields.

14 Duplication of data is known as
(a) data security
(b) data incomplete
(c) data redundancy
(d) None of the above

Ans. (c) Data redundancy means duplication of data. It eliminates replication of data item into different files from a large database.

15 Key field is a unique identifier for each record. It is defined in the form of
(a) rows   (b) columns
(c) tree   (d) query

Ans. (b) Key is a data item that allows you to uniquely identify individual occurrences which is defined as the column or set of columns.

16 Which of the following fields will not make a suitable primary key?
(a) A customer's account number
(b) A date-field
(c) An auto number field
(d) A student's admission number

Ans. (b) From the given options, data field can not be set as a primary key because it can't be fixed for an object.

17 When you define a field for a table, which of the following parameters do access always consider optional?
(a) Field Name   (b) Data Type
(c) Field Size   (d) Description

Ans. (d) Description field of table is optional, as it depends on database designer that he/she wants to describe field or not.

18 Which of the following is not a data type?
(a) Picture/Graphic   (b) Date/Time
(c) Text   (d) Number

Ans. (a) From the given options, Date/Time, Text and Number are the data types.

19 The default data type for a field is
(a) Number
(b) Auto Number
(c) Currency
(d) Text

Ans. (d) Text that allows to store text or combination of text and numbers.

20 For what, Memo data type is used?
(a) To add table
(b) To store objects created in other programs
(c) For long text entries
(d) For short text entries

Ans. (c) As we know, Memo provides character upto 65536 so, it is used for long text entries.

21 What data type should be chosen for a zipcode field in a table?
(a) Text   (b) Number
(c) Memo   (d) All of these

Ans. (b) Number data type should be chosen for a zipcode field in a table.

22 You create a table in MS-Access. You decided to create two fields RollNo and Date of Birth, what will be the data type of Date-of-Birth column?
(a) Number   (b) Text
(c) Yes/No   (d) Date/Time

Ans. (d) Date/Time will be the data type for Data of Birth because it allows to store date and time format.

23 Which data type helps you to handle input column that is in boolean format?
(a) OLE Object   (b) Attachment
(c) Yes/No   (d) None of these

Ans. (c) Yes/No data type will allow boolean value.

24 Which of the following commands is not a Data manipulation language?
(a) Select   (b) Insert
(c) Update   (d) Alter

Ans. (d) Data manipulation language commands are used to access and manipulate data in existing database. e.g. Select, Insert, Update etc.
While Alter is a Data Definition Language command.

Fill in the Blanks

1 .... is a collection of related information.

Ans. Database

2 .... are the basic building blocks of a database.   **[CBSE Textbook Page no. 257]**

Ans. Tables

3 Table is also known as.......... .

Ans. file

4 In a tables, columns are called .... and rows are called ....

Ans. fields, records

5 A field in a table is also called as ....

Ans. column

6 A set of related data item is called as ....

Ans. record

7 .... is the smallest part of a table in which one data item can be kept.

Ans. Field

8 A .... enables users to view, enter and change data directly in database objects such as tables. **[CBSE Textbook Page no. 262]**

Ans. form

9 The different objects supported by MS-Access are tables, queries .... and reports.

Ans. forms

10 The database is managed by a software package known as ....

Ans. DBMS

11 In database, all the data are stored at a .... location.

Ans. centralised

12 Three popular DBMS software are ...., ... & ....   **[CBSE Textbook Page no. 243]**

Ans. MYSQL, MS-Access, Oracle

13 Primary key is used to .... identify the record in a table.

Ans. uniquely

14 The candidate key, which is not used as primary key is called .... key.

Ans. alternate

15 A foreign key is a reference of the .... key in another table.

Ans. primary

16 .... is a field which is used as a primary key and numbers each record sequentially.

Ans. AutoNumber

17 To store object like image, you need to create a field in a table, having field type as ....

Ans. OLE Object

18 In a Text type data field, we can enter a maximum of .... characters.

Ans. 255

19 A .... is a language that enables users to access and manipulate data in a database.   **[CBSE Textbook Page no. 249]**

Ans. Data Manipulation Language (DML)

20 TCL commands are used to manage .... in database.

Ans. transaction

21 ..... statement is used to add one or more records to a database.   **[CBSE Textbook Page no. 268]**

Ans. Insert

22 .... command is used to retrieve data from a database.

Ans. SELECT

True and False

1 A database can have only one table.

Ans. **False** No, database does not have a limit on number of tables. It depends on the disk space.

2 Database is a collection of logically non-related data.

Ans. **False** A database is a collection of integrated and logically related data.

3 Field contains set of characters.

Ans. **True** It is an individual sub-component of one record that contains set of characters which have a proper meaning.

4 A relationship cannot be created with the help of a table.

Ans. **False** A relationship is a connection between two tables of data.

5 A query is used to retrieve data, from the database based on one of more criteria. This database object is not supported by MS Access 2017.

Ans. **False** Because MS-Access 2007 supports the database object query.

6 A report allows you to represent data, retrieved from one or more tables so that, it can be analysed and printed if required.

Ans. **True** When you want to print those records which are fetched from your database then, reports are more useful for this purpose.

7 Primary key field gives us permission to record duplicate entry.

Ans. **False** A primary key is a key which identifies records uniquely in a table so it does not give us permission to record duplicate entry.

8 A table can have multiple primary keys.

Ans. **False** If we create multiple primary keys in a table, then primary key will be unable to find the unique key value.

9 A primary key field does not allow numbers.

Ans. **False** Primary key has to identify a unique value which can be present in a table, in a number form also. It means, primary key field allows number too.

10 A primary key value can be NULL.

Ans. **False** The primary key of table is used to uniquely identify each and every row in the table. So, its all keys and columns must be defined as NOT NULL.

11 If a piece of data (field value) is stored in two places in the database, then storage space is wasted and changing the data in one place will not cause data inconsistency.

Ans. **False** If a piece of data is stored in two places in the database, then storage space is wasted and changing the data in one sport will cause data inconsistency.

12 A foreign key is a primary key in another table.

Ans. **True** When a table's primary key field is added to a related table in order to create the common field which relates two tables, it is called a foreign key in the related table.

13 A Text data type cannot allow number entry.

Ans. **False** As, Text data type can include both texts as well as numbers.

14 Memo data type allows you to store character type values in a table.

Ans. **True** Memo data type allows upto 65536 characters.

15 Memo data type allows you to store only 255 characters in the table.

Ans. **False** Memo data type is used when character size is more than 255.

16 The Datasheet View displays the data in a table in tabular format.

Ans. **True** A datasheet view is a simple view of data arranged in rows and columns.

17 Design View allows users to enter data in the table.

Ans. **False** Because Design View is used to edit the table design only.

Very Short Answer (VSA) Type Questions

1 What is database? Give an example.

Ans. A collection of related information organised as tables is known as database e.g. INGRES, MySQL etc.

2 What is the difference between 'Rows' and 'Columns' in a table?

Ans. In a table, rows are called records and columns are termed a fields. A row stores complete information of a record whereas column stores only similar data values for all records.

3 What is field in database? Give an example.

Ans. A field is an area, reserved for a specific piece of data. It is also known as attribute. e.g. Customer Name.

4 Define forms and what is the need of using them?

Ans. A form is a window or screen that contains numerous fields or spaces to enter data. Forms can be used to view and edit your data. It is an interface in user specified layout.

5 Mention any two integer data types of a table field in database. **[CBSE SQP Term-II]**

Ans. TINYINT, SMALLINT are the two integer data type of a table field in database.

6 Name the relationship in which one column of the primary key table is associated with all the columns of the associated table and *vice-versa*. **[CBSE SQP Term-II]**

Ans. One-to-many or many-to-one

7 How is data organized in a RDBMS?
[CBSE Textbook Page no. 243]

Ans. A relational database is a type of database. It uses a structure that allows us to identify and access data in relation to another piece of data in the database. Data in a relational database is organized into tables.

8 Write the purpose of DBMS.

Ans. DBMS is used to store logically related information at a centralised location. It facilitates data sharing among all the applications requiring it.

9 Write any two uses of database management system.

Ans. (i) DBMS is used to store data at a centralised location.
(ii) It is used to minimise data redundancy and data inconsistency.

10 Write any two advantages of using database.

Ans. (i) It can ensure data security.
(ii) It reduces the data redundancy.

11 Define Reports of a database.
[CBSE SQP Term-II]

Ans. Reports are the ways to produce the data stored in databases and tables in a printed form. Report is a database object, like a table, query or form.

12 A table named School (containing data of students of the whole school) is created, where each record consists of several fields including AdmissionNo (Admission Number), RollNo (Roll Number), Name. Which field out of these three should be set as the primary key and why?

Ans. AdmissionNo should be set as primary key because admission numbers are unique for each and every students of the school, which is not possible in the case with Roll No and Name.

13 When Memo data type is preferred over Text data type for a field?

Ans. When the length of the field is more than 255 characters. Text data type is not capable to store the project description because its length cannot be more than 255 characters so, Memo data type is preferred over Text data type.

14 What happens when text is entered in a Number type field?

Ans. When we enter text in a Number field and press Enter or press Tab key, MS-Access displays a message that "The value you entered does not match the Number data type in this column."

15 List datatypes available in Numeric datatype.
[CBSE Textbook Page no. 248]

Ans. Datatypes available in Numeric datatype are TINYINT, SMALLCINT, MEDIUMINT, INT and BIGINT.

16 List datatypes available in Date datatype.
[CBSE Textbook Page no. 248]

Ans. Date datatype is available in Date datatype.

17 Write one example of data field for which you would set the Required property to Yes?

Ans. In a table, when we declare a field as a primary key, then the field's Required property must be set to yes because in a primary key field, we need to enter data always.

18 How Entry Required and Default Value properties of a table field in a database are different from each other? **[CBSE SQP Term-II]**

Ans. **Entry Required** If it sets to yes then it will be necessary for the user to insert the value in the field, which means that field cannot be left blank.

While, **Default Value** It can be set for a field, if user don't provide any value while entering the values in the table.

19 What is Referential Integrity? Explain its two(any) purposes. **[CBSE SQP Term-II]**

Ans. Referential Integrity is a property of data stating that all its references are valid. In the context of relational databases, it requires that if a value of one attribute of a relation references a value of another attribute, then the referenced value must exist.

A referential integrity is a database concept that is used to build and maintain logical relationships between tables to avoid logical corruption of data. It is a very useful and important part in RDBMS. Usually, referential integrity is made up of the combination of a primary key and a foreign key.

20 How can you create table using Create command?

Ans.
```
CREATE TABLE table_name
(
column_A name1 data_type (Size),
column_A name2 data_type (Size),
:
);
```

21 Create a table of Student based on the following table instance.

Column Name	Data Type	Length
ID	integer	
Name	varchar	15
Stream __Id	integer	

Ans.
```
CREATE TABLE STUDENT (ID Integer, Name varchar (15),
Stream-Id Integer);
```

22 Write a SQL command to create the table BANK whose structure is given below :

Field Name	Datatype	Size	Constraint
ID Number	integer	10	Primary key
Name	varchar	20	
B_date	date		
Address	varchar	50	

Ans. The SQL command to create a table as per given structure is as follows :

```
MySQL> CREATE TABLE BANK (ID__Number integer
(10) PRIMARY KEY, Name varchar (20), B__date
Date, Address varchar (50));
```

23 Insert some information into a table COLLEGE, whose structure is given below :

Roll_no	Name	Class	Branch

Ans. (i) MySQL>INSERT INTO COLLEGE (ROLL__NO, NAME, CLASS, BRANCH) VALUES (2, 'VIKAS',12, 'SCIENCE');

(ii) MySQL>INSERT INTO COLLEGE (ROLL_NO, NAME, CLASS, BRANCH) VALUES (3, 'RAJ', 10, 'SCIENCE');

24 Identify the columns and data types of a table: Airlines. Mention at least four columns with data type. **[CBSE 2022 Term-II]**

Ans.

Columns	Datatype
Flight_No	Text
No_of_Passengers	Integer
Airlines	Text
Arrival_Time	Date/Time
Departure_Time	Date/Time
Fares	Float

Short Answer (SA) Type Questions

1 Distinguish between data and information.

Ans. Distinguish between data and information are as follows:

Data	Information
It is a raw facts.	It is a process form of data.
It considers facts, symbols, images for reference or analysis.	It considers knowledge derived from study, experience or instruction.
e.g. 23 is a data.	e.g. age=23 is information

2 What are the main purposes of a database system?

Ans. (i) Storage of information
(ii) Retrieval of information quickly.
(iii) Sorting, selecting data that satisfies certain and readable format.
(iv) Produce the report in some standardised and readable format.

3 How are fields, record and a table related to each other? Explain with the help of an example.

Ans. Fields are one type of information. A record contains logically related fields.
A table Emp name contains logically related records.

EmpNo	Name	Salary
1	Shridhar	20,000
2	Raghav	40,000

Here, EmpNo, Name and Salary are three different fields. 1, Shridhar, 20,000 represents one complete record.

4 Define query in the context of database.

Ans. A query is an inquiry into the database using the SELECT statement. These statements give you filtered data according to your conditions and specifications indication the fields, records and summaries which a user wants to fetch from a database.

5 What do you mean by data integrity?

Ans. Refer to text page no 109.

6 What is the utility of primary key in database? Write distinct features of primary keys.

Ans. Primary key is used to uniquely identify the record in a database. It can be a column or a set of columns in the table. Main features of primary key are as follows :
(i) It must contain a unique value for each record of table.
(ii) It does not contain null values.

7 State the relationship and difference between a primary and foreign key.
[CBSE Textbook Page no. 248]

Ans. Relationship between primary key and foreign key :
A foreign key is a column or set of columns in one table that references the primary key columns in another table.

Difference between primary key and foreign key :
Primary key can't accept null values whereas foreign key can accept multiple null value.

8 Define the following data types
(i) AutoNumber
(ii) Currency
(iii) Text

Ans. (i) **AutoNumber** It allows to store numbers that are automatically generated for each record. It increases the number automatically.

(ii) **Currency** It allows to store monetary values that can be used in calculations accurate upto 15 digits on L.H.S and 4 digits on R.H.S of decimal points.

(iii) **Text** It allows to store text or combination of text and numbers, as well as numbers that don't require calculations such as phone numbers.

9 Distinguish between Text and Memo data types.

or How are field types Text and Memo different from each other? Explain with the help of an example.

Ans. Distinguishing between Text and Memo are as follows:

Text	Memo
It is used for relatively short entries.	It is used for long text paragraphs.
It can store upto 255 characters only.	It can store upto 65536 characters.
It uses field size property to control the number of characters.	It does not use field size property.
e.g. Emp__name	e.g. Emp__description

10 A text field is initially 40 characters long and one record has an entry in this field in MS-Access database. The field value contains 28 characters, including spaces. Now, you have reduced the length of the field to 20 characters. What will happen to the field value?

Ans. Since, the new field length is 20 characters long. So, this field will contain only left 20 characters including spaces and the remaining data will be discarded. Thus, the data from the right side of the field will be lost.

11 What do you mean by Entry Required field information?

Ans. Entry Required field information decides whether entering data in the field is necessary or not. So, if Entry Required is set to Yes, then that field must have some value in it. By default, Entry required is set to Yes.

12 When is AutoNumber data type preferred over Numberdata type?

Ans. When you want to increment the number automatically as you add or delete the records. AutoNumber data type is preferred. Also, if the table does not have a primary key, then AutoNumber uniquely identifies the record.

13 How to insert a field into a table in Datasheet view?

Ans. Refer to text on Page no. 115.

14 Write the steps to create a form using Split Form command.

Ans. Refer to text on Page no. 118.

15 What do you mean by UPDATE command?

Ans. UPDATE command is used to update a single record or multiple record in a table. The UPDATE command is used to modify the existing rows in a table.

Syntax

```
UPDATE <table_name> SET<Column1>
=<value 1>, <Column 2>=<value 2>,.....
WHERE <condition>;
```

16 Write SQL command to create the table VEHICLES with given constraint and also add some information in it.

Column Name	Data_type (Size)	Constraint
Reg_No	char (15)	Primary Key
Reg_Date	date	
Owner__Name	varchar (20)	
Address	varchar 40	

Ans. To create a table using the CREATE TABLE command

```
mysql> (CREATE TABLE VEHICLES (Reg_No
char(15)Primary key, Reg_Date date,
Owner_ Name varchar (20), Address varchar (40));
```

To add information using the INSERT command

```
mysql>INSERT INTO VEHICLES(Reg_No, Reg_Date,
Owner_Name, Address) VALUES (100, 12-12-13,
'VIKAS', 'MEERUT');
```

Long Answer (LA) Type Questions

1 Discuss the components of a database.

Ans. Refer to text on Page no. 107.

2 Distinguish between a record and a field in a table with an example.

Ans. Distinguish between a record and a field in a table are as follows:

Record	Field
It is a collection of data items which represent a complete unit of information about a thing or a person.	It is an area with in the record reserved for a specific piece of data.
A record refers to a row in the table.	A field refers to a column in the table.
Record is also known as tuple.	Field is also known as attribute.
e.g. If Employee is a table, then entire information of an employee is called a record.	e.g. If Employee is a table, then empId, empName, department, Salary are the fields.

3 Define Database Management System. Write two advantages of using database management system for school.

Ans. Database Management System (DBMS) is a collection of programs that enable users to create, maintain database and control all the access to the database. The primary goal of the DBMS is to provide an environment that is both convenient and efficient for user to retrieve and store information. The advantages of using DBMS for school are as follows:

(i) In school, DBMS is used to store the data about students, teachers and any other related things at a centralised location.

(ii) It provides security to the personal information of the school, stored in it.

4 List the data types used in a DBMS/RDBMS.

[CBSE Textbook Page no. 248]

Ans. Refer to text on Pages no. 110, 111, 112.

5 Write one example of each field, for which you would use

(i) Text data type   (ii) Memo data type

Ans. (i) **Text data type** It allows to store text or combination of text and numbers as well as numbers that don't require calculations such as phone number. This data type allows maximum 255 characters to store.

e.g. If Employee is a table and Emp_No, Name and Description are fields, then name will be a Text field. Because, Name is a character entry field.

(ii) **Memo data type** It allows long blocks of text that uses text formatting. e.g. In the Employee table, the field Description will be of Memo data type, because the length of description of employee may be large.

6 Distinguish between Number and Auto Number data type field. Give example of each.

Ans. Distinguishing between Number and AutoNumber data type field are as follows:

Number	AutoNumber
It holds numeric values which are used for calculations.	It allows to store numbers that are automatically generated for each record.
The field length of the data type is 1, 2, 4, 8 or 16 bytes.	The field length of this data type is 4 bytes.
It does not support field property New values.	It supports the field property New values.
Number type can store any integer/float value depending on decimal precision specified.	Autonumber will have values calculated by system.
e.g. In a table Employee, Salary is a Number type field.	e.g. In a table Bank, the Account No is a Auto Number field as, for every new customer, this field will automatically increase and will provide a new number.

7 Explain Data Manipulation Language in SQL database?

Ans. Refer to text on Page no. 113.

8 How to design a report using Report Wizard?

Ans. Refer to text on Page no. 122-123.

9 Define the following terms.

(i) Insert Command   (ii) Select Command

(iii) Delete Command   (iv) DCL Command

(v) Template

Ans. (i) **Insert Command** It is used to add a single record or multiple records into a table.

Syntax
```
Insert into <table_name> (col1, col2.....)
values (val1, val2);
```

(ii) **Select Command** It is used to query or retrieve data from a table in the database.

Syntax
```
Select column_list from table_name;
```

(iii) **Delete Command** To discard unwanted data from a database, the delete command is used.

Syntax
```
Delete from <table_name> WHERE <condition>;
```

(iv) **DCL Command** DCL commands are used to assign security levels in database which involves multiple user setups. They are used to grant defined role and access privileges to the users.

(v) **Template** It is a complete tracking application with predefined tables, forms, reports, queries, macros and relationship.

10 Write SQL queries for the questions from (a) to (e) on the basis of table class.

No	Name	Stipend	Subject	AvgMark	Grade
01	Vikas	1200	Medical	67	B
02	Boby	1400	Humanities	78.4	B
03	Tarun	1000	Medical	64.8	C
04	Varun	1600	Non-medical	84	A
05	Atul	1800	Non-medical	92	A

(a) Select all the non-medical stream students from the class table.
(b) List the names that have grade A sorted by stipend.
(c) Arrange the records of class name wise.
(d) List the records whose grade is B or C.
(e) Insert the new row with the following data. (06, 'Jack', 2800, 'Humanities', 98, 'A')

Ans. (a) mysql> SELECT * FROM Class WHERE Subject= 'Non-medical';
(b) mysql> SELECT Name FROM Class WHERE Grade='A' ORDER BY Stipend;
(c) mysql> SELECT * FROM Class ORDER BY Name;
(d) mysql> SELECT * FROM Class WHERE Grade IN ('B', 'C');
(e) mysql> INSERT INTO Class VALUES (06, 'Jack', 2800, 'Humanities', 98, 'A');

11 Write SQL commands for the questions from (a) to (e) on the basis of table SHOP.

S_NO	P_Name	S_Name	Qty	Cost	City
S1	Biscuit	Priyagold	120	12.00	Delhi
S2	Bread	Britannia	200	25.00	Mumbai
S3	Chocolate	Cadbury	350	40.00	Mumbai
S4	Sauce	Kissan	400	45.00	Chennai

(a) Display all products whose quantity in between 100 and 400.
(b) Display data for all products sorted by their quantity.
(c) To list S_Name, P_Name, Cost for all the products whose quantity is less than 300.
(d) To display S_NO, P_Name, S_Name, Qty in descending order of quantity from the SHOP table.
(e) Give S_Name for products whose name starts with 'B':

Ans. (a) mysql> SELECT * FROM SHOP WHERE Qty BETWEEN 100 and 400;
(b) mysql> SELECT * FROM SHOP ORDER BY Qty;
(c) mysql> SELECT S_Name, P_Name, Cost FROM SHOP WHERE Qty <300;
(d) mysql> SELECT S_NO, P_Name, S_Name, Qty FROM SHOP ORDER BY Qty DESC;
(e) mysql> SELECT S_Name FROM SHOP WHERE P_Name LIKE 'B%';

12 Write the SQL commands for the questions from (a) to (e) on the basis of table Employee?

Emp_no	E_name	Profile	Manager	Hire_date	Salary	Commission	Dept_no
8369	SMITH	CLERK	8902	1990-12-18	8000	NULL	20
8499	ANYA	SALESMAN	8698	1991-02-20	16000	300.00	30
8521	SETH	SALESMAN	8698	1991-02-22	12500	500.00	30
8566	MAHADEVAN	MANAGER	8839	1991-04-02	29850	NULL	20
8654	MOMIN	SALESMAN	8698	1991-09-28	12500	1400.00	30
8698	BINA	MANAGER	8839	1991-05-01	28500	NULL	30
8882	SHIVANSH	MANAGER	8839	1991-06-09	24500	NULL	10
8888	SCOTT	ANALYST	8566	1992-12-09	30000	NULL	20
8839	AMIR	PRESIDENT	NULL	1991-11-18	50000	NULL	10
8844	KULDEEP	SALESMAN	8698	1991-09-08	15000	0.00	30

(a) Display Employee Name and Salary of those employees whose salary is greater than or equal to 22000?

(b) Display details of employees those are not getting commission.

(c) Display employee name and salary of those employees who have their salary in range of 2000 to 4000?

(d) Display the name, profile and salary of employee (s) who doesn't have manager?

(e) Display the name of employee whose name contains "A" as fourth alphabet.

Ans. (a) mysql>SELECT E_name, Salary FROM Employee WHERE Salary> = 22000;

(b) mysql>SELECT * FROM Employee WHERE Commission IS NULL;

(c) mysql>SELECT E_name, Salary FROM Employee WHERE Salary BETWEEN 2000 and 4000;

(d) mysql>SELECT E_name, Profile, Salary FROM Employee WHERE Manager IS NULL;

(e) mysql>SELECT E_name FROM Employee WHERE E_name LIKE '_ _ _ A%';

Application Oriented Questions

1 Consider the following table

Employee

EmpNO	EmpName	Designation
1	Shail	A
2	Anup	B
3	Mansi	A
4	Pooja	B

(i) Which of the above field can be selected as a primary key?

(ii) EmpName field also has unique values for all the records. Can it be made primary key? Give answer with reason.

Ans. (i) EmpNo can be selected as a primary key.

(ii) EmpName is having unique values, but there is no guarantee that if more employees are included then there would not be multiple people with similar names.

So, in future its values may be duplicate. Thus, it cannot be made as a primary key.

2 The following table named SummerCamp shows part of the information kept on children attending the SummerCamp in Shimla.

Child ID	First Name	Last Name	DOB	Gender	Group
109	Vedansh	Gupta	30/06/10	M	2A
214	Mack	Tyagi	09/12/08	M	1B
115	Aditi	Thakur	13/04/09	F	1A
108	Vikrant	Chauhan	02/02/09	M	2A
141	Swati	Saini	06/05/10	F	2B
233	Vishakha	Tyagi	01/08/10	F	3A
274	Madhur	Gupta	06/03/10	M	3B

(i) State the number of fields in the above table.

Ans. (i) Number of fields-6

(ii) Number of records-7

(iii) If a new child joins the SummerCamp, then SummerCamp would add a record in the table.

(iv) If a child is shifted from one group to another, then SummerCamp would edit a record in the table.

(v) If any child leaves the SummerCamp then SummerCamp would delete a record of that child from the table.

(vi) Text and Date/Time.

3 Damini is a programmer in an institute and is asked to handle the records containing information of students. Suggest any 5 fields name and their data type of students database.

Ans.

Field Name	Data Type
RollNo	Number
Name	Text
Class	Text
Section	Text
Gender	Text

4 Consider the following database:

[CBSE SQP Term II]

Product Code	Product Name	DateofSale	QtySold	Customer Name	Amount
P001	Pencil	05/10/11	5	Himanshu	25
P002	Eraser	04/01/12	4	Ali	8
P003	Sharpner	09/12/11	6	Deepak	12
P004	Whitener	25/04/11	2	Ankit	30
P005	Glue Pen	20/07/12	3	Ruchi	30

Answer the following questions:

(i) Write the name of the field that contains numeric data.

(ii) Identify the primary key field in the database.

(iii) Identify the field type of the DateofSale field.

(iv) Identify the names of the fields that contain textual data.

(v) The given table contains how many fields and records?

Ans. (i) QtySold and Amount

(ii) ProductCode

(iii) Date/Time data type

(iv) ProductCode, ProductName and CustomerName

(v) 6 fields and 5 records

5 Consider the table TEACHERS.   [CBSE SQP Term II]

Table : TEACHERS

NUMBER	NAME	AGE	SUBJECT	DATEOFJOIN	SALARY	GENDER
1	JUGAL	34	COMPUTER	10/01/2019	12000	M
2	PRATIGYA	31	SCIENCE	24/03/2019	20000	F
3	SANDEEP	32	MATHS	12/12/2019	30000	M
4	SANGEETA	35	SCIENCE	01/07/2020	40000	F
5	SATTI	42	MATHS	05/09/2020	25000	M
6	SHYAM	50	SCIENCE	27/06/2021	30000	M
7	SHIV OM	44	COMPUTER	25/02/2021	21000	M
8	SHALAKHA	33	MATHS	31/07/2020	20000	F

Write SQL commands

  (i) To show all the information about IT teachers.

  (ii) To list the details of all the teachers, who are getting salary between 20000 to 35000.

  (iii) To display the subject of all the teachers, whose age is more than 40 years.

  (iv) To display the list of names of all the teachers in alphabetical order.

Ans. (i) SELECT * FROM TEACHERS WHERE SUBJECT = "COMPUTER";

   (ii) SELECT * FROM TEACHERS WHERE SALARY >= 20000 AND SALARY <= 35000;

   (iii) SELECT SUBJECT FROM TEACHERS WHERE AGE > 40;

   (iv) SELECT * FROM TEACHERS ORDER BY NAME;

Self Assessment

Multiple Choice Questions

1. Which part of a database holds only one type of information?
   (a) Report   (b) Field   (c) Query   (d) Record

2. In a relational database, if the primary key in one table is used as the link to another table, what is the term used to describe the field in the second table?
   (a) Secondary key   (b) Alternate key   (c) Candidate key   (d) Foreign key

3. How many views of a table are in MS-Access?
   (a) Three   (b) Seven   (c) Two   (d) Four

Fill in the blanks

4. A row in a table is also known as a ....

5. No two rows can contain same value in the .... field.

6. All SQL statements should end with a ....

True or False

7. A form enables user to enter or view data in the database easily.

8. Data in a database is stored in a query.

9. The property allows that zero length can be applied to the data type number.

Very Short Answer (VSA) Type Questions

10. Define candidate key.

11. What is the need of setting relationship between tables?

12. Why is the data type OLE object used?

Short Answer (SA) Type Questions

13. Distinguish between form and report.

14. List the key features of DBMS.

15. What are steps to create a table in Design view?

Long Answer (LA) Type Questions

16. Write the conditions, which would help to choose a primary key for your database table? Define the term primary key.

17. Explain the use of validation property.

18. Identify the required data types in MS-Access for each column.

Table Employee

ENo	Employee Number
EName	Employee Name
EAddress	Employee Address
ESalary	Employee Salary
EDESIGNATION	Employee Designation

Application Oriented Type Questions

19. Look at the given table called Item and answer the questions.

ItemId	ItemName	ItemStock	ItemDOP	QualityPurchased

 (i) Suggest the data types of all the fields.

 (ii) Which two fields can act as the primary key from the above table.

20. Consider the following database Student.

RollNo	FirstName	LastName	Class	Marks Obtained	Scholarship Awarded (₹)
1205	Mohan	Garg	12th	99.9	50000
1009	Dushyant	Singh	10th	98.7	45000
1101	Swati	Rana	11th	95.4	30000
945	Ravindra	Saini	9th	97.5	35000
1015	Ritika	Thakur	10th	98.6	400000

 (i) The marks obtained by the student with RollNo 1101 is?

 (ii) What is the name of the student, who has got the highest marks and what is the amount of scholarship awarded to him/her?

 (iii) How many records are there in the table?

 (iv) How many fields are there in the table?

Web Applications and Security

A web application (web app) is an application program that is stored on a remote server and delivered over the Internet through a browser interface.

Common web applications include webmail, online retail sales and online auction.

Working with Accessibility Options

Accessibility features are designed to help people with disabilities use technology more easily. For example a text-to-speech feature may read text out loud for people with limited vision, while a speech-recognition feature allows users with limited mobility to control the computer with their voice.

Launching Accessibility Options

To launch accessibility options, follow the given steps:

Step 1   Click on Start button → Control Panel. Control Panel window will appear on your screen with various category.

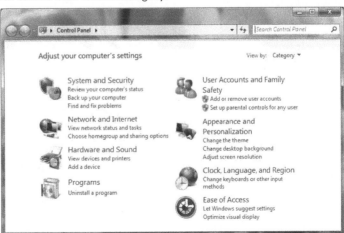

Step 2   Click on Ease of Access category. After this, Ease of Access window will appear.

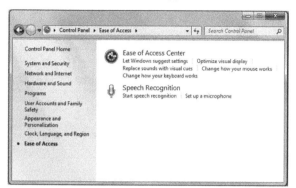

Step 3   In the Ease of Access Center, click on Let Windows suggest settings.

Step 4   A window will provide in which you can change settings of keyboard, mouse etc.

Step 5   You can choose any options under Select all statements that apply to you:

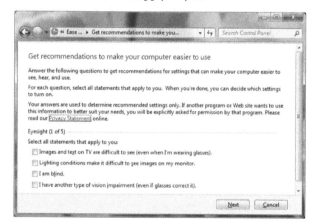

Step 6   Click on Ease of Access Center option. A window will appear.

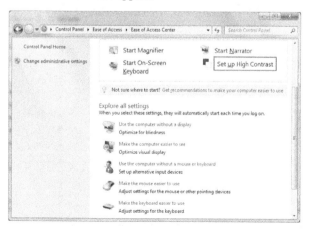

Step 7   In this window, four options are given as :

- **Start Magnifier** a display utility that makes the computer screen more readable by creating a separate window that displays a magnified portion of the screen.
- **Start Narrator** a text-to-speech utility that reads what is displayed on the screen–the contents of the active window.
- **Start On-Screen Keyboard** displays a virtual keyboard on the computer screen that allows people to type data by using a pointing device.
- **Set Up High Contrast** a window showing settings for color and contrast of display.

Explore All Settings

Instead of looking for accessibility settings in various places on your computer, windows bring all those settings together and organises them into categories that you can explore in Ease of Access Center. Some of them are

(i) Make the Computer Easier to Use

If you occasionally have trouble seeing items on your screen, you can adjust the settings to make text and images on the screen appear larger, improve the contrast between items on the screen.

You can adjust many of these settings on the make the computer easier to see page in the Ease of Access Center.

Open the Ease of Access Center, then select the options that you want to use.

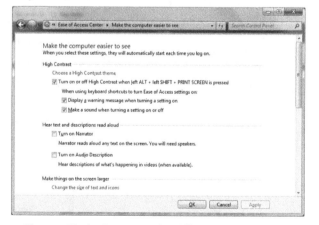

- **Choose High Contrast** This allows you to set a high-contrast color scheme that heightens the color contrast of some text and images on your computer screen.
- **Remove Background Images** This turns off all unimportant, overlapped content and backgroup images to help make the screen easier to use.

(ii) Make the Mouse Easier to Use

You can change how the mouse pointer looks, and turn on other features that can help make it easier to use your mouse.

You can adjust these settings on the Make the mouse easier to use page in the Ease of Access Center.

Open the Ease of Access Center, then select the options that you want to use :

- **Change the Color and Size of Mouse Pointer** You can use these options to make the mouse pointer larger or change the color to make it easier to see.

- **Turn on Mouse Keys** You can use this option to control the movement of the mouse pointer by using the numeric keypad.

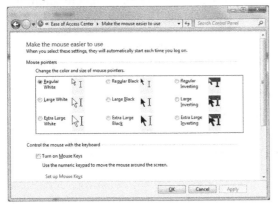

(iii) Make the Keyboard Easier to Use

You can use your keyboard to control the mouse and make it easier to type certain key combinations. You can adjust these settings on the Make the keyboard easier to use page in the Ease of Access Center.

Open the Ease of Access Center, then select the options that you want to use:

- **Turn on Sticky Keys** This option sets Sticky Keys to run when you log on to windows. Instead of having to press three keys at once (Ctrl, Alt, Delete), you can use one key by turning on Sticky Keys and adjust settings.

- **Turn on Toggle Keys** This option sets Toggle Keys to run when you log on to windows. These keys can play an alert each time you press the Caps Lock, Num Lock or Scroll Lock Keys.

(iv) Use Text or Visual Alternatives to Sounds

Windows provide settings for using visual cues to replace sounds in many programs.

You can adjust these settings on the use text or visual alternatives for sounds page in the Ease of Access Center.

Open the Ease of Access Center, then select the options that you want to use:

- **Turn on Visual Notifications for Sounds** This option sets sound notifications to run when you log on the windows. You can also choose how you want sound notifications to warn you.

- **Turn on Text Captions for Spoken Dialog** This option causes windows to display text captions in place of sounds to indicate that activity is happening on your computer.

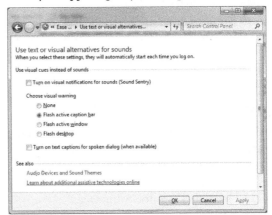

Check Point 01

1. Common web applications include
   (a) webmail   (b) online retail sales
   (c) online auction   (d) All of these

2. How to open Ease of Access Center?

3. Which option is used to set for color and contrast of display?

Networking Fundamental

A **network** can be defined as an interconnected collection of autonomous computers. A 'computer network' or simply a 'network' is a collection of computers and other hardware devices, interconnected by communication channels (satellites or cables) that allow sharing of resources and information. A computer networking is the practice for exchanging information/services between two or more computer devices together for the purpose of sharing data. The speed of a network is measured in Mbps (Megabits per Second).

Benefits of Networking

Computer network is very useful in modern environment, so some of the benefits of networking are discussed here :

- **File Sharing** Networking of computers helps the users to share data files.
- **Hardware Sharing** Users can share devices such as printers, scanners, CD-ROM drives, hard drives, etc.
- **Application Sharing** Applications can be shared over the network and this allows to implement client/server applications.
- **User Communication** This allows users to communicate using e-mail, newsgroups, video conferencing within the network.
- **Access to Remote Database** By networking, we are able to access to the remote database. It is easy for any person using his PC to make reservations for aeroplanes, trains, hotels, etc., anywhere in the world with instant confirmation within the network.

Types of Network

A network refers to a group of interconnected computers which are capable of sharing information and communication devices.

On the basis of coverage or geographical spread, a network can be divided into following types:

LAN (Local Area Network)

When a group of computers and its devices are connected in a small area, then this network is said to be a LAN. Computers or users in a local area network can share data, information, software and common hardware devices such as printer, modem, hard disk, etc. A LAN typically relies mostly on wired connections for increased speed and security but wireless connection also be a part of LAN. LAN are used within office building, school, etc.

WAN (Wide Area Network)

The network which connects the different countries network is known as WAN. It can be a group of LANs. The largest existing WAN is Internet. For example, a network of ATMs, BANKs, National Government Offices spread over a country or continents are examples of WANs.

Comparison between LAN, MAN and WAN

Basis	LAN	MAN	WAN
Speed	11 to 54 Mbps	11 to 100 + Mbps	10 to 384 Kbps, 1.83 to 7.2 Mbps
Range	Upto 5 km	5 km to 15 km	Upto 1000 km
Applications	Enterprise networks	Even replacement last mile access	Mobile phones, Cellular data

PAN (Personal Area Network)

PAN refers to a small network of communication. The range of a PAN is generally 10 metres. PAN may be wired using USB cables or wireless using wireless network technologies such as bluetooth, wireless USB, 2-wave and ZigBee. Bluetooth personal area network is also called a **piconet**. It can be composed of upto eight devices in a master-slave relationship.

Network Devices

Network devices are the components used to connect computer and other electronic devices together, so that they can share files or resources like printers or fax machines. The most common type of network devices used by the public to setup a Local Area Network (LAN) are hub, switch, repeater and if online access is desired, a high-speed modem is required.

Some of them are described below:

Hub

A hub is a device, which is used with computer systems to connect several computers together. It acts as a centralised connection to several computers with the central node or server. It is a multi-port device, which provides access to computers.

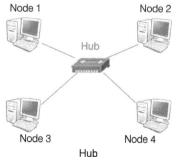

Hub

Switch

A switch is a hardware device, which is used to connect devices or segment of network with smaller subsets of LAN segments. The main purpose of segmenting is to prevent the traffic overloading in a network.

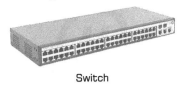

Switch

Repeater

Repeater is a hardware device, used to amplify the feable signals, when they are transported over a long distance. When the signal is transmitted over a line, then due to resistance and other causes it accumulates noise.

Due to this noise, the quality of signal degrades. The basic function of a repeater is to amplify the incoming signal and retransmit it to the other device.

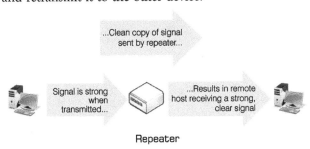

Repeater

Gateway

A gateway is a device which is used to connect dissimilar networks. The gateway establishes an intelligent connection between a local network and external networks, which are completely different in structure. Infact, the gateway is a node that routes the traffic from a workstation to outside network. The gateway also acts as a proxy server and a firewall, which prevents the unauthorised access.

Gateway

Bridge

Bridge serves a similar function as switches. A bridge filters data traffic at a network boundary. Bridge reduces the amount of traffic on a LAN by dividing it into two segments. Traditional bridge supports one network boundary, whereas switches usually offer four or more hardware ports.

Switches are sometimes called **multipart bridges**.

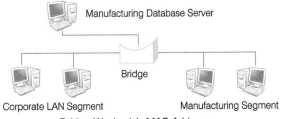

Bridge Work with MAC Addresses

Router

A hardware device designed to take incoming packets, analyse the packets, move the packets to another network, convert the packets to another network interface, drop the packets, direct packets to the appropriate locations, etc. A router functions similar to a bridge. However, unlike a bridge, a router passes data packets from one network to another network based on their IP addresses not MAC addresses.

Modem (Modulator/Demodulator)

Modem is a device that converts digital signal to analog signal (modulator) at the sender's site and converts back analog signal to digital signal (demodulator) at the receiver's end, in order to make communication possible *via* telephone lines.

> ### When are modems required?
> When a network contains largest number of system/computer, it needed modem.

NIC (Network Interface Card)

NIC stands for Network Interface Card. NIC provides the physical connection between the network and the computer workstation. With most LAN's cables, NIC is used for their connectivity.

Network Topologies

The network topology refers to the arrangement or pattern of computers, which are interconnected in a network. Commonly used network topologies are as follows:

Bus Topology

It is a type of network in which the computers and the peripheral devices are connected to a common single length data line.

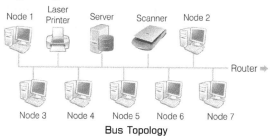

Bus Topology

All the computers or devices are directly connected to the data line.

The data is transmitted in small blocks, known as **packets.**

Ring or Circular Topology

In this type of topology, each node is connected to two and only two neighbouring nodes. The data travels in one direction only from one node to another node around the ring. After passing through each node, the data returns to the sending node.

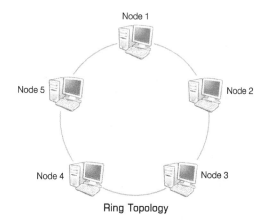

Ring Topology

Star Topology

In this topology, there persists a central node called **server** or **hub**, which is connected to the nodes directly.

If a node has to take information from other node, then the data is taken from that node through the central node or server.

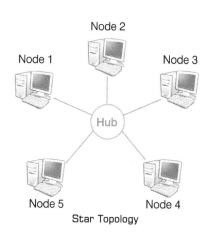

Star Topology

Mesh Topology

In this topology, each node is connected to more than one node, so that it provides alternative route, in case, if the host is either down or busy. It is also called a completely interconnected network. We can also call it as a extension to **P2P network**.

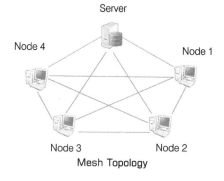

Mesh Topology

Tree Topology

It is an extension and variation of bus topology. Its basic structure is like an inverted tree, where the root acts as a server. In tree topology, the node is interlinked in the form of tree. If one node fails, then the node following that node gets detached from the main tree topology.

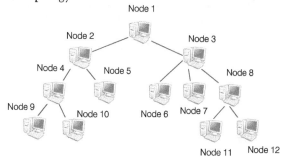

Tree Topology

Models of Computer Networking

There are mainly two models of computer networking as follows:

Peer-to-Peer Network

It is also known as P2P network. This computer network relies on computing power at the edges of a connection rather than in the network itself. P2P network is used for sharing content like audio, video, data or anything in digital format.

In P2P connection, a couple of computers is connected *via* a Universal Serial Bus (USB) to transfer files. In peer-to-peer networking, each or every computer may be worked as server or client.

Client-Server Network

The model of interaction between two application programs in which a program at one end (client) requests a service from a program at the other end (server).

It is a network architecture which separates the client from the server. It is scalable architecture, where one computer works as server and others as client. Here, client acts as the active device and server behaves as passively.

Data Transfer on Network

Switching techniques are used for transmitting data across networks. Different types of switching techniques are employed to provide communication between two computers. These are

Circuit Switching

It is a methodology of implementing a telecommunication network in which two network nodes establish a dedicated communication channel (circuit), first through the network and then the message is transmitted through the channels.

The main advantage of circuit switching is guaranteed delivery. The circuit switching guarantees the full bandwidth of the channels and remains connected for the duration of the communication session.

The defining example of a circuit switched network is the early analog telephone network.

When a call is made from one telephone to another, switches within the telephone exchanges create a continuous wire circuit between the two telephones for as long as the call last.

Message Switching

It is a network switching technique, in which data is routed entirely from the source node to the destination node. In this technique, no physical path is established between source and destination in advance. During message routing, every intermediate switch in the network stores the whole message.

If the entire network's resources are engaged or the network becomes blocked, the message switched network stores and delays the message until some resource become available for effective transmission of the message.

Packet Switching

In packet based networks, the message gets broken into small data packets. These packets are sent out from the computer and they travel around the network seeking out the most efficient route to travel as circuits become available.

This does not necessarily mean that they seek out the shortest route. The main advantage of packet switching is that the packets from many different sources can share a line, allowing for very efficient use of the communication medium.

Check Point 02

1 The speed of a network is measured in
   (a) Mbps   (b) bytes
   (c) KHz   (d) None of these
2 Which type of network is spreaded over a city?
3 What do you mean by router?
4 What is the main advantage of circuit switching?

Internet

The Internet has gained popularity and emerged as an important and efficient means of communication. The term Internet is derived from the words 'interconnection' and 'networks'. A network is a collection of two or more computers, which are connected together to share information and resources.

The Internet is a world wide system of computer networks, i.e. **network of networks**. Through Internet, computers become able to exchange information with each other and find diverse perspective on issues from a global audience. Most of the people use Internet for sending and receiving e-mail and net surfing for retrieving information.

Network of Networks

Connecting to the Internet

There are mainly three ways of connecting to the Internet, which are as follows:

Dial-up Connection

It is a temporary connection, set up between your computer and ISP server.

Dial-up connection uses the telephone line (Public Switched Telephone Network (PSTN) and modem to connect to the Internet. The modem connects the computer through the standard phone lines, which serves as the data transfer medium. When a user initiates a dial-up connection, user needs to enter the password and specify a username and modem dials a phone number of an Internet Service Provider (ISP) that is designated to receive dial-up calls.

DSL broadband service providers in India are BSNL, Airtel, Reliance, MTNL and Tata Indicom etc.

The ISP then establishes the connection, which usually takes about 10 sec and is accompanied by several beeping and buzzing sounds.

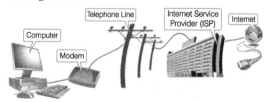

Dial-up Connection

Broadband Connection

The term broadband commonly refers to high speed Internet access that is always ON and faster than the traditional dial-up access. It is the short form of broadband width, that uses a telephone line to connect to the Internet. Speed of broadband connection is measured in Mbps (Megabits per Second). Broadband access allows users to connect to the Internet at greater speed than a standard 256 Kbps (Kilobits per Second) modem or dial-up access. Broadband access requires the use of a broadband modem.

Broadband includes several high speed transmission technologies, which are as follows:

(i) **Digital Subscriber Line** (DSL) It is a popular broadband connection which provides Internet access by transmitting digital data over the wires of a local telephone network. It uses the existing copper telephone lines for Internet access.

A special modem is necessary in order to be able to use a DSL service over a standard phone line.

Faster forms of DSL, typically available to businesses are as follows:

- High data rate Digital Subscriber Line (HDSL)
- Very High data rate Digital Subscriber Line (VHDSL or VDSL)
- Asymmetrical Digital Subscriber Line (ADSL)
- Symmetrical Digital Subscriber Line (SDSL)

(ii) **Cable Modem** This service enables cable operators to provide broadband using the same co-axial cables, that deliver pictures and sound to your TV set. A cable modem can be added to or integrated with a set-top box that provides your TV set for Internet access. They provide transmission speed of 1.5 Mbps or more.

(iii) **Broadband over Power Line** (BPL) It is the delivery of broadband over the existing low and medium voltage electric power distribution network. Its speed is generally comparable to DSL and cable modem speeds. BPL can be provided to homes using existing electrical connections and outlets. It is also known as power-**band**.

BPL is good for those areas where there are no broadband connections, but power infrastructure exists. e.g. in rural areas.

- ◆ **ARPANET** was the world's first operational packet switching network.
- ◆ **ISP** (Internet Service Provider) is a company that provides individuals and other companies access to the Internet. Internet Service Provider is used to join the Internet. Internet services typically provided by ISPs include Internet access, Internet transit, domain name registration, web hosting, usenet service and colocation. ISP does not provide e-mail address. e.g. MTNL, BSNL, Airtel etc.

Gigo

Wireless Connection

Wireless broadband connects a home or business to the Internet using a radio link between the customer's location and the service provider's facility. Wireless broadband can be mobile or fixed. Unlike DSL and cable, wireless broadband requires neither a modem nor cables. The distance between the devices connected to each other through a wireless Internet connection does not affect the rate of data transfer between them.

Some ways to connect the Internet wirelessly are as follows:

(i) **Wireless Fidelity** (Wi-Fi) It is a universal wireless networking technology that utilises radio frequencies to transfer data. Wi-Fi allows high speed Internet connections without the use of cables or wires.

Wi-Fi networks can be designed for private access within a home or business. It can be used for public Internet access at 'hotspots' that offers Wi-Fi access such as restaurants, coffee shops, hotels, airports, convention centres and city parks.

Wi-Fi Network

(ii) **Worldwide Interoperability for Microwave Access** (WiMAX) Today, it is one of the hottest broadband wireless technology. These systems are expected to deliver Broadband Wireless Access (BWA) services upto 31 miles (45 km) for fixed stations and 3-10 miles (5-15 km) for mobile stations.

WiMAX would operate similar to Wi-Fi but at higher speed, over greater distances and for a greater number of users. It has the ability to provide services even in areas that are difficult for wired infrastructure to reach. Also, it has the ability to overcome the physical limitations of traditional wired infrastructure.

WiMAX Network

Satellite

Satellites which are orbiting around the Earth, provide necessary links for telephone and television service. They can also provide links for broadband. Satellite broadband is another form of wireless broadband and is also useful for serving remote or sparsely populated areas.

Terms Related to Internet

World Wide Web (WWW)

It is a system of Internet servers that supports hypertext and multimedia to access several Internet protocols on a single interface. It is often abbreviated as the Web or WWW. It is a way of exchanging information between computers on the Internet, trying to tie them together into a vast collection of interactive multimedia resources. It is only a portion of what makes up the Internet, but it is the fastest growing part of the Internet.

Web Page

The backbone of the World Wide Web is made up of files or documents called **pages** or **web pages**, that contain information and links to resources both **text** and **multimedia**. It is created using HTML (Hyper Text Markup Language).

CBSE Web Page

Website

A group of related web pages that follow the same theme and are connected together with hyperlinks is called a Website. In other terms, "A website is a collection of digital documents, primarily HTML files, that are linked together and that exist on the web under the same domain." Each website is accessed by its own address known as **URL** (Uniform Resource Locator).

e.g. http://www.carwale.com is a website, while http://www.carwale.com/new/ is a Web page.

Two terms that are associated with a website are as follows:

(i) **Home Page** The initial, main or first page of a website is known as **home page**. It can help the viewers to find out what they can find on particular site.

(ii) **Web Portal** It is a web page that combines useful information and links.

Web Browser

It is a software application that is used to locate, retrieve and display some content on the World Wide Web, including web pages. These are programs used to explore the Internet. It is an interface that helps a computer user to gain access over all the content on the Internet. We can install more than one web browsers on a single computer. The user can navigate files, folders and websites with the help of a browser.

There are two types of web browsers, which are as follows:

(i) **Text Web Browser** A web browser that displays only text-based information is known as **text web browser**. e.g. Lynx.

(ii) **Graphical Web Browser** A web browser that supports both text and graphic information is known as **graphical web browser**.

e.g. Internet Explorer, Firefox, Netscape, Safari (for Apple), Google Chrome, Opera etc.

Web Server

It is a computer program that serves requested HTML pages or files from the web client.

A web client is the requesting program associated with the user. The web browser is a client that requests HTML files from web servers. Every web server that is connected to the Internet is associated with a unique address, i.e. IP address which is made up of a series of four numbers between 0 to 255 separated by periods. e.g. 68.178.157.132 or 68.122.35.127.

Web Address/URL

Web is a collection of documents (web pages) stored on computers around the world. Each web page has an address describing where it can be found. This address is known as **Web Address** or **URL (Uniform Resource Locator)**. A web address identifies the location of a specific web page on the Internet, such as

```
http://www.learnyoga.com
```

On the web, web addresses are called URLs. It is the web address for a website or a web page. The URL specifies the internet address of a file stored on a host computer connected to the internet.

Parts of URL

The URL contains three parts, which are as follows:

(i) The name of the protocol to be used to access the file resource.

(ii) A domain name that identifies a specific computer on the Internet.

(iii) A path name with hierarchical description that specifies the location of a file in that computer.

e.g.

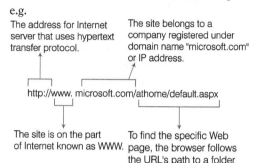

E-mail Address

E-mail stands for 'Electronic Mail'. It is a paperless method of sending messages, notes, pictures and even sound files from one place to another using the Internet as a medium. It is an individual name, which is used to send and receive e-mail on the Internet. It is used to specify the source or destination of an e-mail message.

e.g.   arihant@gmail.com

Check Point 03

1 The term ..... is derived from words interconnection and networks.

2 Which network connection is also known as power-band?

3 What is the full form of Wi-Fi?

4 ..... is a way of exchanging information between computers.

Introduction to Instant Messaging

Instant Messaging (IM) is an Internet service that allows people to communicate with each other in real time through an instant messaging software. Unlike e-mail, instant messaging allows messages from one person to appear right away on the other person's computer screen right after the send button is pressed.

Instant Messaging allows effective and efficient communication, allowing immediate receipt of acknowledgement or reply. However, IM is basically not necessarily supported by transaction control.

Many instant messaging services offer video calling features, voice over IP and web conferencing services. Web conferencing service can integrate both video calling and instant messaging abilities.

Instant Messaging Account

Messaging to each other participants need to be signed in to the same instant messaging software. To use instant messaging software, a user must have a valid instant messaging account. These accounts are differ in formats. Some IM software such as Yahoo! Messenger, Windows live messenger use email addresses for managing the account and software such as Skype use standard names.

Instant Messaging Service

Here are services of instant messaging:

- Accepts instant messages from external sites.
- Determines the user to which the message should be delivered and routers it accordingly.
- Accepts instant messages from internal hosts.
- Determines the destination system to which the message should be delivered and routes it accordingly.

Key Features of an Instant Messaging

Key features of an Instant Messaging are as follows:

- Video calling
- Language translation (IM has an in-built translator).
- Going invisible (Your status can be shown as offline to your IM contact list).
- Encrypted messages (Text sent disappears from the receiver's phone automatically after they read it).
- In-built lock.
- Save messages for future reference.

Popular Instant Messaging Software

There are two kinds of instant messaging software:

Application Based

This type of instant messaging software are downloaded from Internet and installed on user's computer.

These are :

- Whatsapp
- Viber
- Skype
- Facebook Messenger
- Google Talk
- WeChat

Web Based

This type of software is accessed using browsers such as google chrome etc. These are :

- Meebo
- eBuddy
- MSN Web Messenger
- Yahoo! Web Messenger
- AIM Express
- MessengerFX

Google Talk Instant Messenger

Google Talk is also known as Gtalk, developed by Google. It is an instant messaging services that provides both text and voice communication developed by Google Inc. This is a free service from Google which requires users to have a google or gmail account to use the client. Gtalk follows in the company's tradition of keeping things simple. All our contacts are automatically loaded from your gmail account, the first time you launch the client. You can start a conversation in a click and keep all of your different chats in separate windows. Although, Google Talk does not allow you to phone call , it will let you talk with other google users and even send voice mail if they are offline.

Launching Google Talk

To launch Google Talk, follow the given steps:

Step 1 Click on **Start** button.

Step 2 Click on **All Programs**. A sub menu will appear.

Step 3 Click on **Google Talk** and then click on Google Talk.

Or

Step 4 Double click on **Google Talk** icon which appear on desktop.

For chatting, you need to have contact list. You can add your contact from gmail account by sending an invitation. But, if you do not have any gmail account, first create a gmail account because you need to sign-in with gmail account to use Google Talk.

To Sign in, into your Google Talk Account

To sign in, into your Google Talk account, follow given step:

Step 1   Use your Gmail account's username and password.

Step 2   Then click on **Sign in** button to sign into Google Talk.

After Sign in into Google Talk account, you can see window as display below.

Chatting on Instant Messenger

Chatting on Google Talk

Here are the steps to chat with a contact on Google Talk:

Step 1 You can start chatting with your contact by double click on Google Talk. After this, a pop-up window will appear on the screen.

Step 2 Chat window has text box. In this box, you can type message and press **Enter** key.

Step 3 Message will sent to other person. He/She will read this message and reply your message if he/she wants.

To use Group Chat, just start a conversation with a contact, then click the drop–down on the right of the chat window and select Group Chat.

From there, you can add as many contacts which you want. Group Chat is far from innovative. There are some etiquettes and rules while chatting on Google Talk, as follows:

- When starting a conversation with someone over Instant Messaging (IM), you should always say 'Hi' or 'Hello'.

- Use of all caps sentences is a bad. In written language, capitalised sentences stand for shouting.

- First thing you should check is, if the person in front of you is 'available' or 'busy'. If a status message says 'busy', you should not disturb him/her.

- Take care to use correct grammar and spelling.

- Appropriate abbreviation should be use by you e.g. 'LOL' (Laugh Out Loud), 'np' (no problem) or 'u' (you) etc.

- Once the conversation ends, say 'thanks' or 'thank you'.

- It is simply rude to keep some one hanging when they are expecting an answer from you. So, the polite thing would be to respond.

Chatting on Gmail

Besides sending and receiving e-mail, gmail users have access to a range of additional features that can be quite useful. One of the most popular features of gmail is chat. Google Chat is gmail's instant messaging feature, which allows you to talk in real time to friends and family.

To chat on Gmail, follow the given steps:

Step 1 Log in to your **Gmail account** with username and password.

Step 2 A window will appear on the screen.

Step 3 Left side of this window, contact list will be display.

Step 4 Double click on the contact name with which you want to start chat.

Step 5 After clicking on the contact name, a small pop-up window will be display on the right bottom side.

Step 6 Here, you can type the message for chatting.

Chatting on Yahoo

With Yahoo Messenger, you can chat and talk with your friends with yahoo accounts easily. You can use the Yahoo Messenger program on your computer or the app on your mobile device to call your friends and talk to them.

To chat on Yahoo, follow the given steps:

Step 1 Open your **Yahoo account** with your Yahoo id and password.

Step 2 Click your Name or Yahoo id in the upper-left corner of the screen and select **Available** to show your contacts that you are online and able to chat.

Step 3 Click the **Minimized Yahoo Messenger** window at the bottom of the screen if it automatically appeared when you went online.

Step 4 This maximizes window and displays any requests you received since the last time you were online. Click **Accept, Decline** or **Block** to act on an add request.

Step 5 Click **Compose Message → Instant Message**, to start a new conversation. Type a message and press **Enter** to send the message.

General rules and etiquettes to be followed while chatting

- The first thing you should check is, if the person in front of you is available or busy.
- It's simply rude to keep someone hanging when they are expecting an answer from you. So, the polite thing would be to respond.
- Don't use offensive language.
- Avoid replying to negative comments with more negative comments.
- You may have to leave your seat for some reason but always inform the person in front that you are going to be away for sometime.

Check Point 05

1 What is the full form of 'LOL' which used in chatting?

2 On which device, you can use Yahoo Messenger program?

3 When you come online on Yahoo Messenger and you receive requests with some options as

(a) Accept   (b) Decline

(c) Block   (d) All of these

Creating and Publishing Web Pages - Blog

A blog is a website or a web page, in which an individual records opinion links to other sites on regular basis. A blog content is written frequently and added in a chronological order. It is written online and visible to everyone.

A typical blog combines text, images and links to other blogs, web pages and other media related to its topic. In education, blogs can be used as instructional resources. These blogs are referred to as **edublogs**. The entries of blog are also known as **posts**. A person who writes a blog or a weblog is known as **blogger**. Blogging is the act of posting content on a blog. There are some popular websites which offer blog service as follows:

- Joomla   - WordPress.com
- Drupal   - Blogger
- Tumblr   - Weebly

Creating a Blog Account on WordPress

WordPress is a free personal publishing platform. It is an easy to use, fast and flexible blog script. It comes with a great set of features, designed to make your experience as a publisher as pleasant as possible. The steps to create a Blog account in WordPress are as follows:

Step 1 Open a **web browser** e.g. Mozilla Firefox, Google Chrome etc., for creating a blog account.

Step 2 Type the URL www.wordpress.com in the address bar and press **Enter** key.

Step 3 Now, click on **Sign Up** button and after this, a page will appear as shown below :

Step 4 Above page shows different fields such as E-mail Address, Username, Password etc.

- **E-mail Address** WordPress will sent an activation link to your e-mail id after clicking on Create Blog button. So, provide a valid e-mail address.
- **Username** This name will manage your blog.

- **Password** You must use strong password for securing purpose. You can use uppercase and lowercase letter with numbers and special symbols.
- **Blog Address** This address is used by viewer to view your blog.
- **Language** Here, you can choose language in which you want to write a blog.

Step 5   Click on **Create Blog** button.

Step 6   Now, you will get an activation link on your e-mail account. Open your e-mail and check to WordPress e-mail.

Step 7   Open that e-mail and click on **Confirm Now** link, your blog will be activated.

Step 8   After activating the blog, **WordPress Blog Account** will appear on your screen.

Adding Context to the Blog

Now, your blog is ready to use. To create a post, follow the given steps:

Step 1   Click on **New Post** from the left side of the window. The following window will appear on the screen.

Step 2   Given the title to your blog in **Add New Page** text box. e.g. Arihant Publication.

Step 3   Type the content about Arihant Publication in content box and click on **Publish** button to publish your post.

Step 4   To view your post, open the web browser and type your blog address in the address bar.

Step 5   Now, you can see your post as well as others. Here, you can also comment on others post by clicking on **Leave a Reply** option.

Step 6   After typing the comment, click on **Post Comment** option.

Check Point 06

1   Blogging is the act of posting content on a blog. State True or False.

2   Write any two popular websites for blog.

3   What is the use of e-mail address field in sign up page?

Using Offline Blog Editors

An offline blog editor is a very useful tool for bloggers because it lets you create blog posts without an Internet connection. So, instead of waiting for an online editor to load, your can just work offline. Offline editors let you create, edit and format your content before you upload it to your website. Some popular free offline blog editors are as follows:

- Windows Live Writer (For Windows)
- BlogDesk (For Windows)
- Qumana (For Windows and Mac)
- MarsEdit (For Mac) free only 30 days trial

Qumana

It is a desktop based blog editor that allows you to create and modify blog posts for more than one blog. It is used for windows and Mac operating system. Qumana works with a variety of blog platforms. They are :

- Blogger
- Diaryland
- WordPress.com
- Drupal
- Blogware
- BlogHarbor

The launch the Qumana, follow the given steps:

Step 1   Click **Start** button → **All Programs** → **Qumana** → **Qumana**

                                    or

Double click on the Qumana icon which is available on the desktop.

Step 2   After clicking, a window will appear on screen as follows:

Step 3   Enter your **WordPress blog address** in textbox and click on **Next** button.

Step 4   After this, a sign in window will appear on the screen with Username and Password fields as shown below :

Step 5 Click on **Next** and then click on **Finish**.

If you have any post in blog, then these posts will be display in Qumana.

To create a new post in Qumana, follow the below steps:

Step 1   Click on **New Post** option.

Step 2   After clicking, a window will appear on the screen as shown below :

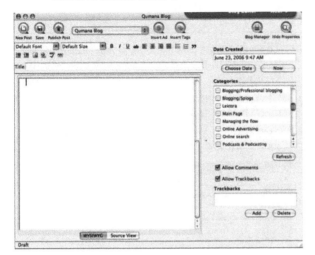

Step 3   Type the suitable title for your post in the **Title field** and content of the post in the box which given below the title field.

Step 4   Click on **Publish Post** button.

This post will be updated to your blog account. If you want to make your blog more attractive, you can also add picture in your blog.

To insert the image in your blog, follow the given steps:

Step 1   Click on **Image** icon. A **Insert Image** window will appear on screen as shown below :

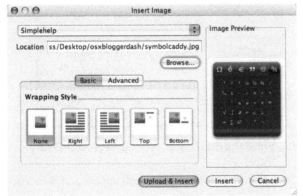

Step 2   Click on **Browse** .... to locate the image which you like to add in your post.

Step 3   After selecting the appropriate image, click on **Upload & Insert** button.

Step 4   Now, click on **Publish Post**.

Check Point 07

1   .... is useful tool for bloggers to create, edit and format your content without an Internet connection.

2   Give any one name of free offline blog editor.

3   What is the use of Qumana editor?

Online Transaction and Online Shopping

Online transaction is a payment method in which the transfer of fund or money happens online over electronic fund transfer. Online shopping is the process of buying goods and services from merchants over the Internet. Books, clothing, household appliances, toys, hardware, software and health insurance are just some of hundreds of products consumers can buy from an online store.

Benefits of Online Shopping

Some benefits of online shopping are as follows:

- Online shopping is very convenient. You can get products at home.
- Online shopping's websites provide million of choices of product.
- They offer huge discount on goods and services.
- Online shops give us the opportunity to shop 24 × 7 and also reward us with cashback.
- Sending gifts to relatives and friends is easy by online shop.

Some Popular Online Websites

- **Amazon** An online shopping portal for buying consumer products.
- **Flipkart** An online shopping portal for buying consumer products.
- **Nykaa** An online shopping portal for beauty products.
- **IRCTC** An online portal for booking train tickets and seeing seat availability.
- **RedBus** An online portal for booking bus tickets.
- **Myntra** An online portal famous for branded clothing.

 COD (Cash on Delivery) is a feature, provided by some websites where the users can pay once they receive the product.

Transaction for Purchasing Goods at Flipkart

To purchase goods on Flipkart, follow the given steps:

Step 1   By web browser, open the **Flipkart** site.

Step 2   **Home page** of Flipkart will appear as shown below.

Step 3   Click on **Login** if you have an account on Flipkart otherwise click on Signup to register on Flipkart.

Step 4   A window will appear on screen with **Enter Mobile Number** field.

Step 5   Enter mobile number and click on **CONTINUE**. A window will be appear as shown below :

Step 6   You will received an **OTP** (One Time Password), enter this number and set password and then click on **Sign up**.

Step 7   Flipkart home screen will appear where different categories are given. You can select any category which you want.

Step 8   For example, select **Sports, Books** and **More**.

Step 9   The sub categories of Sports, Books and More will be display. In this category, select **Books → Indian Writing**.

Step 10   Click on the item which you want to purchase and then click on **Add to Cart**.

Step 11   Now, click on **My Cart** and Cart window will appear as shown below :

Step 12   Click on **Place Order.** A Delivery Address window will appear as shown below :

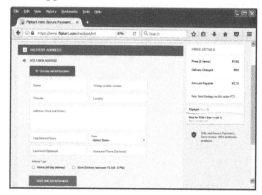

Step 13   Enter the details and click on **Save And Deliver Here**.

Step 14   The order summary page will appear and then click on **Continue** button.

Step 15 **Payment Options** window will appear as shown below. Here is the different payment methods. You can select any one of them. e.g. Cash on Delivery.

Step 16 Enter the characters in the given box and click on **Confirm Order**.

Step 17 After confirmation, a message will be received by you on registered mobile number.

Transaction for Booking Rail Tickets

An E-Ticket or electronic ticket is the digital ticket equivalent of a paper ticket. IRCTC (Indian Railway Catering and Tourism Corporation) is used to book and cancel rail tickets.

To book the ticket on IRCTC, follow the given steps:

Step 1 Open the **IRCTC** site by www.irctc.co.in address. The home page of IRCTC will appear on the screen.

Step 2 Enter in **From** and **To** fields, class type and click on **Find Trains** option.

Step 3 Search the train and click on **Check Availability and Fare** to find the availability of train and book now.

Step 4 The following page will display. If you have an account on IRCTC then enter login name and password otherwise click on **REGISTER** button.

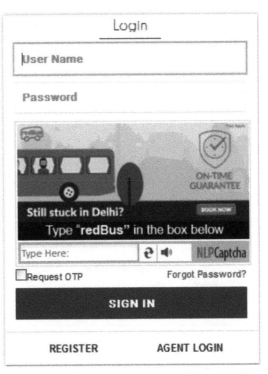

Step 5 Individual Registration page will appear, fill the details and click on **Register** button.

Step 6 After this, a window will appear as shown below

Step 7 Enter the required fields and click on **Continue Booking**.

Step 8 **Travelling Passengers** page will be appear as shown below.

Step 9 Click on **Continue Booking**. Payment options page will be display on the screen. Select the appropriate option and enter details.

Step 10 **Payment Page** will be appear as shown below. Fill your bank details and click on **Proceed** button.

Step 11 E-ticket will be generated on screen as well as sent to your registered e-mail id.

Check Point 08

1 Which products can you buy online?
2 Give any one website which offers service to buy goods.
3 .... is the payment method in which the transfer of fund or money happens online over electronic fund transfer.

Internet Security

It is a branch of computer security that deals specifically with Internet based threats. The Internet security prevents attacks targeted at browsers, networks, operating systems and other applications. The main aim of Internet security is to set up precise rules and regulations that can deflect attacks that arise from the Internet.

Internet security relies on particular resources and criteria for safeguarding the data that is communicated or transferred online.

Best Practices for Internet Security

There are various best practices for Internet security, as follows:

Use Secure Password

Your passwords are the most common way to prove your identity when using website, e-mail accounts and your computer itself. The use of strong password is therefore essential in order to protect your security and identity.

Do the following to choose the best password:

- To create a strong password, simply choose three random words.
- You can use numbers, symbols and combination of uppercase and lowercase.
- Choose a password with atleast eight characters.
- Do not use your username, actual name or business name as password.
- Avoid to keep commonplace, dictionary word, your birthday date etc.
- Avoid to use the word 'Password' and numerical sequence for password.

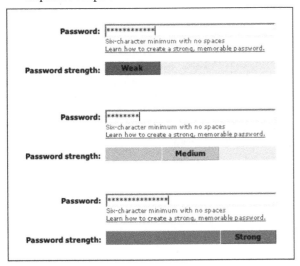

Install Anti-Virus Protection

Only install an anti-virus program from a known and trusted source. Keep virus definitions, engines and software upto date to ensure your anti-virus program remains effective.

Keep Software upto Date

Installing software updates for your operating system and programs in critical. Always install the latest security updates for your device.

- Turn on automatic updates for your operating system.
- Use web browser such as Google Chrome etc. that receive frequent, automatic security updates.
- Make sure to keep browser plug-ins up to date.

Always Keep your Firewall Active

Every computer is protected by a firewall. This firewall controls the flow of data over any network. Though firewall is the most secure feature in data protection. The firewalls provided mainly by the anti-virus developing companies are used.

Always use Secure Network Connection

Avoid doing crucial transaction over a public network. Any network other than your home or work network is an insecure network. Before using any connection other than trusted networks, always make sure that you secure the connection using appropriate VPN (Virtual Private Network) settings.

Backup your Data

Backup on a regular basis, if you are a victim of a security incident, the only guaranteed way to repair your computer is to erase and re-install the system.

Do not Share Personal Information

You should never share your personal information on unknown or unauthorised site, because they can use your personal information for illegal work.

Use Encryption Software

Always use encryption software for protecting your personal data from unauthorised user.

Remove Unnecessary Programs

Uninstall any software and services which you are not using from long time.

Beware of E-mail or Attachments from Unknown People

Never open an attachment you were not expecting and if you do not know the sender of an attachment, delete the message without reading it.

Do not Click Random Links

Do not click any link that you cannot verify. If you doubt link's validity, ask for more information from the sender.

Never Share Passwords

Never share your passwords even with friends, family or computer support personal.

Clearing Cache and Cookies on Web Browser

Follow the steps below for how to clear web history on the Mozilla Firefox browser:

Step 1 Click on the upper right of the browser toolbar.

Step 2 Click **History**.

Step 3 Click Clear **Recent History**.

Step 4 Click the drop-down menu next to Time range to clear and select **Everything**.

Step 5 Place a checkmark next to the following options under **Details:**

- Browsing and Download History
- Form & Search History
- Cookies
- Cache
- Active Logins
- Offline Website Data
- Site Preferences

Step 6 Click on **Clear Now** button.

The window will close and the items you have selected will be cleared.

Check Point 09

1 What is the aim of Internet security?

2 Why do we should remove unnecessary programs?

3 Which of the following is/are best practice(s) for Internet security?
   (a) Use secure password
   (b) Use encryption software
   (c) Keep software upto date
   (d) All of the above

SUMMARY

- A web application (web app) is a computer program that utilizes web browsers and web technology to perform tasks over the Internet.
- Accessibility features are designed to help people with disabilities to use technology more easily.
- A computer network is a group of computer systems and other computing hardware devices that are linked together through communication channels to facilitate communication and resource sharing.
- A network topology is the arrangement with which computer systems or network devices are connected to each other.
- Switching techniques are used for transmitting data across networks, such as circuit switching, packet switching and message switching.
- Internet is a global network connecting millions of computers.
- Wireless connection uses waves to transfer data, i.e. no cables are needed to guide the signals.
- The World Wide Web (WWW) is a combination of all resources and users on the Internet that are using the Hyper Text Transfer Protocol (HTTP).
- An Internet Service Provider (ISP) is an organisation or business that provides Internet access and other related services to users.
- Instant Messaging (IM) is a form of text communication between two or more people in real time while online.
- Google Talk or Gtalk is an instant messaging service that provided both text and voice communication.
- Google chat is gmail's instant messaging feature which allows you to talk to friends and family.
- A blog is a web page in which an individual records opinion links to other sites on regular basis.
- WordPress is an open source software that you can use to create a website or blog.
- Offline blog editor helps to write post while you are offline.
- Online shopping is the activity or action of buying products or services over the Internet.
- Internet security is a broad term that refers to the various steps individuals and companies take to protect computers or computer networks are connected to the Internet.

Exam Practice

Multiple Choice Questions

1 Which of the following is an application program that is stored on a remote server and delivered over the Internet?
(a) Web application
(b) System application
(c) Internet application
(d) None of the above

Ans. (*a*) A web application is an application program that is stored on a remote server and delivered over the Internet. It includes web mail, online auction and online retail sales etc.

2 Computer connected with LAN
(a) work fast
(b) go online
(c) can e-mail
(d) can share information or peripheral devices

Ans. (*d*) Computer connected with LAN can share information or peripheral devices.

3 A group of computers connected together with the help of cables within an office building is called
(a) PAN   (b) WAN
(c) MAN   (d) LAN

Ans. (*d*) Using LAN, we can connect computers within a building only.

4 Network formed between computers which are spread across the continents is called
(a) LAN   (b) WAN
(c) MAN   (d) WLAN

Ans. (*b*) Across the continents, computers can be connected using WAN only.

5 Digital information is converted into analog information by the modem at
(a) destination computer
(b) source computer
(c) Both (a) and (b)
(d) Neither (a) nor (b)

Ans. (*b*) Digital information is converted into analog information by modem at source computer.

6 Modulation and demodulation are performed by
(a) microwave   (b) satellite
(c) modem   (d) fibre optic

Ans. (*c*) Modulation and demodulation are performed by modem.

7 A modem is connected in between a telephone line and a
(a) computer
(b) serial port
(c) network
(d) communication adapter

Ans. (*a*) Modem is a device that enables computers and other equipments to communicate with each other using telephone lines.

8 Which of the following is not a transmission medium?
(a) Telephone lines   (b) Co-axial cable
(c) Modem   (d) Microwave

Ans. (*c*) Telephone lines, co-axial cable and microwave are transmission medium but modem is a network device that converts analog signal to digital signal and *vice-versa*.

9 What can you do with the Internet?
(a) Exchange information with friends and colleagues
(b) Access pictures, sounds, video clips and other media elements
(c) Find diverse perspective on issues from a global audience
(d) Internet exchange information, access pictures, find diverse perspective on issue from a global audience.

Ans. (*d*) Internet exchange information, access pictures, find diverse perspective on issues from a global audience.

10 The first network was
(a) ARPANET   (b) Internet
(c) NSFnet   (d) NET

Ans. (*a*) The Advanced Research Projects Agency NETwork (ARPANET) was the world's first operational packet switching network.

11 Which of these services will not be provided by a typical Internet Service Provider (ISP)?
(a) An e-mail address
(b) Modem
(c) A connection to the Internet
(d) Technical help

Ans. (*a*) ISP refers to a company that provides Internet services, modem, connection and technical help but it does not provide an e-mail address.

12 To join the Internet, the computer has to be connected to a
(a) Internet architecture board
(b) Internet society
(c) Internet Service Provider
(d) None of the above

Ans. (*c*) Internet Service Provider is used to join the Internet.

13 Wireless broadband can be
(a) mobile   (b) fixed
(c) Both (a) and (b)   (d) None of these

Ans. (*c*) Wireless broadband can be mobile or fixed. It does not require modem or cable.

14 Nick connects to the Internet at home using a laptop computer with a wireless connection.

Nick is going to change to a desktop computer using a 1 Gbps ethernet cable connection.

Which of these should be the result of making the changes?
(a) Increased portability and decreased speed
(b) Decreased portability and increased speed
(c) Increased portability and increased speed
(d) Decreased portability and decreased speed

Ans. (*b*) If Nick is going to change to a desktop computer using a 1 Gbps ethernet cable connection then it decreased portability and increased speed.

15 A collection of web pages linked together in a random order is
(a) a website   (b) a web server
(c) a search engine   (d) a web browser

Ans. (*a*) A website is a collection of web pages linked together in a random order and displays related information on a specific topic.

16 Home page helps viewers to find out what they can find on the particular site? Home page is the
(a) first page of a website   (b) index page
(c) about page   (d) None of these

Ans. (*a*) Home page refers to the initial or main or first web page of a website, sometimes called the front page. It can help the viewers to find out what they find on particular site.

17 Which client software is used to request and display web pages?
(a) Web server   (b) Multimedia
(c) FTP   (d) Web browser

Ans. (*d*) A Web browser is a program that your computer runs to communicate with web servers on the Internet, which enables you to download and display the web pages that you request.

18 .... is an example of text-based browser which provides access to the Internet in the text-only mode.
(a) Mozilla Firefox   (b) Lynx
(c) Internet Explorer   (d) All of these

Ans. (*b*) Lynx is a highly configurable text-based web browser.

19 In URL, http://www.arihant.com/index.htm, which component identifies the website?
(a) http   (b) www.arihant.com
(c) /index.htm   (d) All of these

Ans. (*b*) www.arihant.com, because domain name identifies the website.

20 In URL, http://www.arihant.com/index.htm, which component identifies the path of a web page?
(a) http   (b) www.arihant.com
(c) /index.htm   (d) All of these

Ans. (*c*) /index.htm, because path name identifies the path of a web page.

21 A web page is located using a
(a) Universal Record Linking
(b) Uniform Resource Locator
(c) Universal Record Locator
(d) Uniformly Reachable Links

Ans. (*b*) URL (Uniform Resource Locator) specifies the location of a specific web page on the Internet.

22 Instant messaging service accepts instant messages from
(a) external sites   (b) internal sites
(c) Both (a) and (b)   (d) None of these

Ans. (*a*) Instant messaging is an internal service that accepts instant messages from external sites.

23 Which of the following is an application based instant messaging software?
(a) Google Talk   (b) eBuddy
(c) Meebo
(d) MSN Web Messenger

Ans. (*a*) Instant messaging are the types of software as application based and web based. Google Talk is an application based software.

24 A blog consists of
(a) images   (b) text
(c) links   (d) All of these

Ans. (*d*) A blog consists of images, text and links.

25 .... is the act of posting content on a blog.
(a) Edublog   (b) Posting
(c) Blogging   (d) Blogger

Ans. (*c*) Blogging is the act of posting content on a blog.

26 Which of the following offers a blog service?
(a) Drupal   (b) Joomla
(c) WordPress.com   (d) All of these

Ans. (*d*) Various softwares are there which offer blog services such as WordPress. com, WordPress.org, Joomla, Drupal, Blogger, Weebly etc.

27 Qumana is an offline blog editor which is used for .... operating system(s).
(a) Windows   (b) Mac
(c) Both (a) and (b) (d) None of these

Ans. (*c*) Qumana is a desktop based blog editor that allows you to create and modify blog post. It is used for Windows and Mac both operating system.

28 Which of the following websites is used for booking train tickets?
(a) Nykaa
(b) IRCTC
(c) RedBus
(d) Myntra

Ans. (*b*) IRCTC (Indian Railway Catering and Tourism Corporation) is an online portal for booking train tickets and seeing seat availability.

Fill in the Blanks

1 .... is used to text-to-speech utility that reads what is displayed on the screen.

Ans. Start Narrator

2 .... is the formation of networks.

Ans. Networking

3 The acronym yo LAN is ....**[CBSE Text book]**

Ans. Local Area Network

4 The small area network created around a bluetooth device is called ....

Ans. PAN (Personal Area Network)

5 .... serves a similar function as switches.

Ans. Bridge

6 The digital signals to analog signals are carried out by ...., so that data can travel over telephone lines.

Ans. modem

7 In .... topology, each node is connected to two and only two neighbouring nodes.

Ans. ring

8 In packet based networks, the message gets broken into small ....

Ans. data packets

9 .... key is an accessibility function which is designed for people who have vision impairment or cognitive disabilities.
[CBSE SQP Term-II]

Ans. Toggle key

10 Networks in which certain computers have special dedicated tasks, providing services to other computers (in the network) are called .... networks.   **[CBSE SQP Term-II]**

Ans. Client-Server

11 .... is a universal wireless networking technology that utilises radio frequencies to transfer data.

Ans. Wireless Fidelity

12 Satellite which are orbiting around the ...., provide necessary links for telephone and television service.

Ans. Earth

13 Three types of wireless Internet connectivity are ...., ... & ...., .   **[CBSE Textbook]**

Ans. Wi-fi, WiMAX, Satellite

14 In WWW, a client is called .... and a server is called ....

Ans. web browser, web server

15 Safari is a web browser developed by ....

Ans. Apple

16 Web based type of software is accessed using ....

Ans. browsers

17 .... is a computer program that provides services to other computer programs.

Ans. Server

18 The address of location of the document on WWW is called ....

Ans. URL

19 In URL, http://www.cbse.nic.in/ , ... is a protocol.

Ans. http

20 A router passes data packets from one network to another network based on their .... not MAC address.

Ans. IP address

21 abc@mnc.co.in represents an ....

Ans. E-mail address

22 .... is a form of communication over the Internet that offers an instantaneous transmission of text based messages from sender to receiver.   **[CBSE Textbook]**

Ans. Instant Messaging

23 Appropriate abbreviation should use .... for no problem.

Ans. 'np'

24 Educational blogs are referred to as ....

Ans. edublogs

25 Blog Desk is an offline blog editor which is used for .... operating system.

Ans. Windows

26 ...... is an online portal famous for branded clothing.

Ans. Myntra

27 You should uninstall any .... and services which you are not using from long time.

Ans. software

28 Browsing and download history, cookies, cache etc are available in .... option.

Ans. Details

True and False

1 A computer connected to a network is known as stand-alone computer.

Ans. **False** A computer connected to a network is known as host or node.

2 Networking of computers helps the users to share data files.

Ans. **True** One of the benefits of networking is to help the users to share data files.

3 A separate printer will be needed in a network for all connected computers.

Ans. **False** Computers connected to a LAN can share information through a common printer.

4 MANs are the computer networks confined to a localised area such as an office building, school etc.

Ans. **False** LANs are the computer networks confined to a localised area such as an office building, school etc.

5 MAN provides communication services upto 5 km.

Ans. **False** MAN provides communication services upto 100 km.

6 Hub is a single-port device, which provides access to computers.

Ans. **False** Hub is a multi-port network device, which provides access to computers.

7 The repeater establishes an intelligent connection between a local network and external networks.

Ans. **False** The gateway establishes an intelligent connection between a local network and external networks, which are completely different in structure.

8 In star topology, there persists a central node called server or hub.

Ans. **True** In star topology, there persists a central node called server or hub, which is connected to the nodes directly.

9 Circuit switching is guaranteed delivery.

Ans. **True** The main advantage of circuit switching is guaranteed delivery.

10 DSL can be provided to homes using existing electrical connection and outlets.

Ans. **False** BPL can be provided to homes using existing electrical connections and outlets. It is also known as power-band.

11 WWW is an Internet service.

Ans. **True** The World Wide Web (WWW) is a set of programs, standards and protocols that allows the multimedia and hypertext files to be created, displayed and linked on the Internet.

12 Web pages and websites are same.

Ans. **False** Website is the collection of web pages.

13 HTML is used to create web pages.

Ans. **True** HTML is a markup language which is used to create web pages.

14 Home page is the server page of a website.

Ans. **False** Home page is the first web page of a website. When a website is opened, its home page is displayed.

15 Website can be accessed by URL.

Ans. **True** Each website is accessed by its own address known as URL.

16 Graphical web browser supports only graphics information.

Ans. **False** Graphical web browser supports both text and graphic information. e.g. Google Chrome, Opera etc.

17 URL is an Internet machine.

Ans. **False** URL is the web address for a website or a web page.

18 WeChat, Skype and Viber are web based instant messaging softwares.

Ans. **False** WeChat, Skype and Viber are application based instant messaging softwares.

19 Google chat is gmail's instant messaging feature.

Ans. **True** Google chat is gmail's instant messaging feature which allows you to talk your friends and family.

20 In professional, blogs can be used as instructional resources.

Ans. **False** In education, blogs can be used as instructional resources. These blogs are referred to as edublogs.

21 Online shopping's websites provide million of choices of products.

Ans. **True** Online shopping's websites provide million of choices of products and also offer us huge discount.

22 Internet security prevents attacks targeted at browsers.

Ans. **True** Internet security prevents attacks targeted at browsers, network, operating systems and other applications.

Very Short Answer (VSA) Type Questions

1 Name the term defined by given below statement: "A group of computers connected to each other by a link."

Ans. Computer network is defined as a group of computers connected to each other by a link that allows sharing of resources and information.

2 What is the definition of networking?
[CBSE Textbook]

Ans. A computer networking is the practice for exchanging information/services between two or more computers together for the purpose of sharing data.

3 What are the main types of computer networks.

Ans. Following are the three main types of computer networks, based upon the geographical area as follows:
  (i) Local Area Network (LAN)
  (ii) Metropolitan Area Network (MAN)
  (iii) Wide Area Network (WAN)

4 What is the main purpose of switch?

Ans. A switch is a hardware device which is used to connect devices or segment of network with smaller subsets of LAN segments.

5 Identify the following devices :
  (i) A device that is used to connect different types of networks. It performs the necessary translation so that the connected networks can communicate properly.
  (ii) A device that converts data from digital bit stream into an analog signal and vice-versa.

Ans. (i) Router   (ii) Modem

6 What is the advantage of mesh topology?

Ans. In mesh topology, each node is connected to more than one node, so that it provides alternative route, in case, if the host is either down or busy.

7 Give the names of models of computer networking.

Ans. There are mainly two models of computer networking as follows:
  (i) Peer-to-Peer network (ii) Client-server network

8 How many techniques are used for transmitting data across network?

Ans. There are three techniques used for transmitting data across network : circuit switching, packet switching and message switching.

9 Why Internet is called a network of networks?

Ans. Internet is called a network of networks because it connects several large and all heterogeneous networks together into a bigger network.

10 Write two advantages of using Internet.

Ans. Advantages of using Internet are as follows:
  (i) It is used for communication, entertainment, searching information and for providing many types of services.
  (ii) It provides the facility of e-mail.

11 Name any five DSL broadband service providers in India.

Ans. BSNL, Airtel, Reliance, MTNL and Tata Indicom are the five DSL broadband service providers in India.

12 Differentiate between wired and wireless access. Give one example for each type.
[CBSE SQP Term-II]

Ans.

Wired	Wireless
A wired setup uses physical cables or wires which is used to transfer data between devices and computer systems.	A wireless setup does not use wires or cable in order to access the Internet.
Examples of wired access are: Dial-up connection, DSL or Cable Internet Access.	Examples of wireless access are Wi-Fi and WiMaX.

13 Name the device that converts digital signal to analog that can travel over phone lines.
[CBSE SQP Term-II]

Ans. Modem is the device that converts digital signal to analog that can travel over phone lines. The full form of Modem is MOdulator-DEModulator.

14 Ramya wants to connect all the computers of her office wirelessly in order to avoid clumsy cables. Which wireless technology would be best suitable for her office?

Ans. Wi-Fi technology would be best suitable for her office to avoid cabling. Because, it allows high speed Internet connections without the use of cables or wires.

15 Write the full form of following terms.
   (i) WiMAX   (ii) BPL

Ans. (i) WiMAX - Worldwide Interoperability for Microwave Access.
   (ii) BPL - Broadband over Power Line.

16 What can a user do with WWW?

Ans. Using WWW (World Wide Web), a user can download files, listen to music, view video files and jump to other documents or websites by using hypertext links.

17 List any four advantages associated with networking.   **[CBSE SQP Term-II]**

Ans. Four advantages of networking are as follows
   (i) **User Communication** Network allows users to communicate using emails, social networking sites, video conferencing, etc.
   (ii) **File Sharing** By using networking, data or information can be shared or transferred from one computer to another.
   (iii) **Media and Entertainment** Most of the companies and TV channels use network to broadcast audio and video including live radio and television programmes.
   (iv) **Hardware Sharing** Hardware components such as printers, scanners, etc., can also be shared. For example, instead of purchasing 10 printers, one printer can be purchased and shared among multiple users thus, saving cost.

18 Mr. Lal owns a factory which manufactures automobile spare parts. Suggest him the advantages of having a web page for his factory.

Ans. The web page provides the information to the clients about his factory of spare parts. Moreover, he can receive the order on the Internet from the clients using the web page.

19 Name two web browsers of Internet.

Ans. Internet Explorer and Google Chrome are the two web browsers of Internet.

20 Can we use URL to access a web page? How?

Ans. Yes, as a location on a web server, which is called a website and each website has a unique address known as URL. So, an URL can be used to access a web page.

21 What is URL?

Ans. URL means Uniform Resource Locator. It is a unique address of a web page on the Internet. It specifies the Internet address of a file stored on a host computer connected to the Internet.

22 Identify Web addresses and E-mail addresses from the following.
   (i) www.scrapbook.com
   (ii) aba@scrapbook.com
   (iii) www.countrywide.co.in
   (iv) 123@hotshot.co.in

Ans. Key features of an Instant Messaging are :
   (i) and (iii) are web addresses.
   (ii) and (iv) are e-mail addresses.

23 Write any two key features of an Instant Messaging (IM).

Ans. Key features of an Instant Messaging are :
   (i) Video calling
   (ii) Language translation

24 List any five application based instant messaging software.   **[CBSE Textbook]**

Ans. Whatsapp, Viber, Skype, WeChat, Google Talk

25 Who is blogger?

Ans. A person who writes a blog or a weblog is known as blogger. Blogging is the act of posting content on a blog.

26 List any 5 websites that provide blog service.   **[CBSE Textbook]**

Ans.
- Joomla
- WordPress.com
- Drupal
- Blogger
- Tumblr

27 Explain the purpose of a blog.
[CBSE Text book]

Ans. The main purpose of blog is to convey messages about events, announcements, need, review etc. Blogs are usually managed using a web browser and this requires active internet connection.

28 What do you understand by ISP with respect to web applications? Name any two connection types that home users use. **[CBSE SQP Term-II]**

Ans. An Internet Service Provider (ISP) is an organisation which provides you with access to the Internet *via* wired or wireless connection. To use the Internet, you need an Internet connection. Internet connections are provided by the Internet Service Providers (ISPs) such as Bharat Sanchar Nigam Limited (BSNL), MTNL, Airtel, Vodafone, Reliance, Tata Indicom, etc.

The home users use cable modem(type of broadband connection) and Wi-Fi(Wireless Fidelity). It is a popular technology that allows an electronic device such as computer or mobile phone to exchange data wirelessly over a network.

29 Explain the purpose of online transactions. **[CBSE Textbook]**

Ans. Online transaction helps us to save many things like paper which is used for making notes, time which is spend in transaction and counting.

30 List any five websites that allow online transactions. **[CBSE Textbook]**

Ans.
- Myntra
- IRCTC
- RedBus
- Amazon
- Flipkart

31 What do you mean by Cash on Delivery?

Ans. Cash on Delivery (COD) is a feature provided by some websites where the users can pay once they receive the product.

Short Answer (SA) Type Questions

1 Write down any three points of differences between LAN, MAN and WAN.

Ans. Three major points of differences among LAN, MAN and WAN are as follows:

Basis	LAN	MAN	WAN
Geographic Area	Generally within a building	Within a city	Across the continents
Distance	Upto 5 km	Upto 160 km	Unlimited
Speed	11 to 54 Mbps	11 to 100+ Mbps	10 to 384 Kbps, 1.83 to 7.2 Mbps

2 Explain the LAN and WAN. **[CBSE Textbook]**

Ans. **LAN** A Local Area Network (LAN) is a computer network covering a small geographical area like a home, office or small group of buildings such as buildings in a school. Computers connected to a LAN can share information and peripheral equipments.

WAN A Wide Area Network (WAN) is used to connect LANs and other types of network together, so that users and computers in one location can communicate with users and computers in other locations.

3 What is the use of repeater in a network?

Ans. In a network, repeater receives a weak signal coming from a source and amplifies it to its original strength and then again forwards it to the destination. Basically, repeaters are used in a network so that a signal can travel longer distance.

4 When the computer network uses telephone lines as communication channel then MODEM is used as a data communication device. Now, explain the working of MODEM.

Ans. MODEM performs the task of modulation at sender's site and demodulation at the receiver's site. Basically, our computer generates data in the form of digital signals which need to be forwarded to the receiver through telephone lines. Since, telephone lines can carry only analog signals. So, digital signals need to be converted to analog signals at sender's site this is called modulation. At receiver's site, again analog signals should be converted back to the original digital signals, then this is called demodulation.

5 What are the differences between star topology and bus topology of network?

Ans. Differences between star topology and bus topology are as follows :

Star Topology	Bus Topology
All the nodes are directly connected with the central node or server.	There is a single length of transmission medium, on which various nodes are attached and the server can be anywhere in the transmission cable.
Faults can be easily detected.	Faults cannot be easily detected.
It is fast in transmission.	Becomes slow with increase in node.

6 What do you mean by tree topology?

Ans. Refer to text on Page no. 142.

7 Difference between circuit switching and packet switching.

Ans. Differences between circuit switching and packet switching are as follows :

Circuit Switching	Packet Switching
Initially designed for voice communication.	Initially designed for data transmission.
Inflexible, because once a path is set all parts of a transmission follows the same path.	Flexible, because a route is created for each packet to travel to the destination.
It is connection oriented.	It is connectionless.

8 Elucidate the following terms.

(i) PAN   (ii) WiMAX   (iii) Satellite

Ans. (i) **PAN** It stands for Personal Area Network. It is a computer network used for communication among computer and different technological devices close to it.

(ii) **WiMAX** It stands for Worldwide Interoperability for Microwave Access. It is a wireless transmission of data using a variety of transmission modes.

(iii) **Satellite** Which are orbiting around the Earth, provide necessary links for telephone and television service.

9 How many types of web browsers? Explain them.

Ans. Refer to text on Page no. 146.

10 Why do we use instant messaging?

Ans. Instant messaging is a set of communication technologies used for text based communication between two or more participants over the Internet or other types of networks. Many instant messaging services offer video calling features, voice over IP and web conferencing services.

Web conferencing services can integrate both video calling and instant messaging abilities.

11 How can you launch Google Talk?

Ans. To launch Goole Talk, follow the given steps:

(i) Click on Start button → All Programs

(ii) Click on Google Talk and then double click on Google Talk.

12 Write the steps to create a new post in Qumana.

Ans. To create a new post in Qumana, follow the below steps:

(i) Click on New Post option. A window will appear.

(ii) Type the title and content of the post in respective fields.

(iii) Click on Publish Post button.

13 What are the benefits of online shopping?

Ans. Some benefits of online shopping are:

(i) It provides the products with better prices.

(ii) It can give us an opportunity to shop 24×7.

(iii) We can get more varieties of product.

(iv) We can send gifts more easily to our relatives and friends.

(v) We can also buy older products at lesser price.

(vi) There is no crowd while online shopping.

14 What is Internet security? Also explain their uses.

Ans. Refer to text on Page no. 154.

Long Answer (LA) Type Questions

1 How to make the computer easier to use in windows?

Ans. Refer to text Page no. 138.

2 What is a computer network? Why do we need networking in our system?

Ans. Computer network is a collection of computers and other hardwares interconnected by communication channels, which allows sharing of resources and information. We need networking for many reasons, which makes it fast and easy. Some of them are given below:

(i) **File Sharing** Data files can be shared.

(ii) **Hardware Sharing** It can share devices, such as printer, scanner, CD-ROM devices etc.

(iii) **Application Sharing** We are able to share the applications of different system within a network.

(iv) **User Communication** It allows users to communicate easily.

(v) **Access to Remote Database** It allows users to access the database from any system in the network.

3 How can you transfer data on network?

Ans. Refer to text on Page no. 143.

4 Why is Internet called 'Network of Networks'?

Ans. Internet is called 'Network of Networks' because it is global network of computers that are linked together by cables and telephone lines making communication possible among them. It can be defined as a global network over a million of smaller heterogeneous computer networks.

The network which consists of thousands of networks spanning the entire globe is known as Internet. The Internet is a world wide collection of networked computers, which are able to exchange information with each other very quickly.

Mostly people use the Internet in two ways, E-mail and World Wide Web. In Internet, most computers are not connected directly, they are connected to smaller networks, which in turn are connected through gateways to the Internet backbone.

A gateway is a device that connects dissimilar networks. A backbone is central interconnecting structure - that connects one or more networks.

5 Explain the following term.
(i) World Wide Web   (ii) Website
(iii) Wep Page   (iv) Web Browser
(v) Web Server

Ans. For (i), (ii), (iii) Refer to text on Page no. 145 and for (iv), (v) Refer to text on Page no. 146.

6 Give an example of E-mail address and explain each part of it.

Ans. The example of an E-mail address is abc@gmail.com. The format of E-mail address is username@hostname or domain name. So, as per the above example of E-mail address abc is the username and gmail.com is the name of hosting server or host (domain) name. Thus, we can say that E-mail address has two parts separated by '@' symbol.
(i) **Username** On the left side of separator @ is the user name. A user name cannot have blanks.
(ii) **Domain Name for the Host Server** The portion to the right of @ identifies the server or host network that services your E-mail. It is also known as E-mail server.

7 What do you mean by Instant Messaging? Also explain one Instant Messaging software. **[CBSE Textbook]**

Ans. Instant Messaging (IM), form of text based communication in which two persons participate in a single conversation over their computers or mobile devices within an Internet based chatroom.

Various softwares provide instant messaging services as Whatsapp, Google Talk, Skype, Meebo, eBuddy etc.

Google Talk

It is an instant messaging and VoIP service developed by Google. This client lets you to log in to the service to chat and hold video-conferences with your friends from the Windows desktop.

Google Talk is more than just a regular chat, you can also make free PC to PC VoIP calls and even leave voice messages like an answering machine. If your contacts are also using the Google Talk client, you can send files too.

Google Talk was integrated into gmail where users could send instant messages to other gmail users. As it worked within a browser, the Google Talk client did not need to be downloaded to send instant messages to gmail users.

8 How to create a blog account on WordPress?

Ans. Refer to text on Page no. 149-150.

9 How can anyone book the ticket online?

Ans. Refer to text on Page no. 154.

10 Internet security deals specifically with Internet based threats. Explain any three best practices of Internet security.

Ans. Refer to text on Page no. 154-155.

Application Oriented Type Questions

1 The following paragraph describes the term computer network.

A computer network is a group of (i) .... that are (ii) .... to each other for the purpose of (iii) .... A computer (iv) .... allows computers to communicate with many other computers and to (v) .... resources and information.

Fill in the blanks with words from the list below:

Connected, Computers, Sending, Communication, Network, Share.

Ans. (i) computers   (ii) connected
(iii) communication   (iv) network
(v) share

2 Manoj has to set up a network between his devices at home which included a smart phone, a laptop and a personal computer. What type of network he would be setting up for the same?
(i) PAN   (ii) MAN   (iii) WAN

Ans. Manoj would be setting up a PAN (Personal Area Network) which is best suited for set up involving a computer, a cell phone and/or a handheld computing device such as a PDA.

3 Laluma Chakradhar wants a broadband connection to access her mails and stay informed about the latest happening in the field of Biotechnology. Can you suggest two Internet Service Providers (ISPs) of India to be approached for the same?

Ans. BSNL and Airtel.

4 Anila works in a Multi National Company (MNC) and needs to work online from home also. She requires fast Internet connection. Which type of Internet connection in your view would be best suited for her?

Ans. Anila should prefer broadband connection.

5 The following sentences describe the term web browser.

Web browsers are programs used to explore the (i) .... A web browser is an interface that helps a computer user gain access to all the content that is on the Internet and the hard disk of the computer.

It can view (ii) ...., text documents, audio and video files, games etc. More than one (iii) .... can also be installed on a single computer. The user can navigate through files, folders and (iv) .... with the help of a browser. When the browser is used for browsing (v) ...., the pages may contain certain links which can be opened in a new browser. Multiple tabs and windows of the same browser can also be opened. An example of web browser is (vi) ....

Fill in the blanks with words from the list given below:

Internet	TCP	Images
Web browser	Photos	Websites
SMTP	Web pages	
Google Chrome		

Ans. (i) Internet   (ii) images
(iii) web browser   (iv) websites
(v) web pages   (vi) Google Chrome

6 Now-a-days people can communicate to each other with the help of e-mail facility. It is gradually replacing other communication means such as telephone, post.
(i) What is meant by the term e-mail?
(ii) Which one of the following is an advantage of using e-mail compared to using post?
  (a) Same delivery time anywhere in the world.
  (b) The e-mail can contain pictures.
  (c) You can send it anywhere.

Ans. (i) E-mail means Electronic Mail. It is a basic Internet service for sending or receiving messages electronically over the Internet.
(ii) (a) Same delivery time anywhere in the world.

7 Sharvan Joshi is a student of Political Science and is a keen researcher of political issues related to various countries and states. He wants to share his research and his own opinions on these issues on day-to-day basis with everyone on World Wide Web (WWW).

He is also interested in collecting views of others to enhance his research and knowledge related to his area of interest. He belongs to a middle class family and can not afford his own website. Also being a non-technical person he can not create a dynamic website to deal with day-to-day inputs.

Suggest an easy way for Sharvan to achieve the same.

Ans. Sharvan should develop a blog.

8 Rahul and Amit are working on a school project assigned to them by their teacher. They have to send instant messages to each other and also do video conferencing after school hours in order to complete the project on time.
(i) Suggest any 4 good instant messaging software that they can use.
(ii) Apart from computers, list 4 hardwares that Rahul and Amit need for video conferencing.
[CBSE SQP Term-II]

Ans. (i) Instant Messaging (IM) is a form of communication over the Internet that offers an instantaneous transmission of text-based messages from sender to receiver. Google hangouts, Skype, Windows Live Messenger, Zoom are the good instant messaging softwares.
(ii) For video conferencing, you should have microphones, headsets speakers and web cameras.
  (a) Using **Microphone**, the speaker can convey their messages.
  (b) **Web camera** is used to have a real-life image of the person.
  (c) **Speakers** are used to listen to the words of the speaker.
  (d) Headsets are used to listen to the speaker without disturbing anyone nearby.

9 Rahul has purchased some stationary items from an online site. He has to make online payment for the items to complete the transaction. Help by answering his following queries.
(i) Suggest any two options that he can use to make payment of his bill on the online shopping website.
(ii) Name any 2 situations where online shopping could be useful.
(iii) Name any 2 popular online transaction websites.
(iv) Write full form of COD in reference to online shopping. **[CBSE SQP Term-II]**

Ans. (i) Credit, debit card or by Internet banking, etc are the options that he can use to make payment of his bill on the online shopping website.
(ii) (a) They offer huge discount on goods and services.
  (b) Online shopping saves time and efforts in order to buy product of one's choice.
(iii) Flipkart, Amazon are two popular online transaction websites.
(iv) COD stands for Cash On Delivery. Cash on delivery is the sale of goods by mail order where payment is made on delivery rather than in advance.

Self Assessment

Multiple Choice Questions

1. Which of the following is the benefit of computer network?
   (a) File sharing
   (b) Hardware sharing
   (c) User communication
   (d) All of these

2. It is an interface that helps computer user to gain access over all the content on the Internet.
   (a) Website   (b) Web browser
   (c) Web page   (d) Web server

3. Which of the following is not web based instant messaging software?
   (a) eBuddy   (b) Meebo
   (c) Messenger FX   (d) Facebook Messenger

Fill in the blanks

4. With ...., you can chat and talk with your friends with Yahoo accounts easily.

5. The entries of blog are also known as ....

6. .... is used by viewer to view your blog.

True or False

7. Qumana blog editor works with blogware platform.

8. Online shopping offers us no discount on goods and services.

9. Every computer is not protected by a firewall.

Very Short Answer (VSA)
Type Questions

10. Which network is often used to connect several LANs together to form a bigger network?

11. What is the use of URL?

12. Write any two instant messaging service.

Short Answer (SA)
Type Questions

13. How can you sign in into your Google Talk account?

14. What do you mean by blog?

15. Expain Qumana in brief.

Long Answer (LA)
Type Questions

16. How can you purchase goods on online websites?

17. Give any five best practices for Internet security.

18. Explain the following.
    (i) Gateway
    (ii) Web page
    (iii) Offline blog editor
    (iv) Online shopping
    (v) Online Transaction

Application Oriented
Type Questions

19. Shivani works in an MNC and needs to work online from home also. She requires fast Internet connection. Which type of Internet connection in your view would be best suited for her? Apart from browsing on the Internet she will require uploading/downloading of files to/from remote sites. Which protocol will help her to perform this activity?

20. Mr. Praveen has offices in three cities. He wants to connect his computers at various offices. He is unable to decide whether he should go for three LANs for different offices or should also create a WAN connecting these three LANs.

    Help him decided by suggesting what should he go for. Support your answer proper justification.

Abbreviation and Glossary

Abbreviation

ADSL	Asymmetric Digital Subscriber Line
AMV	Animated Music Video
ARPANET	Advanced Research Projects Agency NETwork
ASCII	American Standard Code for Information Interchange
ATM	Automated Teller Machine
B2B	Business to Business
B2C	Business to Consumer
Bcc	Blind carbon copy
B2G	Business to Government
BPL	Broadband over Power Lines
BWA	Broadband Wireless Access
C2B	Consumer to Business
CBI	Computer-Based Instruction
CBT	Computer-Based Training
C2C	Consumer to Consumer
Cc	Carbon copy
CGI	Common Gateway Interface
CPU	Central Processing Unit
CSS	Cascading Style Sheets
DNS	Domain Name System
DSL	Digital Subscriber Line
E-Banking	Electronic Banking
E-Commerce	Electronic Commerce
E-Governance	Electronic Governance
E-Groups	Electronic Groups
E-Learning	Electronic Learning
E-mail	Electronic Mail
E-Reservation	Electronic Reservation
E-Shopping	Electronic Shopping
EULA	End User License Agreement
FAQ	Frequently Asked Questions
FOI	Freedom of Information
FTP	File Transfer Protocol
GBPS	Gigabits Per Second
GPL	General Public License
GUI	Graphical User Interface
HDSL	High-bit-rate Digital Subscriber Line
HTML	HyperText Markup Language
HTTP	HyperText Transfer Protocol
IAB	Internet Architecture Board
IBT	Internet-Based Training

ICT	Information and Communication Technology
IE	Internet Explorer
IETF	Internet Engineering Task Force
IIS	Internet Information Server
IMAP	Internet Message Access Protocol
InterNIC	Internet Network Information Center
IP	Internet Protocol
IPR	Intellectual Property Rights
IPS	Internet Protocol Suite
IRTF	Internet Research Task Force
ISBN	International Standard Book Number
ISOC	Internet Society
ISDN	Integrated Services Digital Network
IT	Information Technology
ISP	Internet Service Provider
Kbps	Kilobits per second
Mbps	Megabits per second
NNTP	Network News Transfer Protocol
NSFnet	National Science Foundation Network
OOS	Open Source Software
PC	Personal Computer
PDA	Personal Digital Assistant
PHP	Personal Home Page/Hypertext Preprocessor
POP	Post Office Protocol
PSTN	Public Switched Telephone Network
RTI	Right to Information
SDSL	Symmetric Digital Subscriber Line
SET	Secure Electronic Transaction
SMTP	Simple Mail Transfer Protocol
SSL	Secure Sockets Layer
TCP	Transmission Control Protocol
URL	Uniform Resource Locator
VHDSL	Very High-bit-rate Digital Subscriber Line
VoIP	Voice over Internet Protocol
WBT	Web-Based Training
Wi-Fi	Wireless Fidelity
WiMAX	Worldwide Interoperability for Microwave Access
WWW	World Wide Web
W3C or WWWC	World Wide Web Consortium

Glossary

Anchor tag Mark the text as hyperlink.

Animation project It is a project that generally consists of a sequence of images of the motion of objects to create a video.

Application programmer An individual who writes application programs in a user organisation.

ARPANET First operational packet switching network.

Ask Block This block allows users to input any text they want it is widely used when a user must communicate with the project.

Asymmetric Digital Subscriber Line Technology that enables faster data transmission over copper telephone line.

Attributes Provide additional information about the tag in HTML.

Backup Copy of file or other item of data made in case the original is lost or damaged.

Blog Discussion or informational site consisting of discrete entities displayed in reverse chronological order.

Blogger A person who writes a blog.

Blogging Act of posting content on a blog.

Broadband connection It is a high speed Internet connection.

Broadband over Power Line It is a method of power line communication that allows relatively high speed digital data transmission over the public electric power distribution wiring.

Bulletin board system Computer or an application dedicated to the sharing of messages on a network.

Cascading Style Sheets It is a style sheet language used for describing the presentation of a document written in a markup language like HTML.

Chat Real time informal communication between two users *via* Internet.

Chat rooms Area on Internet that allows users to communicate with each other through instant messaging.

Client Application run on a personal computer.

Colspan This attribute defines the number of columns a table cell should span.

Combo Box It is used to display a drop-down list of some options from which one can be selected.

Communication Activity of exchanging information.

Computer program Sequence of instructions written to perform a specified task with a computer.

Container tag Tag that requires a starting as well as ending tag.

Copyright It is a legal right created by the law of a country that grants the creator of an original work exclusive rights to its use and distribution, usually for a limited time.

Cyber fraud Crime involving the use of Internet to obtain money.

Cyber ethics It refers to a code of safe and responsible behaviour for the Internet community.

Data sharing It is the ability to share the same data resource with multiple applications or users.

Definition list It is a list of terms and corresponding definitions. These are typically formatted with the term on the left with the definition following on the right or on the next line.

Dial-up connection Uses a standard phone line and modem to access the Internet at data transfer rates of upto 56 kbps.

Digital Subscriber Line It is a family of technologies that are used to provide Internet access by transmitting digital data over telephone lines.

Domain name Unique name that identifies an Internet resource.

Domain Name System Hierarchical distributed naming system for any resource connected to the Internet.

Download Copy from server computer to client computer over the Internet.

Draft folder Contains messages you started to write but not sent.

E-Banking Method of banking in which the customer conducts transactions electronically *via* Internet.

E-Commerce Buying and selling products and services over the Internet.

E-Governance Governing of a Country/State using Information and Communication Technology.

E-Group Group of persons who come together for a specific purpose over the Internet.

E-Learning Use of electronic educational technology in learning and teaching.

E-Mail Electronic method of sending and receiving messages.

E-Mail Address It identifies an E-mail box to which E-mail messages are delivered.

Emoticons Metacommunicative pictorial representation of a facial expression.

Empty tag Element that only has a starting tag but not ending tag.

End User It is the person that a software program or hardware device is designed for.

E-Reservation Reservation *via* Internet.

E-Shopping Form of electronic commerce which allows consumers to directly buy goods or services from a seller over the Internet.

F

File processing system Collection of files and programs that access/modify these files.

Freedom of Information It refers to a citizen's right to access information that is held by the state.

FTP Protocol used to transfer files between server and client.

H

Hacking It is the gaining of access to a computer and viewing, copying or creating data without the intention of destroying data or maliciously harming the computer.

Hardware Physical components that make up a computer system.

High-bit-rate Digital Subscriber Line One of the earliest form of DSL, it is used for wideband digital transmission within a corporate site and between the telephone company and a customer.

Home page First or main page of the Website.

HTML It is used for creating and visually representing a Web page.

HTTP It is the underlying protocol used by the WWW.

Hyperlink It is a word, phrase or image that you can click onto jump to a new document or a new section within the current document.

HyperText Text that links to other information.

I

Identifier It is a name used to identify a variable, function, class, module or other object.

IMAP It is a protocol for E-mail retrieval and storage.

Inbox folder Contains incoming E-mails.

Information Facts provided or learned about something or someone.

Information and Communication Technology It refers to technologies that provide access to information through telecommunications.

Intellectual Property Rights It refers to a general term for the assignment of property rights through patents, copyrights and trademarks.

Internet Global system of interconnected computer networks.

Internet backbone It refers to one of the principle data routes between large, strategically interconnected networks and care routers on the Internet.

Intranet Network that uses IP technology to share information or service within an organisation.

IP address Numerical address assigned to each device participating in a computer network.

ISP It is a company that provides Internet services.

Iteration It means repetition of a set of statements, depending upon a test condition.

K

Keywords These are reserved words that cannot be used as ordinary identifiers.

M

Markup language Way of writing layout information within documents.

Message It is a discrete unit of communication intended by the source for consumption by some recipient or group of recipients.

N

Nested list A list item that can contain another entire list.

Netiquettes It is a code of good behaviour on the Internet.

Net surfing Exploration of WWW.

Newsgroup Internet based discussion about a particular topic.

O

Operators These are special symbols in program that carry out arithmetic or logical computation.

Ordered list A number list of items.

Outbox folder Contains outgoing E-mails or text messages.

P

Packet It is the unit of data that is routed between an origin and destination on the Internet.

Packet Switched Telephone Network It is the aggregate of the world's circuit-switched telephone networks that are operated by national, regional or local telephony operators providing infrastructure and services for public telecommunication.

Plagiarism It is the act of copying or stealing someone else's ideas or information and presenting them as your own.

Piracy It refers to the unauthorised duplication of copyrighted content that is them sold at substantially lower prices in the market.

Pixel It is one of the small units that make up an image on a computer or television screen.

POP It is a protocol used by local E-mail clients to retrieve E-mail from a remote server.

Post Entries of blog.

Privacy It is the state of being free from public scrutiny or from having your secrets or personal information shared.

Programmer A person who writes computer programs.

Protocol Set of rules for data exchange within or between computers.

Python It is an interpreted high-level programming language for general purpose programming.

 Radio button A radio button or option button is a graphical control element that allows the user to choose only one of a predefined set of mutually exclusive options.

Repeat ( ) block It is a control block and a C block. Blocks held inside this block will loop a given amount of times, before allowing the script to continue.

Rowspan This attribute specifies the number of rows a cell should span.

 Satellite Artificial object which has been intentionally place into orbit.

Scratch It is a free programming environment that runs in your web browser.

Search engine Software system that is designed to search for information on the WWW.

Search engine algorithm Algorithm applied to Web pages in the search engine idea to determine what are the more relevant pages.

Sent mail folder Contains sent mails or messages.

Server Computer or computer program which manages access to a centralised resource or service in a network.

SMTP It is an Internet standard for E-mail transmission.

Social networking sites Online platform that allows users to create a public profile and interact with other users on the Website.

Software Set of instructions.

Software License It is a license agreement that gives an individual, company or organisation permission to use a software program.

Spam folder Contains junk E-mails or unsolicited E-mails.

Sprite In Scratch, it performs functions controlled by scripts.

Symmetric Digital Subscriber Line It is a type of DSL, which is used for transferring data over copper telephone lines.

 Table Set of data elements using a model of vertical columns and horizontal rows, the cell being the unit where a row and a column intersect.

Tag Refers to a string enclosed within angular brackets (<and>).

TCP/IP It is the suit of communications protocols that is used to connect hosts on the Internet.

Telnet It is a network protocol that is used on the Internet or LAN to provide a bi-directional interactive text-oriented communication facility using a virtual terminal connection.

Template Complete tracking application.

Token It is the smallest element in a Python program that is meaningful to the compiler. It represents a sequence of characters that can be treated as a single logical unit.

Tempo In a project, it controls how fast or slow the instrumental blocks in Scratch play notes and drum beats.

Trash folder Contains deleted E-mails.

 Unordered list A bulleted list of items.

Upload Copy from client computer to server over the Internet.

URL It is the global address of documents and other resources on the WWW.

User A person who uses a computer or network service.

User friendly Easy to use, operate and understand.

 Variable It is a reserved memory location to store values.

Very High-bit-rate Digital Subscriber Line It is a DSL technology that providing data transmission faster than ADSL over a single flat untwisted or twisted pair of copper wires and on co-axial cable.

VoIP It is a technology that allows you to make voice call using a broadband connection.

 Web address Internet address of a Website, file or document. It is also known as URL.

Web browser Software for retrieving, presenting and traversing information resources on the WWW.

Web crawler Program that visits Websites and reads their pages and other information in order to create entries for a search engine index.

Web Form A web form or HTML form on a Web page allows a user to enter data that is sent to a server for processing.

Web page Web document that is suitable for the WWW and Web browser.

Web portal Website that offers a broad array of resources and services, such as E-mail forums etc.

Web server Computer system that processes request *via* HTTP.

Website Set of related Web pages typically served from a single Web domain.

while loop This statement repeatedly executes a target statement as long as a given condition is true.

Wi-Fi It is a local area wireless technology that allows an electronic device to exchange data or connect to the Internet using radio waves.

WiMAX Technology supporting long distance wireless broadband.

Wired connection Connection establish using cables.

Wireless connection Connection establish using wireless technology.

WWW It is a system of interlinked hypertext document.

Full Form of HTML Tags/Attributes

A	Anchor		**I**	Italic
ALIGN	Alignment		**IMG**	Image
ALINK	Active Link		**LI**	List Item
B	Bold		**OL**	Ordered List
BGCOLOR	Background Color		**P**	Paragraph
BR	Line Break		**SRC**	Source
DD	Definition Description		**TT**	TeleType
DL	Definition List		**U**	Underline
DT	Definition Term		**UL**	Unordered List
HR	Horizontal Rule		**VLINK**	Visited Link

SAMPLE QUESTION PAPER 1

A Highly Simulated Sample Question Paper for CBSE Class 10

Information Technology

General Instructions

1. Please read the instructions carefully.
2. This Question Paper consists of 21 questions in two sections: Section A & Section B.
3. Section A has Objective Type Questions whereas Section B contains Subjective Type Questions.
4. Out of the given (5 + 16 =) 21 questions, a candidate has to answer (5 + 10 =) 15 questions in the allotted (maximum) time of 2 hours.
5. All questions of a particular section must be attempted in the correct order.
6. Section A : Objective Type Questions (24 Marks)
    (i) This section has 5 questions.
    (ii) Marks allotted are mentioned against each question/part.
    (iii) There is no negative marking.
    (iv) Do as per the instructions given.
7. Section B : Subjective Type Questions (26 Marks)
    (i) This section has 16 questions.
    (ii) A candidate has to do 10 questions.
    (iii) Do as per the instructions given.
    (iv) Marks allotted are mentioned against each question/part.

Time : 2 hours   **Max. Marks : 50**

Section A (Objective Type Questions)

1. *Answer any 4 out of the given 6 questions based on Employability Skills*   (1 × 4 = 4)

    (i) .... is the process in which the receiver interprets and understands the message.   (1)
        (a) Encoding   (b) Decoding   (c) Sender   (d) Receiver

    (ii) .... generates within the human regarding the unreasonable matters.   (1)
        (a) Internal stress   (b) Survival stress   (c) Environmental stress   (d) None of these

    (iii) There are commands that can be used to add more worksheets to the ....   (1)
        (a) document   (b) presentation   (c) workbook   (d) None of these

    (iv) An entrepreneur must establish good relations with .... and its functionaries.   (1)
        (a) customer   (b) government   (c) Both (a) and (b)   (d) None of these

    (v) The overall effects of economic activities on the environment are continuously ....   (1)
        (a) editing   (b) formatting   (c) changing   (d) All of these

    (vi) Energy demand is developing countries will increase to .... times the current levels by 2030.   (1)
        (a) four   (b) six   (c) seven   (d) one

2. *Answer any 5 out of the given 6 questions*   (1 × 5 = 5)

(i) Which allows you to reorder data?   (1)
    (a) Sorting   (b) Filtering   (c) Scenario   (d) Custom sorting

(ii) ...... is used to set tabs, indents and margins for a document.   (1)
    (a) Scroll bar   (b) Ruler   (c) Work bar   (d) None of these

(iii) TCL commands are used to manage ...... in database.   (1)
    (a) data   (b) values   (c) transactions   (d) None of these

(iv) ...... is a network architecture which separates the client from the server.   (1)
    (a) Client Server Network   (b) Peer - to - Peer Network
    (c) Both (a) and (b)   (d) None of these

(v) ...... is a free personal publishing platform.   (1)
    (a) Zoomla   (b) WordPress   (c) Blogger   (d) None of these

(vi) Which of the following component provides additional information in the chart?   (1)
    (a) Legend   (b) Gridlines   (c) Data label   (d) Plot area

3. *Answer any 5 out of the given 6 questions*   (1 × 5 = 5)

(i) Which of the following is not an AutoShape?   (1)
    (a) Line   (b) Circle   (c) Curve   (d) ClipArt

(ii) Which of the following network devices is used to connect dissimilar networks?   (1)
    (a) Gateway   (b) Switch   (c) Bridge   (d) Router

(iii) ...... option changes first letter of every word in capital case.   (1)
    (a) Capitalize   (b) Capitalize Each Word
    (c) Upper Each Word   (d) None of these

(iv) Which of the following charts selects only one range of data series?   (1)
    (a) Line chart   (b) Pie chart   (c) Scatter chart   (d) Bar chart

(v) .... command is used to retrieve data from a database.   (1)
    (a) SELECT   (b) INSERT   (c) UPDATE   (d) None of these

(vi) Web based type of software is accessed using ....   (1)
    (a) web page   (b) website   (c) browsers   (d) None of these

4. *Answer any 5 out of the given 6 questions*   (1 × 5 = 5)

(i) Editing Custom Shapes feature allows ...... of small segments of a drawing.   (1)
    (a) shaping   (b) reshaping   (c) rehearse   (d) None of these

(ii) ...... is found at the top left corner of the window.   (1)
    (a) Micro button   (b) Maximize button   (c) Office button   (d) None of these

(iii) ...... is a collection of related iformation ....   (1)
    (a) Base   (b) Database   (c) Web-base   (d) None of these

(iv) The address of location of the document on www is called ....   (1)
    (a) URL   (b) URI   (c) Both (a) and (b)   (d) None of these

(v) Computer based record keeping system is known as ....   (1)
    (a) Data Manipulation System   (b) Computer Data System
    (c) Computerised Record Keeping System   (d) DBMS

(vi) You should uninstall any .... and services which you are not using from long time.   (1)
    (a) hardware   (b) software   (c) system   (d) None of these

5. *Answer any 5 out of the given 6 questions*   (1 × 5 = 5)

(i) ...... are dividers that break a worksheet into separate pages for printing.   (1)
    (a) Page   (b) Document   (c) Both (a) and (b)   (d) Page breaks

(ii) Line or paragraph spacing is measured in terms of lines or points, which is referred as ....   (1)
    (a) text wrapping   (b) PDF   (c) XPS   (d) leading

    (iii) Which of the following fields will not make a suitable primary key?   (1)
        (a) A customer's account number   (b) A date-field
        (c) An auto number field   (d) A student's admission number

    (iv) ...... is used to text-to-speech utility that reads what is displayed on the screen.   (1)
        (a) Start Narrator   (b) Web page   (c) Website   (d) None of these

    (v) X - axis is a horizontal axis which is also known as ....   (1)
        (a) value axis   (b) category axis   (c) title axis   (d) None of these

    (vi) Instant messaging service accepts instant messages from ....   (1)
        (a) external sites   (b) internal sites   (c) Both (a) and (b)   (d) None of these

Section B (Subjective Type Questions)

Answer any 3 out of the given 5 questions based on Employability Skills. Answer each question in 20-30 words
$(2 \times 3 = 6)$

6. What are the disadvantages of verbal communication?   (2)

7. What do you mean by environment stress?   (2)

8. Write the steps to insert a picture from computer into a slide.   (2)

9. Describe the following functions of an entrepreneur: (2)
    (i) Innovation   (ii) Risk-Taking

10. Explain long lasting development as an importance of sustainable development.   (2)

Answer any 4 out of the given 6 questions in 20-30 words each $(2 \times 4 = 8)$

11. What is hanging indent? Also, give the steps for hanging indent of a paragraph.   (2)

12. How to choose a style set for Word document?   (2)

13. What do you mean by pie chart?   (2)

14. Explain the term relational database management system.   (2)

15. Define router as network device.   (2)

16. Define the following terms: (2)
    (i) Active Cell   (ii) Sheet Tab

Answer any 3 out of the given 5 questions in 50-80 words each $(4 \times 3 = 12)$

17. What do you mean by data control language? Also, give its types.   (4)

18. Define the following: (4)
    (i) Column Chart   (ii) Quick Access Toolbar

19. How to clear web history on the Mozilla firefox browser?   (4)

20. Write the steps for text fitting in Word document. Also, describe its options.   (4)

21. (i) Create a table Student with the following fields: (4)

Column Name	Data Type
Reg _ No	Char(15)
Reg _ Date	Date
Owner _ Name	Varchar(20)
Address	Varchar(40)

(ii) Consider the following table MASTER and write the queries (a) and (b).

Table : MASTER

SNo	Name	Age	Department	Salary
1	Shyam	21	Computer	12000
2	Shiv	25	Maths	15000
3	Rakesh	31	Hindi	14000
4	Sharmila	32	History	20000
5	Dushyant	25	Software	30000

(a) Write a command to update the Salary of the employee to 40000, whose SNo is 3.

(b) Write a query to add a column Date_of_Joining to the table MASTER.

Answers

1. (i) (b) Decoding　　(ii) (a) Internal stress　　(iii) (c) workbook
   (iv) (b) government　　(v) (c) changing　　(vi) (b) six
2. (i) (a) Sorting　　(ii) (b) Ruler　　(iii) (c) transactions
   (iv) (a) Client Server Network　　(v) (b) WordPress　　(vi) (c) Data label
3. (i) (d) ClipArt　　(ii) (a) Gateway　　(iii) (b) Capitalize Each Word
   (iv) (b) Pie chart　　(v) (a) SELECT　　(vi) (c) browsers
4. (i) (b) reshaping　　(ii) (c) Office button　　(iii) (b) Database
   (iv) (a) URL　　(v) (d) DBMS　　(vi) (b) software
5. (i) (d) page breaks　　(ii) (d) leading　　(iii) (b) A date-field
   (iv) (a) Start Narrator　　(v) (b) category axis　　(vi) (a) external sites

6. Following are the disadvantages of verbal communication are:
   - It has no legal validity and hence will lead to problems in certain situations. Emotions are visible and hence leads to trouble in certain cases.
   - It has issues when communicating with distant people.
   - It does not provide permanent record unless it is recorded with modern means of storage.
   - This form of communication is not suitable for lengthy message.

7. Environment stress is a response to happenings around us that cause stress, such as noise, pollution, crowding, pressure of work, family tensions etc. Some of these may be under our control if we try to control them, whereas some may not be controllable by us. Identifying these environmental stresses and learning to avoid them or deal with them will help lower our stress level.

8. The steps to insert a picture from computer into a slide are:
   - Click on Insert tab → Illustrations group → Picture command.
   - A dialog box will open. Navigate to the folder where the picture to be inserted resides.
   - Select the picture and click on Insert command.

9. (i) **Innovation** It includes introducing new products, opening new markets, new sources of raw material and new organisation structure.
   (ii) **Risk-Taking** An entrepreneur has to take risk by choosing one among various alternatives.

10. Sustainable development aims at achieving the goal of economic and social development without destroying the Earth's means and resources. It attempts to create the concept of maintaining the present work for the future and conserving the natural resources for future generation.

11. Hanging indent is the indent, the paragraph except first line. To hanging indent, follow the given points:
   - Open the Paragraph dialog box by dialog box launcher button.
   - In Indentation area, select the Hanging option from the Special drop-down list.
   - Click OK button.

FULLY SOLVED

12. Word supplies you with predesigned style sets that contain styles for titles, subtitles, quotes, headings, lists and more.

    To choose a style set, follow the given steps:
    - Click on Home tab.
    - Click Change Styles in the Styles group. A menu will appear.
    - Select Style Set and a sub menu will appear.
    - You can choose from any of the styles listed on the menu.

13. These types of charts can be 2 or 3-dimensional. They are used to compare the size of the parts with the whole. Only one data series can be plotted, making up 100%. Pie charts within their own window can be made to 'explode' by dragging more pieces of pie away from the centre.

14. RDBMS (Relational Database Management System) is a type of DBMS that stores data in the form of relations (tables). Relational databases are powerful, so they require few assumptions about how data is related or how it will be extracted from the databases.

    An important feature of relational database system is that a single database can be spread across several tables. Base, Oracle, DB2, SAP, Sybase, ASE, Informix, Access etc. are the examples of RDBMS.

15. A hardware device designed to take incoming packets, analyse the packets, move the packets to another network, convert the packets to another network interface, drop the packets, direct packets to the appropriate locations, etc. A router functions similar to a bridge. However, unlike a bridge, a router passes data packets from one network to another network based on their IP addresses not MAC addresses.

16. (i) **Active Cell** The cell with the black outline. Data is always entered into the active cell.

    (ii) **Sheet Tab** The tab at the bottom of a worksheet tells you the name of the worksheet such as Sheet 1, Sheet 2 etc. Switching between worksheets can be done by clicking on the tab of the Sheet which you want to access.

17. DCL (Data Control Language) commands are used to assign security levels in database which involves multiple user setups. They are used to grant defined role and access privileges to the users.

    There are two kinds of user in the schema
    - **Users** They work with the data, but cannot change the structure of the schema. They write data manipulation language.
    - **Admin** They can change the structure of the schema and control access to the schema objects. They write data definition language.

    Basically, the DCL component of the SQL language is used to create privileges that allow to users access and manipulation of the database.

    Two types of DCL commands are :
    (i) **GRANT** Used to give user's access privileges to database.
    (ii) **REVOKE** Used to withdraw access privileges given with the GRANT command.

18. (i) **Column Chart** Values are display in the form of vertical columns in this chart. Many different data series and their values are displaying on X-axis and Y-axis, respectively.

    (ii) **Quick Access Toolbar** It is a customizable toolbar situated at the top-left corner of the window that contains a set of commands that are independent of the tab. These commands are those commands which are mostly used by the user.

19. Follow the steps below for how to clear web history on the Mozilla Firefox browser:
    - Click on the upper right of the browser toolbar.
    - Click History.
    - Click Clear Recent History.
    - Click the drop–down menu next to Time range to clear and select Everything.
    - Place a checkmark next to the following options under Details:
      - Browsing and Download History
      - Form & Search History
      - Cookies
      - Cache
      - Active Logins
      - Offline Website Data
      - Site Preferences
    - Click on Clear Now button.

    The window will close and the items you have selected will be cleared.

20. Several options are available to customise the text-fitting within the shape.
    For text-fitting in the document, follow the steps:
    • Right click on the shape → select Format AutoShape... option from the drop-down menu.
    • The Format AutoShape dialog box will appear.
    • Select the Text Box tab.
    • Select the desired option given below:

Options	Description
Internal margin	Specifies the distance between each edge of your shape and the text contained within it.
Vertical alignment	Changes the vertical placement of your text within the shape.
Word wrap text in AutoShape	Text appears on multiple lines to fit within your AutoShape optimally.
Resize AutoShape to fit text	Resizes the AutoShape to optimally fit your text.
Format Callout...	When working with callouts (e.g. word bubbles), provides options for changing formatting.
Convert to Frame...	Changes your shape to a plain text box.

21. (i) CREATE TABLE Student(Reg_No Char(15), Reg_Date Date, Owner_Name Varchar(20), Address Varchar(40));
    (ii) (a) UPDATE MASTER SET Salary = 40000 WHERE SNo = 3;
         (b) ALTER TABLE MASTER ADD Date_of_Joining Date;

SAMPLE QUESTION PAPER 2

A Highly Simulated Sample Question Paper for CBSE Class 10

Information Technology

> **General Instructions**
>
> See Sample Question Paper 1.

Time : 2 hours   *Max. Marks : 50*

Section A (Objective Type Questions)

1. *Answer any 4 out of the given 6 questions based on Employability Skills*   (1 × 4 = 4)

   (i) .... is essential to complete the cycle of communication.   (1)
     (a) Encoding   (b) Decoding   (c) Feedback   (d) Sender

   (ii) The good stress is called ....   (1)
     (a) eustress   (b) emstress   (c) Both (a) and (b)   (d) None of these

  (iii) .... means to make a duplicate of a file.   (1)
     (a) Deleting   (b) Editing   (c) Pasting   (d) Copying

   (iv) .... describes entrepreneurs as innovators.   (1)
     (a) Howard W. Johnson   (b) Joseph Schumpter   (c) Both (a) and (b)   (d) None of these

   (v) Sustainable development requires the judicious use of ....   (1)
     (a) resources   (b) natural resources   (c) verbal resources   (d) None of these

   (vi) ...... conveys a statement, question, exclamation or command.   (1)
     (a) Sentence   (b) Equation   (c) Formula   (d) None of these

2. *Answer any 5 out of the given 6 questions*   (1 × 5 = 5)

   (i) If you want to locate a range of cells by its name, then you will enter its name in ....   (1)
     (a) formula bar   (b) name box   (c) cell   (d) None of these

   (ii) We can italic the text by ....   (1)
     (a) Ctrl + IT   (b) Shift + I   (c) Ctrl + I   (d) Alt + I

  (iii) ...... command is used to restore database to original since the last COMMIT.   (1)
     (a) REVIEW   (b) SELECT   (c) ROLLBACK   (d) None of these

   (iv) ...... provides the physical connection between the network and computer workstation.   (1)
     (a) LIC   (b) NIC   (c) NC   (d) None of these

   (v) URL is the ...... for a website or a web page.   (1)
     (a) web address   (b) website   (c) web page   (d) Both (a) and (c)

   (vi) How many types of views are available in the spreadsheet?   (1)
     (a) 3   (b) 4   (c) 5   (d) 2

3. *Answer any 5 out of the given 6 questions*   (1 × 5 = 5)

   (i) Which tab of MS-Word contains the Shapes option?   (1)
     (a) Home   (b) Review   (c) Insert   (d) Mailings

(ii) Digital information is converted into analog information by the modem at (1)
  (a) destination computer   (b) source computer   (c) Both (a) and (b)   (d) None of these

(iii) ...... is the indent, the paragraph except first line. (1)
  (a) Left indent   (b) Hanging indent   (c) Right indent   (d) None of these

(iv) The default page orientation in spreadsheet is .... (1)
  (a) landscape   (b) horizontal   (c) portrait   (d) None of these

(v) The key field is a unique identifier for .... (1)
  (a) each column   (b) each record   (c) Both (a) and (b)   (d) None of these

(vi) Every computer is protected by a .... (1)
  (a) firewall   (b) software   (c) server   (d) network

4. *Answer any 5 out of the given 6 questions* $(1 \times 5 = 5)$

(i) ...... is a GUI based software used in the windows environment. (1)
  (a) Word processor   (b) DOS   (c) Both (a) and (b)   (d) None of these

(ii) ...... is referenced by a combination of row number and column letter. (1)
  (a) Data   (b) Work cell   (c) Cell   (d) Document

(iii) ...... leads to data inconsistency. (1)
  (a) Data integrity   (b) Data redundancy   (c) Data sharing   (d) Data recovery

(iv) ...... is a computer program that provides services to other computer programs. (1)
  (a) Server   (b) Client   (c) Network   (d) None of these

(v) Which of the following is not the main building block of a database? (1)
  (a) Lists   (b) Queries   (c) Reports   (d) Forms

(vi) Blog Desk is an offline blog editor which is used for ...... operating system. (1)
  (a) Linux   (b) Unix   (c) Windows   (d) None of these

5. *Answer any 5 out of the given 6 questions* $(1 \times 5 = 5)$

(i) ...... preview displays the page breaks as blue line. (1)
  (a) Break   (b) Page break   (c) Page   (d) None of these

(ii) The .... alignment makes sure that none of the edges of text appear ragged. (1)
  (a) left   (b) right   (c) center   (d) justify

(iii) Key field is a unique identifier for each record. It is defined in the form of (1)
  (a) rows   (b) columns   (c) tree   (d) query

(iv) abc@mnc.co.in represents an .... (1)
  (a) MAC address   (b) URL   (c) E-mail address   (d) None of these

(v) The bar located at the top of the application window is called .... (1)
  (a) title bar   (b) status bar   (c) menu bar   (d) None of these

(vi) A web page is located using a (1)
  (a) Universal Record Linking   (b) Uniform Resource Locator
  (c) Universal Record Locator   (d) Uniformly Reachable Links

Section B (Subjective Type Questions)

Answer any 3 out of the given 5 questions based on Employability Skills. Answer each question in 20-30 words
  $(2 \times 3 = 6)$

6. What are the basic principles of an effective communication? (2)

7. How nature walk does help to manage stress? (2)

8. Write the steps to insert header and footer. (2)

9. Define the following functions of an entrepreneur: (2)
   (i) Establishing relations with Government
   (ii) Establishing contacts with Competitors

10. What are the long term solutions for sustainable development? (2)

Answer any 4 out of the given 6 questions in 20-30 words each $(2 \times 4 = 8)$

11. How to change the prefilled information? (2)

12. What do you mean by chart? (2)

13. Write the steps to format the font size. (2)

14. How to change the type of chart? (2)

15. Explain the term modulator/demodulator. (2)

16. Define the following: (2)
    (i) Text data type   (ii) Memo data type

Answer any 3 out of the given 5 questions in 50-80 words each $(4 \times 3 = 12)$

17. How to apply a picture style in a document? (4)

18. Define the following: (4)
    (i) Star topology   (ii) Web browser

19. Write the steps to sort more than one columns. (4)

20. What are the disadvantages of DBMS? (4)

21. (i) Create a table CUSTOMER with following details: (4)

Column Name	Data Type
CustNo	Varchar(5)
Name	Char(20)
Address	Char(50)

(ii) Consider the following table SummerCamp and write the queries (a) and (b).

Table : SummerCamp

Child ID	First Name	Last Name	DOB	Gender	Group
109	Vedansh	Gupta	30/06/10	M	2A
214	Mack	Tyagi	09/12/08	M	1B
115	Aditi	Thakur	13/04/09	F	1A
108	Vikrant	Chauhan	02/02/09	M	2A
141	Swati	Saini	06/05/10	F	2B
233	Vishakha	Tyagi	01/08/10	F	3A
274	Madhur	Gupta	06/03/10	M	3B

(a) Write a command to insert a new record with the following values:
    (105, 'Shyam', 'Sharma', 07/09/10, 'M', '1A')

(b) Write a query to display all the record of table SummerCamp whose DOB between 02/02/09 and 06/03/10.

Answers

1. (i) (c) Feedback (ii) (a) eustress (iii) (d) copying
   (iv) (b) Joseph Schumpter (v) (b) natural resources (vi) (a) Sentence
2. (i) (b) name box (ii) (c) Ctrl + I (iii) (c) ROLLBACK
   (iv) (b) NIC (v) (a) web address (vi) (c) 5
3. (i) (c) Insert (ii) (b) source computer (iii) (b) Hanging indent
   (iv) (c) portrait (v) (b) each record (vi) (a) firewall
4. (i) (a) Word processor (ii) (c) Cell (iii) (b) Data redundancy
   (iv) (a) Server (v) (a) Lists (vi) (c) Windows
5. (i) (b) Page break (ii) (d) justify (iii) (b) columns
   (iv) (c) E-mail address (v) (a) title bar
   (vi) (b) Uniform Resource Locator

6. The most basic principle for a communication to be effective is that the intended message of the sender and the interpreted message of the receiver are one and the same. Although this should be the goal in any communication, it is not always achieved. Thus, a set of principles needs to be followed to ensure it. The most popular name of these basic principles is known as 7C's of Effective Communication.

7. Nature Walks means walking in the local park or similar such activity. These walks may be done more than once a day for short periods of time during which we indulge in 'thought-stopping', i.e. not to think about our day-to-day activities. Such an activity will help us to avoid 'burn out', promote adequate sleep, ease muscle tension and decrease mental worries.

8. To insert a header or footer, follow these steps :
   • Select the Insert button.
   • Click either Header & Footer command. A drop-down menu will appear.
   • From the drop-down menu, select Blank to insert a blank header & footer, or choose one of the built-in options.
   • The Design tab will appear on the ribbon and the Header & Footer will appear in the document.

9. (i) **Establishing Relations with Government** An entrepreneur must establish good relations with government and its functionaries. His functions are to obtain licences, payment of taxes, selling the product to government, provision for export-import etc.

   (ii) **Establishing Contacts with Competitors** An entrepreneur must form contacts with the competitors to analyse the market. He must be in a position to make opportunities out of the given situation.

10. Following are the long term solutions for sustainable development:
    • Government should make policies against illegal activities.
    • Awareness campaigns should be launched for farmers and industrialists.
    • Ecology must be protected through imposition of taxes and fines.
    • Practice of sustainable agriculture must be promoted such as permaculture, agroforestry, mixed farming, multiple cropping and crop rotation.

11. To change the prefilled information, follow the given steps:
    • Select the Microsoft Office button.
    • Click the Word Options button. The Word Options dialog box will appear.
    • Enter the User name and/or Initials in the Personalise your copy of Microsoft Office section from Popular.
    • Click OK button.

12. A chart is a tool that is used in Excel for representing data graphically. Charts allow anyone to more easily see the meaning behind the numbers in the spreadsheet and to make showing comparisons and trends much easier. It is one of the most impressive features of MS-Excel.
    Endless variations are available, allowing you to produce a chart, edit and format it, include titles and many more.

13. Steps to format the font size of text are as follows:
    • Select the text that you want to modify.

- Click the drop-down arrow next to the Font Size box in the Font group on the Home tab. The Font Size drop-down menu will appear.
- Move your cursor over the various font sizes. A live preview of the font size will appear in the document.
- Choose the Font Size that you want to use.

14. To change the chart type, follow the given steps:
   - Select the chart and click on the Design tab.
   - In the Type group, click on the Change Chart Type command.
   - Change Chart Type dialog box will appear. Select the type of chart, you want to use.
   - Click on the OK button.

15. Modem is a device that converts digital signal to analog signal (modulator) at the sender's site and converts back analog signal to digital signal (demodulator) at the receiver's end, in order to make communication possible *via* telephone lines.

16. (i) **Text data type** It allows to store text or combination of text and numbers as well as numbers that don't require calculations such as phone number. This data type allows maximum 255 characters to store.

   e.g. If Employee is a table and Emp_No, Name and Description are fields, then name will be a Text field. Because, Name is a character entry field.

   (ii) **Memo data type** It allows long blocks of text that uses text formatting. e.g. In the Employee table, the field Description will be of Memo data type, because the length of description of employee may be large.

17. Steps to apply a picture style in a document are as follows:
   - Select the picture.
   - Click the Picture Tools Format tab.
   - Click More drop-down arrow in Picture Styles group to display all the Picture Styles.
   - However, when a cursor moves over different picture styles, the live preview of the style will be displayed on the picture in a document.
   - Choose any style as per the requirement.

18. (i) In star topology, there persists a central node called server or hub, which is connected to the nodes directly. If a node has to take information from other node, then the data is taken from that node through the central node or server.

   (ii) Web browser is a software application that is used to locate, retrieve and display some content on the World Wide Web, including web pages. These are programs used to explore the Internet. It is an interface that helps a computer user to gain access over all the content on the Internet. We can install more than one web browsers on a single computer. The user can navigate files, folders and websites with the help of a browser.

19. To sorting more than one columns, follow the given steps:
   - Select those cells, which you want to sort.
   - Click on Sort & Filter option from Editing group in Home tab. By this, you will get a drop–down menu.
   - From this menu, select Custom Sort option and then Sort dialog box will appear.
   - Click on Add Level button and then select next column (which you want to sort).
   - Click on OK button.

20. There are many advantages of database, but database also have some minor disadvantages. These disadvantages are as follows:
   (i) **Cost of Hardware and Software** Through the use of a database system, new costs are generated due to additional hardware and software requirements.

   (ii) **Complexity** A database system creates additional complexity and requirements.

   (iii) **Database Failures** If database is corrupted due to power failure or it is corrupted on the storage media, then our valuable data may be lost or the system will stop working.

   (iv) **Lower Efficiency** A database system is a multi-user software, which is less efficient.

21. (i) CREATE TABLE CUSTOMER (CustNo Varchar(5), Name Char(20), Address Char(50));
   (ii) (a) INSERT INTO SummerCamp VALUES (105, 'Shyam', 'Sharma', 07/09/10, 'M', '1A');
      (b) SELECT * FROM SummerCamp WHERE DOB BETWEEN 02/02/09 AND 06/03/10;

SAMPLE QUESTION PAPER 3
A Highly Simulated Sample Question Paper for CBSE Class 10

Information Technology

General Instructions

See Sample Question Paper 1.

Time : 2 hours   **Max. Marks : 50**

Section A (Objective Type Questions)

1. *Answer any 4 out of the given 6 questions based on Employability Skills* $(1 \times 4 = 4)$

(i) .... is the actual information that the sender wishes to convey to the receiver.   (1)
  (a) Message   (b) Information   (c) Data   (d) None of these

(ii) .... is identified as a condition in which a person is tensed and worried.   (1)
  (a) Mediation   (b) Stress   (c) Walk   (d) Ceisure

(iii) A header is the .... margin of each document page.   (1)
  (a) left   (b) right   (c) top   (d) None of these

(iv) .... is a software application capable of organising, storing and analysing data in tabular form.   (1)
  (a) Word processor   (b) Spreadsheet   (c) Presentation   (d) Document

(v) A/An .... is the organiser of society's productive resources.   (1)
  (a) entrepreneur   (b) leadership   (c) motivator   (d) None of these

(vi) United Nations Sustainable Development Summit goals are termed as ....   (1)
  (a) Agenda 2030   (b) Agenda 2020   (c) Agenda 2010   (d) None of these

2. *Answer any 5 out of the given 6 questions* $(1 \times 5 = 5)$

(i) Ctrl + N shortcut key is used to create a new blank ....   (1)
  (a) worksheet   (b) workbook   (c) Both (a) and (b)   (d) None of these

(ii) A right aligned paragraph has its .... margin even.   (1)
  (a) left   (b) center   (c) right   (d) up

(iii) The .... command is used to modify the existing rows in a table.   (1)
  (a) UPDATE   (b) SELECT   (c) INSERT   (d) REVIEW

(iv) A person who writes a blog or a weblog is known as ....   (1)
  (a) program   (b) user   (c) blogger   (d) None of these

(v) .... service can integrate both video calling and instant messaging abilities.   (1)
  (a) Web conferencing   (b) Web browser   (c) Web page   (d) None of these

(vi) Two types of page orientation are ....   (1)
  (a) portrait   (b) landscape   (c) Both (a) and (b)   (d) None of these

3. *Answer any 5 out of the given 6 questions* $(1 \times 5 = 5)$

(i) Which of the following is a powerful tool that you can use to create effective documents?   (1)
  (a) Multiplan   (b) MS-Word 2007   (c) Spreadsheet   (d) Presentation

(ii) A collection of web pages linked together in a random order is ....   (1)
  (a) a website   (b) a web server   (c) a search engine   (d) a web browser

(iii) A/An .... is a software package that processes textual matter and creates organised documents. (1)
    (a) processor   (b) Word processor   (c) worksheet   (d) None of these

(iv) Which of the following allows you to change the appearance of a cell? (1)
    (a) Conditional formatting   (b) Formatting   (c) Conditional   (d) None of these

(v) .... acts as an interface between the application program and the data stored in the database. (1)
    (a) Field   (b) Record   (c) DBMS   (d) Column

(vi) .... are used for transmitting data across networks. (1)
    (a) Circuit switching   (b) Switching techniques   (c) Channel   (d) None of these

4. *Answer any 5 out of the given 6 questions* $(1 \times 5 = 5)$

(i) .... break partitions only the body text of the document. (1)
    (a) Page   (b) Section   (c) Both (a) and (b)   (d) None of these

(ii) A/An .... is an equation that calculates the value to be displayed. (1)
    (a) spreadsheet   (b) formula   (c) cell   (d) worksheet

(iii) The candidate key, which is not used as primary key is called .... key. (1)
    (a) primary   (b) foreign   (c) alternate   (d) super

(iv) Wireless broadband can be .... (1)
    (a) mobile   (b) fixed   (c) Both (a) and (b)   (d) None of these

(v) What data type should be chosen for a zipcode field in a table? (1)
    (a) Text   (b) Number   (c) Memo   (d) All of these

(vi) .... is the formation of networks. (1)
    (a) Server   (b) Networking   (c) Client   (d) None of these

5. *Answer any 5 out of the given 6 questions* $(1 \times 5 = 5)$

(i) .... shortcut key is used to hide the selected rows. (1)
    (a) Alt + 8   (b) Alt + 9   (c) Ctrl + 9   (d) Ctrl + 8

(ii) ...... can be used for inserting information at the top of each page automatically. (1)
    (a) Header   (b) Footer   (c) Both (a) and (b)   (d) None of these

(iii) RDBMS provides relational operators to manipulate the data. Here RDBMS refers to .... (1)
    (a) Record Database Management System   (b) Relational Database Management System
    (c) Reference Database Management System   (d) None of theae

(iv) In .... topology, the node is interlinked in the form of tree. (1)
    (a) tree   (b) mesh   (c) star   (d) bus

(v) .... automatically enters the appropriate formula or function into your spreadsheet. (1)
    (a) Sum   (b) AutoSum   (c) Auto   (d) Total

(vi) The speed of a network is measured in .... (1)
    (a) mbps   (b) bytes   (c) kHz   (d) None of these

Section B (Subjective Type Questions)

Answer any 3 out of the given 5 questions based on Employability Skills. Answer each question in 20-30 words
                                                     $(2 \times 3 = 6)$

6. Explain the part of speech. (2)

7. What do you mean by survival stress? (2)

8. Explain the following features of Word processor: (2)
    (i) Text editing   (ii) Word wrap

9. Describe the role of entrepreneurs. (2)

10. What are the uses of sustainable development? (2)

Answer any 4 out of the given 6 questions in 20-30 words each (2 × 4 = 8)

11. How to choose a style for a Word document? (2)

12. Write the steps to freeze the columns. (2)

13. What do you mean by relative cell referencing? (2)

14. Describe various transaction control commands of SQL. (2)

15. Explain the working of message switching technique. (2)

16. Define the following :
(i) Header (ii) Footer

Answer any 3 out of the given 5 questions in 50-80 words each (4 × 3 = 12)

17. How to create a Custom View in spreadsheet? (4)

18. Define the following: (4)
(i) Web based instant messaging software
(ii) Cable modem

19. What are differences between fields and tuples? (4)

20. Explain the different paragraph alignments. (4)

21. (i) Create a table DOCTORS with the following fields: (4)

Column Name	Data Type
DocID	Varchar(5)
DocName	Char(30)
Department	Char(20)
OPD_Days	Date

(ii) Consider the following table ITEMS and write the queries (a) and (b).

TABLE: ITEMS

Code	IName	Qty	Price	Company	TCode
1001	DIGITAL PAD 121	120	11000	XENITA	T01
1006	LED SCREEN 40	70	38000	SANTORA	T02
1004	CAR GPS SYSTEM	50	2150	GEOKNOW	T01
1003	DIGITAL CAMERA 12X	160	8000	DIGICLICK	T02
1005	PEN DRIVE 32 GB	600	1200	STOREHOME	T03

(a) To display the details of all the items in ascending order of item names (i.e., IName)

(b) To display IName and Price of all those items, whose price is in the range of 10000 and 22000.

Answer Key

1. (i) (a),	(ii) (b),	(iii) (c),	(iv) (b),	(v) (a),	(vi) (a)
2. (i) (b),	(ii) (c),	(iii) (a),	(iv) (c),	(v) (a),	(vi) (c)
3. (i) (b),	(ii) (a),	(iii) (b),	(iv) (a),	(v) (c),	(vi) (b)
4. (i) (a),	(ii) (b),	(iii) (c),	(iv) (c),	(v) (b),	(vi) (b)
5. (i) (c),	(ii) (a),	(iii) (b),	(iv) (a),	(v) (b),	(vi) (a)

UNSOLVED

SAMPLE QUESTION PAPER 4

A Highly Simulated Sample Question Paper for CBSE Class 10

Information Technology

General Instructions

See Sample Question Paper 1.

Time : 2 hours   **Max. Marks : 50**

Section A (Objective Type Questions)

1. *Answer any 4 out of the given 6 questions based on Employability Skills*   (1 × 4 = 4)

    (i) .... skills are essential for working in an organisation.   (1)
        (a) Stress   (b) Communication
        (c) Good communication   (d) None of these

    (ii) Awareness about our ...... is not a kind of self-awareness.   (1)
        (a) Biases   (b) Yoga   (c) Mediation   (d) None of these

    (iii) The shortcut key for printing the presentation is ....   (1)
        (a) Alt + P   (b) Ctrl + P   (c) Shift + P   (d) Ctrl + A

    (iv) A/An ...... has a good vision towards the achievement of his goals.   (1)
        (a) entrepreneur   (b) self-confident   (c) goal-oriented   (d) None of these

    (v) ...... is a word for a person, place, thing or idea.   (1)
        (a) Pronoun   (b) Noun   (c) Article   (d) Paragraph

    (vi) Sustainable Forest Management which were developed in Europe during the ...... centuries.   (1)
        (a) 18th and 16th   (b) 20th and 21st   (c) 17th and 18th   (d) None of these

2. *Answer any 5 out of the given 6 questions*   (1 × 5 = 5)

    (i) Which is the descriptive text aimed at helping user to identify the chart?   (1)
        (a) Chart title   (b) Plot area   (c) Chart area   (d) Gridlines

    (ii) A document is a paper with written contents and the process of preparing a document is called ....   (1)
        (a) Page break   (b) Work area   (c) Documentation   (d) None of these

    (iii) The processed form of data is known as ....   (1)
        (a) value   (b) information   (c) knowledge   (d) None of these

    (iv) Quemana works with a variety of .... platforms.   (1)
        (a) Blog   (b) WordPress   (c) Hub   (d) None of these

    (v) The backbone of the www is made up of files called ....   (1)
        (a) web browser   (b) web pages   (c) server   (d) client

    (vi) To insert a .... page break, select the row below where you want to insert the page break.   (1)
        (a) vertical   (b) ruler   (c) horizontal   (d) None of these

3. *Answer any 5 out of the given 6 questions*   (1 × 5 = 5)

    (i) Full form of OLE is   (1)
        (a) Object Link and Embed   (b) Object Linking and Embedding
        (c) Object Linker and Embedding   (d) Objective Linking and Embedding

(ii) HTML is used to create (1)
    (a) browser   (b) server   (c) web pages   (d) None of these

(iii) .... option allows a user to edit picture. (1)
    (a) Edit   (b) Crop   (c) Paste   (d) Format

(iv) Each worksheet contains (1)
    (a) 1048576 rows   (b) 16384 columns   (c) Both (a) and (b)   (d) None of these

(v) Multiple mismatching copies of the same data is known as .... (1)
    (a) data inconsistency   (b) data redundancy   (c) data integrity   (d) None of these

(vi) With most LAN's cables, ... is used for their connectivity. (1)
    (a) PIC   (b) NIC   (c) NIP   (d) None of these

4. *Answer any 5 out of the given 6 questions* $(1 \times 5 = 5)$

(i) .... is a section of the document that appears at the bottom margin of the page. (1)
    (a) Footer   (b) Header   (c) Top   (d) Center

(ii) .... is located on left of the formula bar. (1)
    (a) Formula bar   (b) Name box   (c) Active cell   (d) Ruler

(iii) A/An .... language is a portion of a DML involving information retrieval only. (1)
    (a) DCL   (b) TCL   (c) Query   (d) None of these

(iv) Internet security prevents attacks targeted at .... (1)
    (a) browsers   (b) operating system   (c) network   (d) All of these

(v) A field or a set of fields that uniquely identify each record in a table is known as a .... (1)
    (a) primary key   (b) alternate key   (c) candidate key   (d) foreign key

(vi) .... are web based instant messaging softwares. (1)
    (a) WeChat   (b) Skype   (c) Viber   (d) All of these

5. *Answer any 5 out of the given 6 questions* $(1 \times 5 = 5)$

(i) .... displays worksheets as they would appear if you printed them out. (1)
    (a) Layout   (b) Page layout   (c) Page break   (d) None of these

(ii) Alignments buttons are available on the .... tab. (1)
    (a) Home   (b) Insert   (c) Format   (d) File

(iii) Out of the following, which one is the most appropriate data field in context of employee table, if only one of these is required? (1)
    (a) Age in years   (b) Date of birth   (c) Age in days   (d) Age in months

(iv) The main advantage of circuit switching is .... (1)
    (a) delivery   (b) guaranteed delivery   (c) power band   (d) None of these

(v) The contents of a cell can be changed by pressing .... key on keyboard. (1)
    (a) F5   (b) F3   (c) F2   (d) None of these

(vi) MAN provides communication services upto .... (1)
    (a) 100 m   (b) 100 km   (c) 10 km   (d) None of these

Section B (Subjective Type Questions)

Answer any 3 out of the given 5 questions based on Employability Skills. Answer each question in 20-30 words

$(2 \times 3 = 6)$

6. What do you mean by non-verbal communication? (2)

7. Explain the term self-motivation. (2)

8. How can you create new worksheet in MS-Excel? (2)

9. What do you mean by entrepreneur? (2)

10. What are the importance of sustainable development? (2)

Answer any 4 out of the given 6 questions in 20-30 words each $(2 \times 4 = 8)$

11. How to create a new blank document in MS-Word?   (2)

12. What do you mean by paragraph alignment?   (2)

13. How to unfreeze the rows and columns in workbook?   (2)

14. Explain the term table used in database.   (2)

15. Distinguish between repeater and switch.   (2)

16. Define the following: (2)

    (i) AutoSum function   (ii) Full screen workbook view

Answer any 3 out of the given 5 questions in 50-80 words each $(4 \times 3 = 12)$

17. What is absolute cell referencing?   (4)

18. Explain the following :   (4)

    (i) Modem   (ii) Web page

19. Describe three data manipulation language commands.   (4)

20. What is header and footer? How to insert Date/Time into Header/Footer?   (4)

21. (i) Create the table SummerCamp with the following fields: (4)

Column Name	Data Type
ChildID	Varchar(5)
FirstName	Char(20)
LastName	Char(20)
DOB	Date
Gender	Char(2)
Group	Varchar(5)

    (ii) Consider the following table APPLICANTS and write the queries (a) and (b).

TABLE: APPLICANTS

No.	NAME	FEE	GENDER	C_ID	JOINYEAR
1012	Amandeep	30000	M	A01	2012
1102	Avisha	25000	F	A02	2009
1103	Ekant	30000	M	A02	2011
1049	Arun	30000	M	A03	2009
1025	Amber	40000	M	A02	2011

    (a) To display NAME, FEE, GENDER, JOINYEAR about the APPLICANTS, who have joined before 2010.

    (b) To display the names of all applicants in ascending order of their JOINYEAR.

Answer Key

1. (i) (c),	(ii) (a),	(iii) (b),	(iv) (a),	(v) (b),	(vi) (c)
2. (i) (a),	(ii) (c),	(iii) (b),	(iv) (a),	(v) (b),	(vi) (c)
3. (i) (b),	(ii) (c),	(iii) (b),	(iv) (c),	(v) (a),	(vi) (b)
4. (i) (a),	(ii) (b),	(iii) (c),	(iv) (d),	(v) (a),	(vi) (d)
5. (i) (b),	(ii) (a),	(iii) (b),	(iv) (b),	(v) (a),	(vi) (b)

SAMPLE QUESTION PAPER 5

A Highly Simulated Sample Question Paper for CBSE Class 10

Information Technology

General Instructions

See Sample Question Paper 1.

Time : 2 hours   *Max. Marks : 50*

Section A (Objective Type Questions)

1. *Answer any 4 out of the given 6 questions based on Employability Skills*   (1 × 4 = 4)

   (i) …… allow you to communicate your message clearly and easily to a large audience.   (1)
      (a) Good writing skills   (b) Communication   (c) Document   (d) None of these

   (ii) The feeling of self-awareness enhances our ……   (1)
      (a) mediation   (b) stress   (c) self-confidence   (d) clarity

   (iii) In …… filter, detailed rules are specified as a part of spreadsheet cells.   (1)
      (a) Normal   (b) Advanced   (c) Both (a) and (b)   (d) None of these

   (iv) …… is the process of identifying opportunities in the market place.   (1)
      (a) Decision maker   (b) Management   (c) Entrepreneurship   (d) None of these

   (v) The ecology can be protected through imposition of …… and afforestation.   (1)
      (a) forestation   (b) deforestation   (c) Both (a) and (b)   (d) None of these

   (vi) …… consists of a main clause and sometimes one or more subordinate clauses.   (1)
      (a) Paragraph   (b) Noun   (c) Sentence   (d) All of these

2. *Answer any 5 out of the given 6 questions*   (1 × 5 = 5)

   (i) Which of the following run horizontally in a worksheet and are identified by a number in the row header?   (1)
      (a) Column letter   (b) Row number   (c) Name box   (d) Formula bar

   (ii) Picture Shape option comes under ……… tab.   (1)
      (a) Picture Format   (b) Tools Format   (c) Picture Tools Format   (d) None of these

   (iii) Table is also known as ……… .   (1)
      (a) file   (b) record   (c) field   (d) sheet

   (iv) Web based type of software is accessed using ………… .   (1)
      (a) web server   (b) web browsers   (c) web client   (d) None of these

   (v) In ……… topology, each node is connected to two and only too neighbouring nodes.   (1)
      (a) ring   (b) tree   (c) mesh   (d) star

   (vi) Which of the following is a boundary that specifies that cell is active at particular moment?   (1)
      (a) Formula   (b) Cell pointer   (c) Cell address   (d) None of these

3. *Answer any 5 out of the given 6 questions*   (1 × 5 = 5)

   (i) Which of the following options are available in Office button?   (1)
      (a) New   (b) Open   (c) Save   (d) All of these

   (ii) Which of the following offers a blog services?   (1)
      (a) Drupal   (b) Joomla   (c) WordPress   (d) All of these

(iii) .... shortcut key is used to make the selected text underline. (1)
    (a) Alt + I   (b) Ctrl + I   (c) Ctrl + U   (d) Alt + U

(iv) Which of the following is the oldest spreadsheet package? (1)
    (a) MS-Excel   (b) Quattro-Pro   (c) VisiCalc   (d) All of these

(v) .... view is a simple view of data arranged in rows and columns. (1)
    (a) Datasheet   (b) Design   (c) Table   (d) None of these

(vi) .... is a multi-port network device, that provides access to computers. (1)
    (a) Switch   (b) Hub   (c) Gateway   (d) Bridge

4. *Answer any 5 out of the given 6 questions*   (1 × 5 = 5)

(i) After selecting the text you need to click the .... in the font group to make the font size larger than the current font size. (1)
    (a) size   (b) font size   (c) font   (d) font-style

(ii) Hide and Unhide option is available in .... tab in MS-Excel. (1)
    (a) Edit   (b) Format   (c) Home   (d) Insert

(iii) Database is a combination of .... (1)
    (a) hardware   (b) software   (c) Both (a) and (b)   (d) None of these

(iv) A computer connected to a network is known as .... (1)
    (a) host   (b) data   (c) node   (d) Both (a) and (c)

(v) Database is made up of all the following components except .... (1)
    (a) tables   (b) queries   (c) forms   (d) formula bar

(vi) The .... establishes an intelligent connection between a local network and external networks. (1)
    (a) bridge   (b) router   (c) gateway   (d) hub

5. *Answer any 5 out of the given 6 questions*   (1 × 5 = 5)

(i) While entering a formula, cell address B $ 5 represents .... (1)
    (a) relative referencing   (b) mixed referencing   (c) absolute referencing   (d) None of these

(ii) .... are the tools which are used to produce own drawings. (1)
    (a) Drawings tools   (b) Picture tools   (c) Both (a) and (b)   (d) None of these

(iii) Facilities offered by database are (1)
    (a) the ability to store a large amount of data in a structured format, easy update, sort query, production of reports
    (b) easy edition, spell check, perform calculations, library of mathematical functions, replication
    (c) the ability to rotate images, copy and paste, fill scale
    (d) None of the above

(iv) .... web browser supports only graphics information. (1)
    (a) Text-based   (b) Graphical`   (c) Both (a) and (b)   (d) None of these

(v) Formula for adding values of cell A1 to A5 would be .... (1)
    (a) SUM (A1 : A5)   (b) = SUM (A1 : A5)   (c) = TOTAL (A 1 : A 5)   (d) = SUM (A 1 + A 5)

(vi) Computers connected to a LAN can share information through a common .... (1)
    (a) printer   (b) data   (c) network   (d) None of these

Section B (Subjective Type Questions)

Answer any 3 out of the given 5 questions based on Employability Skills. Answer each question in 20-30 words
    (2 × 3 = 6)

6. Explain the types of barriers to communicate. (2)

7. Explain the four kinds of self-awareness. (2)

8. Write the steps to save a document. (2)

9. What are the advantages of entrepreneurship? (2)

10. Define the solutions for sustainable development. (2)

Answer any 4 out of the given 6 questions in 20-30 words each   (2 × 4 = 8)

11. Write the steps to modify a style in a document.   (2)

12. How to change the layout of the chart?   (2)

13. What do you mean by filtering data?   (2)

14. Explain the term report in a database.   (2)

15. Distinguish between circuit switching and packet switching.   (2)

16. Describe the following in a document :   (2)
  (i) Ruler   (ii) Scroll bar

Answer any 3 out of the given 5 questions in 50-80 words each   (4 × 3 = 12)

17. Describe all methods for saving a document in MS-Word.   (4)

18. Define the following   (4)
  (i) Blog   (ii) Mesh topology

19. What do you mean by mixed referencing?   (4)

20. How to rename a field into a table in a database?   (4)

21. (i) Create the table SHOP with the following fields: (4)

Column Name	Data Type
S_No	Varchar(5)
P_Name	Char(20)
S_Name	Char(20)
Qty	Int
Cost	Float
City	Char(20)

(ii) Consider the following table CUSTOMER and write the queries (a) and (b).

TABLE: CUSTOMER

CID	CNAME	GENDER	SID	AREA
1001	R SHARMA	FEMALE	101	NORTH
1002	M R TIWARY	MALE	102	SOUTH
1003	M K KHAN	MALE	103	EAST
1004	A K SINGH	MALE	102	EAST
1005	S SEN	FEMALE	101	WEST
1006	R DUBEY	MALE	104	NORTH

(a) To display CNAME,AREA of all female customers from CUSTOMER table.

(b) To display the details of all the CUSTOMER in ascending order of CNAME within SID.

Answer Key

1. (i) (a),	(ii) (c),	(iii) (b),	(iv) (c),	(v) (b),	(vi) (c)
2. (i) (b),	(ii) (c),	(iii) (a),	(iv) (b),	(v) (a),	(vi) (b)
3. (i) (d),	(ii) (d),	(iii) (c),	(iv) (c),	(v) (a),	(vi) (b)
4. (i) (b),	(ii) (c),	(iii) (c),	(iv) (d),	(v) (d),	(vi) (c)
5. (i) (b),	(ii) (a),	(iii) (a),	(iv) (b),	(v) (b),	(vi) (a)

UNSOLVED